James McGee

Half House with Irish Authors

James McGee

Half House with Irish Authors

ISBN/EAN: 9783744760546

Printed in Europe, USA, Canada, Australia, Japan

Cover: Foto ©ninafisch / pixelio.de

More available books at **www.hansebooks.com**

GERALD GRIFFIN.

HALF HOURS

with

IRISH AUTHORS.

SELECTIONS

FROM

GRIFFIN, LOVER, CARLETON, AND LEVER.

NEW YORK:
J. A. McGEE, 7 BARCLAY STREET.
1873.

PREFACE.

IN the following extracts from the works of the ablest and best known Irish novelists of the present century, we have endeavored, while giving variety to the selections, to afford the reader an insight into the many-sided character of the people in the several sections of Ireland. Each of the writers put under contribution thoroughly understood the peculiarities, idiosyncrasies, modes of thought, and forms of expression of his countrymen, but mainly so far as he had studied them in his own particular district or province. Hence the Munster peasant of Griffin, and the northern cottier of Carleton, are as different from each other, and from the Leinster wag sketched by Lover, and the rollicking Connaught soldier of Charles Lever, as if they did not belong to the same age and nation; yet all are drawn true to nature, and, locally, with the greatest fidelity.

The numerous works of these authors have

long since been republished, and are still extensively read in this country, and we trust that our present volume, while affording HALF-HOURS' amusement to the public, will further stimulate the popular desire for a more intimate acquaintance with their larger and highly elaborate productions.

NEW YORK, October, 1872.

CONTENTS.

GERALD GRIFFIN.

	PAGE
THE MISTAKE,	9
THE RAVEN'S NEST	37
SIR DOWLING O'HARTIGAN,	61
THE STORY TELLER AT FAULT,	80

SAMUEL LOVER.

BARNEY O'REIRDON,	115
THE PRIEST'S STORY,	174
PADDY THE PIPER,	186
THE WHITE TROUT,	200

WILLIAM CARLETON.

| THE DONAGH | 215 |
| LARRY MCFARLAND'S WAKE, | 262 |

CHARLES LEVER.

THE DOCTOR'S TALE,	281
THE ADJUTANT'S COURTSHIP,	297
THE GHOST,	313
SERVING A WRIT,	325

GERALD GRIFFIN.

THE MISTAKE.

> "Tell why the sepulchre,
> Wherein we saw thee quietly inurned
> Hath oped his ponderous and marble jaws
> To cast thee up again? What may this mean?"
> HAMLET, act i. scene iv.

THERE was no happier man in the wide world than Phelim O'Rourke, from the longest day he could remember until that on which he was married, and, alas! that we should have to record it, no one so miserable ever after. His fate was the more pitiable, that he was unusually cautious in entering on a state which was to fix the good or evil fortune of his future life. He did not embrace it as a mere boy; he was verging fast beyond manhood at the time, he had known the object of his choice from childhood, and he devoted a fortnight of deep contemplation to the affair before Shrovetide. But after the inextricable knot was tied, the grounds upon which his unfortunate attachment rested proved beyond all conception unsubstantial. The gay good-humor of little Anty O'Donnel, the tender look, the glad welcome, and, above all, the winning obsequiousness of manner which first caught his heart, one by one faded like fairy gifts away in the person of Mrs. O'Rourke, until at the end of five or six months he began almost to call in question the fact of their having ever had any existence. He sometimes thought to himself that he must have been juggled by witchcraft, or his imagination deluded by some love potion, perhaps privately administered by Anty. When he went from home in the morning, instead of the fond farewell look which, in his young fancy, he imagined would daily follow him to his early labor, he had to endure the frowning glances of his helpmate, and her oft-repeated charges about his tarrying out after work-time; for the joyous welcome home, he met a reception that would have augured a change for the worse in the wife of Rip Van Winkle; and for the fond anxiety to please in their frequent communings, a total disregard to every wish of his heart, and a determined resolution to have everything her own way.

Phelim was, happily for himself, of a very elastic temperament. If he was easily depressed by his evil fortune, he was also easily elated when his better star seemed to be in the ascendant; and perhaps if the settled cloudiness of Anty's countenance had been ever so rarely visited with a gleam of sunshine, he might have have considered his fate, though a very checkered one, as not quite insupportable. But the season of her ill-humor set in after wedlock like a polar night to the northern mariner—long and hopeless, and with no promise of a future day. "I have heard tell," he used to mutter to himself, in his moments of bitterness, "of a woman's leading a man the life a dog, but sure a dog has a fine life of it compared to mine. He's up with the sun, delighting himself with his sports in the grassy fields, and there's no living eye takes envy at his amusement; he gets his mess in peace in the chimney corner, twice in the day, without toil or trouble, and he sleeps like a kitten by the fireside all night, without dramin' or startin' as I do, thinkin' of the day's doens; if he gets an odd kick or a batin, he knows 'tisn't out of any ill-will, and it doesn't dwell on his mind a minute after the pain is gone; and if he hears a tongue equal to Anty's, 'tisn't expected he'll understand it. Oh! mo leare! the life of a dog is a fine life."

Time, which, it is said, wears down the edge of the sharpest evil, did very little in his weary course for Phelim O'Rourke when the cholera suddenly reached his neighborhood, and committed awful havoc in every direction. There was the greatest consternation throughout the district, and the visitation was met by every one in fear and trembling, except by those for whom misery had already stripped death of his terrors. Phelim could not be altogether placed among the latter class, nor said to be wholly devoid of apprehension, yet anticipating some respite to his torments, from the very natural hope that Anty's temper would be mollified by the universal panic, he was much less depressed than the multitude. Even a furtive smile might be sometimes detected playing about his mouth, on the announcement of some new and appalling stroke of the destroyer, when he observed the smooth and pallid fear overspreading the brow of his partner, and a silence, sudden as the palsy, arresting her conversation. It at length unfortunately attracted Anty's notice, and, as may be conjectured, convinced from that moment that he was felicitating on the prospect of her seizure with the disease, her rage knew no bounds. Every thrill or start of terror she experienced as the danger increased about her furnished new ground for suspicion; his very looks were watched and examined with a metaphysical acuteness, and the faintest expression traced home to its iniquitous source, until all his anticipations of even temporary repose were buried in the darkest disappointment, the spring by which he thought to lie down for awhile and drink the sweet waters of contentment pouring out for him only new draughts of bitterness.

When we mention that five years had already rolled over the heads of this ill-starred pair, and they were still living in one house, and partaking of the same meals in so decorous a manner as to keep their domestic agreements in some degree hidden from the public, it will be admitted that Phelim was a man of the most enduring patience. With whatever amount, however, of Christian resignation he suffered this sort of life, he could not always avoid indications of peevishness and vexation at his lot. He was often heard to say, " I wish to heaven I was taken off at once be the sickness, and 'twould be an ease to me." Sometimes, indeed, it must be confessed, another alternative floated dimly in the perspective, when his wicked angel whispered the question in his ear: " Wouldn't it answer as well, Phelim, if it took off little Anty?" His better feelings, nevertheless, always discountenanced those evil suggestions, as well as the contingent result of such an occurrence, which his busy imagination was ever ready to disport in when permitted to go at large.

It happened one morning, as they were sitting to breakfast, that they heard a cry next door, and, in a few minutes after, a person ran in and informed them that the woman who lived there and her three children had been carried off by the cholera in the night, leaving the disconsolate husband alone in the world. Mrs. O'Rourke's eye, after she had recovered from the shock which the first announcement of the news had occasioned, fixed itself instinctively on Phelim, and again she saw, or fancied she saw, instead of the natural expression of countenance at such awful accounts, a shrouded delight beaming in his looks, which was very badly concealed in his awkward semblance of sympathy for the sufferers. Her ire was instantly kindled, and after a pause of a few minutes, during which she was endeavoring to subdue the up-bursting violence into, what she hoped might even for its newness prove more cutting, a bitter irony, she observed:

"Pleasant news this fine mornin', Misther O'Rourke; the loss of so many poor innocent craythurs at a sweep is enough to delight the heart of any one!"

"What do you mane be that, Anty?" returned Phelim. "'Twould be a strange bizness if I wasn't sorry for poor Davy in his trouble!"

"Trouble enough!" retorted Anty. "I b'lieve you'd give a thrifle to be in his case for all; 'twould be the glory of your heart, you murthering crocodile, if the sickness come into us to-day, and that you saw me dacently laid under the sod in the even. I know your thoughts, you villain, for all your long faces; I know how you laugh in your heart within when you hear of a poor woman dying, hopin' it may come to my turn at last; but I'll disappoint you; wid the blessin' of Heaven, I tell you, I'll disappoint you!"

Phelim in vain protested against these accusations, and much more to the same purport passed between them, until the dispute reached a pitch that he found by experience it was not safe it should long maintain. He accordingly struck his colors, and was hanging his head, after his usual fashion, in profound silence, waiting for the storm to subside, when the suddenness of that occurrence caught his attention, and, looking up into his wife's face, he thought he observed it singularly pale and grave. She was evidently struggling with some sudden terror, and on recovering her speech, which she did at once, from the moment she saw Phelim fix his looks upon her, she exclaimed:

"You have your wish, you murtherer, if 'tis of any good to you, but 'tis your bad angel done it. If you hadn't sold yourself, the wicked longing couldn't thrive with you."

"What's the matter now?" answered Phelim.

"I'm off," cried Anty, "that's all; run for the priest; run, I tell you, and take your eyes off of me."

"Erah, what's the matter, darlin'?" asked the husband again, with as strong an expression of anxiety as he could summon up.

"Don't darlin' me, you villin," returned Anty. "I'm off and you know it—'tis all your doens—'tis out of the passion you put me into I got it—my death will be at your door."

"Got what, avourneen?"

"Lave off your palaveren again, and get me the priest. Oh! the Lord help me. I'm off, I believe —the cramp—the cramp. I'm done for in earnest —rub me—rub me—will any one get me the priest?"

Phelim now clearly saw that she was getting the cholera, for while she was speaking her voice began to grow hoarse and whispering, her face became bluish, and shrunk to half its usual size, her eyes were sinking in her head, like those of a wasted corpse, and a cold sweat was oozing out from every pore. " Rub me, you vagabond, if there's any compassion left for your poor murthered wife. Oh! my leg—my leg—rub me—won't any one rub me—there—there—higher up—oh! my foot—the other foot—won't I get the priest at all, Dheelen?"

A woman happening to come in at the moment, attracted by her cries, the astounded husband left his wife in her care, and darted off for the priest. We shall not venture to analyze his reflections by the way, nor offer a conjecture as to their nature. It is sufficient to say that by the time he reached Father McMahon's residence his countenance had attained a very decorous length, and he was not wanting in a due degree of impatience to hurry back with the worthy man. They left the door together, and though the priest was mounted very tolerably, and pushed on, as in all cases of urgency, at rather a rapid rate, he was far outstript by the anxious Phelim, who stood again by poor Anty's side before it could have been thought possible for him to traverse such a distance.

The neighbors were at the time holding a consultation in an antechamber, to determine what was the best course to be pursued with her.

" Take her to the hospital at once," says one, who thought the further and the sooner she was removed from his own domicile the better.

" 'Tis the best way," says a second, " for she's a gone woman if there isn't something done for her in a hurry."

"Gone or not gone," exclaimed a third, who proved to be a sister of Anty's, "she'll never set foot in the hospital. I'll not have her pisened be the docthors, any way."

"Indeed, 'tis seldom they're throublesome afther comen out of their hands," observed a pedlar, who stood listening in the crowd; "they're the quieter for visiting 'em ever afther, to my knowledge."

"Thrue for him, faix," cried another; "many's the fine young boy or girl I see go into 'em stout and ruddy, and come out in the mornen with their feet foremost."

"Eyeh, don't be runnen 'em down that way," observed a little tailor, who had obtained some reputation as a wit, "they're not so bad after all; go into 'em ever so bare or naked, and they never fails to send you out with a new wooden jacket and steel buttons!"

"Ulaloo! the vagabonds," exclaimed the sister, "they destroy 'em with their physics; sure I seen 'em with my own two eyes in the hospital, changing color as soon as they drank 'em off."

"No wondher," rejoined the pedlar, "when they're paid for it."

"Paid by whom?" exclaimed half a dozen voices simultaneously.

"By the Government," returned the pedlar; "who else? There are too many of us in the country entirely, and we're for ever fighten, and night-walken, and given the world in all of throuble. They thried emigration, and transportation, and turnen us out to starve on the highroads by what they call the Subletting Act, and they thried the treadmill, and even hanging itself, and 'twas to no purpose. So they med up their minds at last to rid the country of us be pisening us like varmin, and when the cholera come, they tuck advantage of the docthors to do it, be way of curen unknownst to us."

"See that why!" ejaculated several.

"'Tis a good hundred pounds to 'em, at any rate, every poor soul they put out of pain," continued the pedlar.

A low "Dheelen!" (God help us!) was heard from the crowd.

The priest had now arrived, and, seeing Mrs. O'Rourke in such a deplorable way that there was not a moment to be lost, recommended strongly that she should be at once removed to the hospital. He met, however, perhaps in consequence of the pedlar's communication, with more opposition than he expected, especially from Anty's sister, a Mrs. Judy O'Leary, of whom we have before made mention. He at length thought it better to refer the dispute to Phelim as the fittest person to give a final decision on the subject.

"I'll take the advice of Father Mac," cried Phelim, in a melancholy tone, "he's the best judge, and, moreover, I have a great opinion of the docthors." Phelim had been attentively listening to the pedlar's account of them.

"I tell you, Phelim," roared Judy, "if you take

her there, she'll never come out of it a living woman!"

"The will of God be done!" replied Phelim. "How can we help it?"

"Be not putting her in there, you neygur," exclaimed the indignant sister. "Is it to get rid of her you want?"

The priest, perceiving that the difference of opinion between the parties was likely to increase, interposed before it reached a climax, and demanded of Judy what she meant by insinuating such imputations against the hospital, where respectable medical gentlemen were risking their lives night and day, amidst the most shocking scenes, in the hope of rescuing even a few lives from the pestilence.

"Eyeh! the notorious thieves of the earth," returned Judy; "'tisn't for nothing they're doen it, and as for recoveren people, ar'n't the hospitals open now as good as a fortnight, and for the hundred that come out in coffins, there isn't one yet come out in his clothes!"

Phelim heaved a deep sigh.

"My good woman," observed the priest, "this is all a foolish prejudice. The disease is a dreadful one, and people must die of it wherever they are; but, independent of any other consideration, I think the safety of the neighborhood should be considered; there will be danger of the sickness extending itself if the poor creature is left here."

"I'll take care of her myself," answered Judy,

"if she's left, and no one else need come near her."

"No, no, Judy a lanive," exclaimed Phelim, a little alarmed, "I'll not have you or the neighborhood in danger by any means. No, no, avourneen, I'd sooner suffer any loss"—and he wiped his eye with the skirt of his coat—"I'd sooner suffer any loss than have the sickness spreading about like wildfire, as it will if poor Anty's left here."

"Thrue for you, Phelim," responded the alarmed crowd, "'twill be through every house on the road before mornen if she's not taken to the hospital."

"They'll be but few of us left to tell it, I'm afeerd," said Phelim. "May Heaven protect us!"

As the sense of the meeting ran entirely with Phelim on the necessity of poor Anty's removal, it was in vain that the persevering Judy still held out and endeavored to convince them that she would so contrive to nurse-tend her sister as to cut off all communication with those residing about her. It was carried by acclamation that she should be taken off to the hospital, and the cholera-cot having been summoned to the spot, she was laid into it, in a state that, without much aid from the doctors, gave a fair promise of her never revisiting her little home again. Phelim followed slowly and with a dejected look in the wake of the cotmen, and they all soon disappeared from the sympathizing eyes of the anxious and apprehensive crowd.

He returned to his cabin alone, and as David wept for his son while he was yet living, but became resigned when hope and anxiety were alike over, so Phelim grieved for little Anty throughout the day, shedding abundance of tears, but at night, when a messenger arrived directing him to bring a coffin to the hospital, the fountain of his sorrows became dried up. " If I was to weep for a hundred years," he observed, "sure 'twouldn't bring her back again to me, poor thing! 'tis only flying in the face of heaven not to submit to my misfortune like a Christian; there's no knowing how soon it may be my own turn." He accordingly attended at the hospital gate with a becoming spirit, and, having delivered in the coffin, received it in his car from the hands of the porter and cotmen again, freighted with the remains of Mrs. Anty O'Rourke, as was testified by the chalk inscription on the cover. He immediately proceeded to the burying-ground, accompanied by the hospital grave-digger, with whose solitary assistance she was consigned to her last resting-place.

Death was a matter of too common occurrence in these days, to leave that deep or permanent gloom after it which it is sure to do where its visits, as in ordinary times, are but few and far between. Individual distress, however great, seemed of small amount, even in the estimation of the sufferer, while the pestilence was still laying life waste in every direction about him. When, at the end of some ten or fifteen days, it at length quitted Phelim's neighborhood, to hunt for prey in some new or untouched district, his misfortune was but an old and ordinary one in public remembrance. He had, indeed, ceased to grieve on the subject himself, though the image of poor Anty, he declared, still haunted his mind, and, however long he lived, could never be effaced from his memory. This assertion, however, very soon came to be doubted by his acquaintances. The living picture of Maggy Fitzgerald, a blooming girl who lived in his vicinity, was seen too frequently by his side to permit the supposition that a rival from among the dead could occupy any very permanent place in his imagination. The truth was that, within three weeks after his late loss, Phelim was once more over head and ears in love. He had forgotten, or ceased to think, of all his troubles and disappointments, and, of such strange materials is the human heart made up, his affections were as fondly and utterly given away in this new attachment as if he had never loved or been deceived by woman.

Fortune, however, seemed now fully disposed to make him amends for the long period of her desertion. His days passed on in uninterrupted dreams of delight, his nights in refreshing slumbers, and the lark welcomed the golden morning with a song less blitheful. The blissful period that was to complete his happiness was at length fixed, and, day after day, the rosy-footed hours kept whispering as they passed of the joys that were approaching;

but, alas! for poor humanity! How uncertain are its hopes!—how fleeting its enjoyments! On the very eve of the wedding, a friend broke the dreadful secret to him, that it was generally rumored through the country Mrs. Anty O'Rourke was still alive! Phelim sprang three feet from his stool at the announcement, clapping his hands and exclaiming " Murther!" as he came to the ground. On recovering his recollection, however, and calming a little, he totally denied the possibility of such an occurrence, described minutely his having himself received the coffin containing her remains from the porter, and his having buried it beneath three feet of earth, with the assistance of the grave-digger; that they even rolled a great rock over the spot afterwards, which no unaided human effort could roll off again, so that, admitting such an absurdity as her returning to life after interment, there was no possible way by which she could extricate herself from the grave. He partly satisfied his informant by these explanations, but by no means removed the hankering suspicion from his own mind, though perfectly at a loss to account for it. Somebody, it was said, had actually seen and spoken to her, and though reports as groundless every day find circulation, this one came too malapropos to be treated with perfect indifference. He pondered and enquired, and pondered again, until the subject took such entire possession of his mind that he felt he could neither rest nor sleep until he had his doubts cleared up in one way or another. He accordingly came to the resolution of visiting the hospital, and investigating the matter most minutely.

On arriving at the gate, he lifted the knocker with a palpitating heart, feeling that his fate depended on the decision of the next few moments. The porter appeared, and demanded his business.

"Will you tell me, if you please," answered Phelim, "do you remember a woman of the name of Anty O'Rourke, that I brought in here sick of cholera, a little time ago?"

"I do well," returned the porter.

"What became of her?"

"She was discharged, cured, about three weeks ago."

"Cured!" ejaculated Phelim, his jaw dropping, and his eyes dilating like saucers.

"Iss, to be sure. Do you think we never cure any one?" returned the porter, with an air of offended dignity.

"I don't mane that," faltered Phelim, "but my—my—wife."

"Oh! ho! she was your wife, was she? Why, then, I never see one take the recovery of his wife so much to heart before."

"She's dead, I tell you," cried Phelim, "'tis a mistake of yours—you—you yourself put her corpse in the coffin for me, five weeks ago, and gev it into my own two hands at this very doore—don't you remember here at this doore? Do, agra, try to remember—'tis as true as daylight."

"I don't remember any sitch thing," answered the porter.

"Oh! murther!" exclaimed Phelim, striking his hands against his forehead.

"May be," continued the porter, " I gev you some one else in a mistake."

"Oh! murther!" roared Phelim again, as, with hands still pressed to his forehead, he moved backwards and forwards before the gate, stamping the ground vehemently at every step.

"Faix, it sometimes happens us for all," continued the porter, " when there's a great number of 'em goes off in the night. The names are pinned on 'em when they're thrun in the dead-house, but sometimes they slips off again, you know, and then we're all at a dead loss, not knowin' one from another, so no wonther a mistake should happen— some one else's wife I giv' you, I suppose!"

Phelim, upon whom some new light seemed to be breaking during this explanation, now started out of his reverie, and, catching the porter's hand with eagerness, exclaimed, " Tell me one thing now, like an honest man, and may the heavens be your bed as you tell me truly: Do ye ever have two people of the same name in the hospital at the same time?"

"Eyeh! plague on 'em for names! to be sure we do, almost every day—there's no pleasing the people at all, 'count of the bother we have with the way they're christened—all Paddys, or Daveys, or Marys, or Peggys, till we can't tell one for another; but, death and age, man!" continued the porter, suddenly elevating his voice. "Why do you squeeze my hand that way?"

"I didn't mane any offence by it, avourneen," responded Phelim; "I'd be sorry to hurt a hair o' your head, but I have one question more to put to you. What sort of a woman was it be the name of Anty O'Rourke that you turned out cured?"

"A handy little skeleton of a creature, then, that no cholera could kill—one that the world couldn't plaze—scold—scolding always, and with looks that ud freeze a turnip when anybody venthured to answer her."

Phelim's heart sank within him again; he summoned courage, however, to continue the investigation.

"E'then, do you know at all, did she get much medicine from the docthors?"

"She couldn't be got to taste as much as a drop for any of 'em," replied the porter.

"Lord help us!" ejaculated Phelim, with a deep sigh.

"But how is it," said the porter, "now I think on it, if she was your wife, that she didn't go home to you?"

"Thrue for you," answered Phelim, rubbing his hands, and brightening up at a thought which had never occurred to him before. "What is it I'm thinking of at all? Sure if she and I were on the living earth, she'd find me out in half the time.

The power av the world ud hardly keep her from me for three whole weeks, that is, if she had her walk and her five senses. I'm the rail fool and not to recollect that at wanst. No! no! poor ooman, she's dead and buried long enough to keep quiet for my day, at any rate! Sure I helped to make the grave and throw the earth on her myself!"

"I'll be bail, then, she has the good winter's coat of it," observed the porter smiling; "you wouldn't like to let the frost to her, poor thing!"

"Eyeh! no matter," returned Phelim, "'tis equal how we lie, when it comes to that with us; but I'm obleeged to you for your information entirely, a good evenen."

"Safe home to you, Misther O'Rourke," cried the porter, the smile still playing about his mouth, "and if I hear anything of Anty's stirren about, I'll not fail to come with the news to you."

Phelim quickened his pace, and pretended not to hear; muttered, however, when he reached a sufficient distance to vent his feelings with impunity, " Wisha asy enough it is with you, that haven't chick nor child, nor anything but your own four bones to throuble you; may be when you marry you'll not have your jokes so ready, and faix when you do, all the harm I wish you is a wife equal to Anty."

On arriving at home, Phelim recovered his spirits, and made every preparation for the wedding. After trying on a new suit of clothes which was made for him by a Limerick tailor, fitting himself with a shining caroline hat, and reviewing his figure, with due particularity, in a broken piece of a mirror which he had neatly set in polished ash, he spent the evening at the bride's. To such as have loved, it is needless to tell that he did not return home until the moon was going to her rest, and that he then lay down on his humble bed to pass away the time in chiding the lazy hours that one by one came slowly to his pillow to tell him of the approaching morning.

At last came the joyous wedding day, and with it, from far and near, the guests came gathering to the merry house of the bride. The weather was unpropitious, for the morning had set in with wind and rain in all the gloom of beginning winter; but the barn in which, for the sake of increased room, the company were assembled was defended by a thick coating of thatch from the power of the storm, and a roaring fire blazing at the upper end gave a fair guarantee against the influence of the cold. The wedding baked meats were set forth, the bagpipes had struck up a merry air, and the priest had already taken his place at the head of the banqueting table, when a loud knocking was heard at the door, and a poor woman, wrapped in a cloak, who sought shelter from the weather, was admitted to a seat by the fireside. The occurrence was too common to occasion much observation, and the feast proceeded. Great and fearful was the destruction on every hand, and stunning was the noise of the delighted multitude. After the meats and other substantial elements of the entertainment had disappeared, and a becoming time was allowed for discussing the punch, they all arose at a signal from the priest, and a little circle was formed at the upper end of the apartment, in the centre of which he placed himself, with Phelim and Maggy before him. The important ceremony was now about to take place which was to make them happy for ever, and an anxious silence reigned throughout the room, broken only by the whisper of some of the elders to one another, or the suppressed titter of some sly maiden at the bashful bearing of the bride. Just as the priest took the book, a loud cough was heard from the stranger. No one took notice of it, except Phelim; but as soon as he heard it, he started as if he had been electrified, and let fall Maggy's hand from his own; then, looking towards the fireplace where the old woman was sitting, a cold shivering came over him, and large drops of perspiration hung glistening on his forehead.

"What's the matter with you, darlen?" exclaimed Maggy, terrified at the change which came over him.

"Nothing, achree," replied the bridegroom, " but a weakness that came upon me when I heerd that cough from the ind of the room; it was so like the sound of one that I was once used to, but that can never be heard in this world again."

Scarcely had he uttered the words, when another cough resounded in the same direction, and again a sudden terror seized upon Phelim, his teeth began to chatter, his limbs to tremble, and he kept looking up towards the fireplace, like one that was fairy-stricken.

"Heaven purtect us!" he ejaculated, in a faint whisper to himself.

"Phelim—Phelim, honey!" cried Maggy, dreadfully alarmed.

"Sure," muttered he, heedless of the voice of the bride, and gazing vacantly in the one direction, "I berried her with my own two hands!"

"What ails you, Phelim?" exclaimed the priest, shaking him by the shoulder, to arouse him out of the stupor which seemed to oppress him. "Are you ill? Or what is all this strange proceeding about?"

"I'm not well, indeed, your reverence," replied Phelim, recovering himself, "I don' know what's the matter, but I'm sure I'll be quite well when this business is over. Let us go on."

He took Maggy's hand again, and the priest proceeded, but when Phelim commenced to repeat the customary words after him, "I take thee, Margaret Fitzgerald, for my wedded wife," his eyes instinctively fixed itself on the little woman at the fireplace, when, to his utter horror, he saw her slowly rising from her stool, and, throwing back the cloak from her head, turned round to the company. A general scream acknowledged the presence of Mrs. Anty O'Rourke! She settled her look steadily on Phelim, and walked slowly towards him. He staggered back two or three steps, and would have fallen, had he not been supported by those about him. Her person seemed to grow taller as she advanced, her countenance more ferocious than he had ever seen it, and she was struggling with suppressed passion to such a degree as for some moments to impede her utterance. When her feelings at length found vent in words, she shook her clenched fist at him, at once relieving the party from all suspense as to her spectral character. " You villin!" she exclaimed, " you thought you got rid of me, did you ? You thought you had three feet of the sod over me, and that you might get on wid your pranks as you pleased yourself, but I'll spoil your divarsion for you. I'll trait you wid a wife, so I will, you unnatural dog. Your darlen, indeed! (courtesying to Maggy). Your Maggy, achree! So, ma'am—hem. Nothen ud satisfy you but to be Mrs. O'Rourke—Mrs. O'Rourke, enagh! Why you unmoral, unproper character, would you have the man marry two wives? Would you have him scandalize the whole country? O you rail Turk (to Phelim), I have been watching every turn of you, these three weeks back; I've seen your doens—your coorten, and dearen, and drinken. What's become av the pig, you hangman? The pig that I reared from a bonnive wid my own hands. Yes, two hands—look at em—not so white as Maggy's, may be, but belonging to Mrs. O'Rourke for all that, thankee. Where's my pig, again, you born villin?"

Poor Phelim, somewhat aroused by the fury of this attack, endeavored to collect his scattered senses and get out of so awkward a business as decently as he could, but the greater his anxiety to appease her indignation, the longer his explanations; the more abject his apologies, the higher Anty's wrath mounted, until at length, in the climax of a violent fit, she fell on the floor perfectly insensible.

The interest was now suddenly changed. The feelings of the party, which a moment before ran altogether in Phelim's favor, now set back in a returning tide of pity for the unfortunate Anty. All was anxiety and readiness to assist her, and no effort suggested for her recovery was left untried. Water was splashed in her face, feathers burnt under her nose, and attempts were even made at opening a vein by a skilful farrier who happened to be among the guests, but everything they managed to do for her relief proved for a time fruitless. While the crowd was still pressing round her, Phelim lay in a chair by the fireside, overcome with suspense and agitation, but after a lapse of some twenty or thirty minutes, suspecting from various exclamations which reached him from time to time from the group around his wife that there were hopes of her coming to, he roused himself up, and, beckoning Davy Dooley, an old companion of his, to the door, he addressed him with a look full of meaning and in a gentle undertone.

"Isn't this a purty business, Davy?"

"The quarest I ever seen in my born days," replied Davy; "she's coming to, I believe."

"We must have a docthor, Davy," rejoined the husband, eyeing his friend with the same intent look.

"Eyeh! plague on 'em for docthors; hadn't they her ondher their hands before?"

"They weren't to blame, any way, Davy, she gev 'em no fair play either for death or recovery. The porter tould me she wouldn't taste a dhrop of their medicines if they were to flay her alive for it."

"'Twas like her cuteness," observed Davy.

"Well, but listen to me," continued Phelim, and, stooping over, he muttered something into the ear of his friend.

"No better on Ireland ground," exclaimed Davy, slapping his hands in approval of the communication—"a kind, tender-hearted man, that never keeps poor craythurs long in pain. Oh! begannies, he's the real docthor."

"Away with you then, arragal," cried Phelim, "I hear her voice getten stronger; offer him any money. Run, aroo! Oh! mavrone!"

"Where's Davy going?" enquired the priest, as he saw him hastily leaving the door.

"Sending him off for the docthor I am, your reverence," answered Phelim, "for I'll never let her set foot in the hospital again. They neglected her there entirely, them rogues of nurse-tenders, and so I'll have her attended at home now, where she'll be made take every whole happerth the docthor orders for her."

"You're an honest and a sensible man, Phelim," observed the priest, "and I admire your behavior very much in all this strange business. I'm glad to find, too, you're not giving way to that foolish and wicked prejudice against the docthors, which has been so prevalent since the cholera commenced."

"I'd be sorry to undervalue the gentlemen, your reverence," returned Phelim; "sure what ud I do at all now without 'em, and poor Anty is so bad. I wondher is there any chance for her?"

"Very little, I fear, Phelim; it appears like an apoplectic attack."

"Is it anything of a lingering dizaze, your reverence?" continued the husband, in a faltering tone.

"Not at all," replied the priest, "it is generally a very sudden one."

"Ove! ove! the poor craythur! I believe she's a gone woman?" observed Phelim again enquiringly.

"Indeed I fear so," answered the priest, "unless the doctor can do something for her."

As he spoke, Davy came running in; the doctor followed at a more dignified pace. He had met with him by good fortune a few perches from the cabin, and immediately secured his attendance.

On examining the patient, the doctor shook his head despondingly.

"A bad case," he half muttered to himself—"a bad case; too far gone for medicine."

"Thry something, your honor," exclaimed Phelim earnestly, " she was as bad or worse before, and she recovered of it."

"Not so bad as she is now," replied the doctor despondingly. "However, I must do the best I can." And, writing a few words on a scrap of paper, he directed Phelim to take it to the dispensary, where he would get two powders, one of which he was to give his wife as soon as ever he returned, and the second at five o'clock, if she lived so long.

The people cast ominous looks at one another as he concluded, and the doctor and priest departed together. Davy, meantime, started off afresh for the medicine, and, as soon as he got back, took care to see it administered strictly as the doctor ordered. At ten minutes to five precisely Mrs. Anty O'Rourke took her departure for another world.

"She's dead!" whispered Davy, as he laid his hand on Phelim's shoulder, who was hanging drowsily over the dying embers on the hearthstone.

"Dead!" ejaculated Phelim, springing from his seat, as if half astounded at the news—"dead all out, is she, Davy?"

"Dead as a door-nail," returned Davy, "and 'tis just on the stroke of five!"

"Think 'o that, Davy," uttered Phelim faintly, and squeezed the hand of his friend.

"Faix, he was very exact in his business," rejoined his companion significantly. "Oh! mo leare! they're the dearies for doctors!"

"Say nothen, Davy—say nothen," observed the widower, "sure he did as he was taught at the univarsity. He was a kind man, so he was, and I'll not forget it to him."

Phelim was as good as his word; the week after the decease and funeral of poor Anty, he had the doctor invited to another wedding feast, at which the affair between himself and the blooming Maggy was concluded without any further interruption, and he was ever after his most intrepid defender, when any of the old women in his neighborhood ventured to tamper with his reputation. He was, indeed, often heard to declare, "he'd go to the world's end for the docthor—do anything for him—anything in life—but take his medicine."

HOME OF GERALD GRIFFIN.

THE RAVEN'S NEST.

> Her sire an earl—her dame of prince's blood,
> Bright as her hue, and Geraldine she hight.
> *Sonnet on the Countess of Lincoln.*

THE Fabii make not a more distinguished figure in the history of the ancient Roman, or the Medici in that of the modern Tuscan, State, than do the family of the Geraldines in the troubled tale of Ireland's miseries. Whenever the annals of the island shall be treated by a competent pen, they will not fail to be classed by all impartial judges amongst the most remarkable families in history. Their errors, and perhaps in many instances their crimes, were great; but their undaunted courage, their natural eloquence, their vigorous genius, and their hereditary open-heartedness are qualities which will be as certain of awakening admiration as their misfortunes of exciting pity. The story of the earls of Kildare constitutes such a piece of history as Sallust might be proud to write, and the genius of Plutarch would have delighted in the pithy sayings, heroic actions, and touches of character in which the annals of the family abound.

During the reign of the Tudors, a deadly feud had raged for many years between one of the earls of Kildare and a chieftain—a branch of the Geraldines, residing in a distant part of Munster. The Geraldine conceived his rights, as well as those of his country, invaded by the excessive rigor and even injustice with which Kildare (who was Lord Deputy) administered the government; and the earl was so highly incensed by what he called the turbulence and malice of his kinsman that he protested his determination not to lay down his arms until he had compelled him to make submission. " Albeit, he should have him as a common borderer, cut off by the knee." In this resolution he received the entire sanction of the English government, who seldom bore hard upon their deputies for an excess of zeal.

Outworn by continual defeats, and feeling deeply for the sufferings which his fruitless resistance had brought on his dependents, the gallant Geraldine testified at length his willingness to make terms, and offered to come in person to the metropolis in order to make a formal submission to the viceroy. He was not so despicable an enemy that even the haughty earl was not rejoiced at his proposal. He was received in Dublin with the highest ceremonies of respect and joy. The earl gave splendid entertainments, to which many, not only of the substantial citizens of the Pale, but of the native Irish chieftains, were invited; and the public places of the city for several days were thronged with a motley company of revellers, mingling with a confidence as enthusiastic as if they had not been for centuries as bitter enemies as oppression on the one, and hate and outrage on the other, side could make them.

On the second night after the arrival of the Geraldine in Dublin, a party of horse, bearing the marks of long travel in the jaded carriage both of the animals and their riders, appeared upon the borders of the Pale, which they had entered by one of the northern roads. They were commanded by a young man of an appearance at once delicate and martial. The peasants and humble artisans doffed their bonnets as they passed him on the road, and the sentinels saluted and suffered him to go unquestioned. As they approached the city, the sounds of rejoicing which were distinctly heard in the calm air awakened the attention and curiosity of the group.

"Ride on before, Thomas," said the young officer, addressing the page who bore his shield and helmet, "and ask what feasting is toward in the city."

The page spurred on his horse, and, after making enquiry at the booth of a rosy-looking vender of woollen stuffs, returned to say that the Geraldine was in the city.

"The Geraldine! what! hath he taken it, then?"

"Nay," cried the page, "if it were so, I question whether the Pale would be so orderly. He has come to make submission to the king."

"To make submission! The Geraldine make submission!" repeated the young man. "This seems a tale no less improbable than the other. Alas! such wisdom is rare in a Geraldine. The poor isle has suffered deeply to the pride of the Fitzgeralds. Poor, miserable land! Give me the helmet. We must not pass the Geraldine unarmed. How long is it now since this quarrel has begun?"

"Near sixteen years, my lord."

"Thou sayest aright. I remember to have heard of it on my mother's knee. I well remember how Kildare returned to the castle on an autumn evening, all black with dust and sweat, and how she flew to meet him, while I marked his rusty javelin, and puzzled my brains to comprehend its use. I am not so ignorant now. Ill-fated country! How many lives, dost thou compute, have already fallen in this feud?"

"It is thought, my lord, some seventy or eighty soldiers of the Pale, with about seventeen thousand of the Irish, in various encounters; besides, castles sacked, about fifty; towns and villages demolished to the number of nineteen; and private dwellings of the common sort, to the amount of some thousand roofs. The Pale, too, suffered loss of property; a woollen-draper's booth destroyed, besides some twenty cabins in the suburbs, laid in ashes."

"I pray you, Thomas, who might be your accountant?"

"My cousin Simmons, my lord, the city bailiff; your lordship may remember him?"

"Ay, I thought the computation had been made within the Pale. And what was the beginning of the strife?"

"The insolent Geraldine, my lord, had the audacity to turn a troop of the Lord Deputy's horse—"

"Out of a widow's house upon his holding, where they would have taken up their quarters for a fortnight in the scarce season. The insolent Geraldine! I long to see the disloyal knave. Know you if the lady Margaret, his daughter, be with him in the city?"

"My lord, the woollen-draper spoke not of her."

"I long to know them both. Report speaks loudly of her, no less than of the Geraldine himself. But here's the city. Good-morrow, masters! Thank you heartily, thank you all! O'Neil is quiet in the north, my masters! Long live the King! Huzza!"

The last sentences were spoken as the young warrior passed the city gate, where he was recognized and hailed by a holiday throng of the loyal citizens, with shouts of welcome that made the houses tremble around them. "Kildare for ever! Long live the King! Huzza!" was echoed from the city gate to the very drawbridge of the castle. The young nobleman, who had, amid all his gallantry and gaiety, a certain air that showed him to be above the reach of party spirit, received their congratulations with spirit and cheerfulness, but without losing a moment's time either to speak or hear. The streets as he passed presented an appearance singular and altogether new to his eye. The Irish green hanging-bonnet seemed as common as the cap of the Pale; kernes who spoke not a syllable of English were gaping at the splendor of the city; and citizens standing in their booths stared with no less amazement at the unshorn locks, wild looks, and woodland attire of their new allies. Passing on to St. Thomas's Court, where the Lord Deputy at that time transacted the business of the goverment, Sir Ulick Fitzgerald, the young knight whose course we have been following, alighted from his horse, and sent one of the officers to inform the Lord Deputy of his arrival. He was received by Kildare, in the king's chamber; and gave an account of the state of affairs in the North, where he had for some months past occupied the place of Lord Deputy himself.

"Thou art welcome, Ulick, from the North," said Kildare, reaching his hand to his son, who kissed it with reverence and affection. "And now, how hast thou done thy work, my lad?"

"Like a true soldier of the Pale, my lord," replied Sir Ulick. "I taught the rascals what it was to have to do with a friend of England. Thou and our royal master I am sure will love me for it."

"What said O'Neil at the conference?"

"O my good father! bid me not repeat his insolence. He said his lands and castles were in the keeping of his ancestors, before the very name of Ireland had sounded in the ear of a Plantagenet; that we used our power cruelly. (We, my lord, cruel! We! And I could aver, upon mine honor as a knight, we have not piked above twelve score of the rascal's Irishry, except on holidays, when we wanted exercise for the hobbelers. We cruel!) He complained also of trespass on the property of his dependents. (What! had we touched their lives, my lord?) He said all men were naturally free; that he derived his possessions from his progenitors, not from the royal gift; and many things beside, for which I would have set his head upon his castle's gate, but, as your lordship recommended clemency, I only hanged a cousin of his whom we caught in the camp after dark."

"Ulick," said the earl, "thou art a bantering villain; and I warn thee, as the Geraldines stand not overwell with Tudor, how thou sufferest such humors to appear, and before whom. It has been remarked, and by those who might not pierce thine irony, that thou art rather a favorer of these turbulent insurgents. Thou art overmild with the rebels."

"It is a mending fault, my lord," said Sir Ulick; "in the service of Tudor it will soon wear off."

"I tell thee," said the earl, "it is thought by many that thine heart is less with the people of the Pale than might become the descendant of those who have grown old in the royal confidence and favor, and transmitted both as a legacy to their posterity. Thou hast learned the language of these rascal Irishry."

"I confess my crime, my lord," replied the knight; "I know my country's tongue."

"Thou lovest their braggart poetry, and villanous antiquities; and art known to keep in thy train a scoundrel harper, who sings thee to sleep at night with tales of burnings and rapines, done by their outlaw chiefs upon the honest subjects of the crown."

"I confess my fault, my lord. I love sweet music."

"Thou hast even been heard at times," continued the earl, "to sing a verse of their howling ditties in the very precincts of the castle."

"Nay, nay, good father," cried the knight, "if you will impute my tuneful voice as treasonous, blame Nature and not me, for I had it of her. I confess myself guilty in that point also. There is a rebel melody in my voice that I cannot well be rid of."

"Ay, banter, banter, villain," said the Lord Deputy. "I tell thee, in a word, to treasure up what I have said, nor presume so far upon thy loyal deeds to excuse disloyal words. Princes are jealous of a smile. Thou must bear in mind that it is a conquered race thou hast to deal withal, and add a ferule to the rod of government."

"I shall learn, my lord, I hope, as aptly as my

predecessors. Ere I am twice Lord Deputy, I shall amend."

"And now," said the earl, "to thy chamber, and prepare to meet the Geraldine at evening. In a few days, he makes formal submission to the King, before the Lords of Council at Kilmainham Castle; and to-night he must here be entertained as becomes a Geraldine of his birth and breeding. Farewell!"

Spirited, lively, and yet filled with generous affections, the young knight was no less calculated to attract admiration in the hall than in the field. He was early at the festival, and met the Geraldine in his father's presence. The latter was a swart, stout-built man, with a brow that spoke of many dangers braved, and difficulties withstood, if not overcome. Unaccustomed to the polished raillery of a court, the stubborn chief was somewhat disposed at first to be offended with Sir Ulick, who addressed him in a tone of ironical reproof, and upbraided him in eloquent terms with the unreasonableness and selfishness of his withholding from the conquerors, possessions and immunities which he and his ancestors had now so long enjoyed, and which it was but fair that they should yield at least to those poorer adventurers whose services the Tudors had no other means of rewarding. "Did the Geraldine, or his confederates, consider what the Tudors owed those men, to whom they were indebted for the subjugation of so large a province? And would they be so ungenerous as to withhold from the sovereign the means of recompensing so palpable a public service, etc. ?"

The Geraldine, who did not understand irony, was observed two or three times to bend his brows upon the youth, but had his ire removed by some gracious turn in the harangue, introduced with timely promptitude. The hall of the festival was now thrown open; and Sir Ulick, standing at the farther end, summoned to his side his favorite attendant, Thomas Butler, from whom he enquired the names and quality of such guests as, in entering, had attracted his attention.

"I pray thee, gentle Thomas," said Sir Ulick, "what man is that with a cast in his right eye, and a coolun as thick and bushy as a fox's tail, and as carroty-red withal, and a sword that seems at deadly feud with its owner's calves?"

"Who? he, my lord? That is O'Carroll, who thrashed MacMorrough at the Boyne, for burning his cousin's castle and piking his children in the bog."

"And who is she who hangs upon his arm?"

"His daughter Nell, my lord, who ate the tip of MacMorrough's liver, with a flagon of wine, for dinner, on the day after the battle."

"Sweet creature! And that round, short, flashy, merry little man, with his chain?"

"That is the Mayor, my lord."

"And the lofty lady who comes after, like a grenadier behind a drummer?"

"The lady-mayoress, my lord, who took her husband upon her shoulders, and ran off with him to the city, when he would fain have fought single-handed with an enormous O'Toole, who set upon them as they were taking a morning walk to Cullenswood."

"Her stature stood him in good stead. And who are they who follow close behind?"

"Burke of Clanricard, and O'Moore, who hanged and quartered the four widows in Offally for speaking against the cosherings on the poor."

"And the ladies?"

"Their wives and daughters, who were by at the quartering."

"A goodly company. But, hush!"

"What is it, my lord, that you would ask?"

"Hush! hush! Canst thou tell me, Thomas, what lady is that in yellow, as far beyond the rest in beauty of person as in the graceful simplicity of her attire?"

"That, my lord," said the attendant, "is your cousin, Margaret Fitzgerald, and the only daughter of the Geraldine."

"Fame, that exaggerates all portraitures, fell short in hers. My cousin Margaret! Away, good Thomas, I care not to learn more."

Approaching the circle, of which the fair Geraldine formed a chief attraction, Sir Ulick was introduced to his young relative. The evening passed happily away in her society; and before many days they were better friends than, perhaps, themselves suspected, or the parents of either could have readily approved. Both freely communicated their thoughts and wishes on the condition of their families and country. Both mourned the divided interests that distracted the latter, and the wretched jealousies which seemed destined to keep the well-wishers of the island for ever disunited in themselves, and, therefore, utterly incapable of promoting her advantage. Such themes as these formed the subject of conversation one evening, while the dance went gaily forward, and the hall of the banquet seemed more than usually thronged with brilliant dresses.

"Now, at least, cousin Margaret," said Sir Ulick, in a gentle voice, "we may promise ourselves better times. Our fathers seem better agreed at every interview; and so nearly do their tempers harmonize that I am sure it needed but an earlier intimacy to render them as fervent friends as they have been strenuous—Hark! What is that noise?"

While he spoke, the sounds of mirth were interrupted in a startling manner by loud and angry voices at the end of the hall which was occupied by the Lord Deputy and other chieftains of every party. Before time was given for question or reply, the wordy clamor was exchanged for the clash of weapons, and in an instant the scene of merriment was changed to a spectacle of horror and affright. The music ceased, the dance was broken up, and the women shrieked; while of the men, some joined the combatants, whom others thought to separate by flinging cloaks, scarfs, caps, and various articles of dress across the glancing weapons. A truce was thus enforced; and Sir Ulick learned with indignation that the hot-blooded Geraldine had struck his father. The news soon spread into the streets, where a strife began that was not so easily to be appeased. The followers of the Geraldine, whose hearts were never with the treaty of submission, seemed glad of the occasion given to break it off. They fell upon the citizens, who were not slow in flying to their weapons, and a scene of tumult ensued which made the streets re-echo from the riverside to the hills. The Geraldines were driven from the city, not without loss, and their chieftain found himself on horseback without the walls, and further from the royal countenance than ever. He was with difficulty able to rescue his daughter, who, on the first sound of strife, had immediately placed herself by his side.

The war now recommenced with redoubled fury. The Lord Deputy received orders from London to have the Geraldine taken, dead or alive, and set his head, according to the fashion of those times, upon the castle gate. In obedience to these instructions, which needed not the concurrence of his own hearty good-will, Kildare marched an army to the south, and, after several engagements, laid siege to Geraldine in one of his strongest castles. The ruins still occupy a solitary crag, surrounded by a rushy marsh, at a little distance from New Auburn. The place was naturally strong; and the desperation of the besieged made it impregnable. After several fruitless efforts, attended by severe loss to the assailants, to possess themselves of the castle by storm, it was placed in a state of blockade, and the Lord Deputy, encamping in the neighborhood, left famine to complete the work which his arms had failed to accomplish.

With different feelings, Sir Ulick, who held a subordinate command in the army of his father, beheld the days run by, which were to end in the surrender, or (as was more probable, from the well-known character of the Geraldine) in the destruction and death of the besieged. Two months rolled on, and there appeared no symptom on the part of the latter that indicated a desire to come to terms. Such, likewise, was the fidelity with which those feudal chiefs were served by their followers, that not a single deserter escaped from the castle to reveal the real state of its defenders. They appeared upon the battlement as hearty and as well accoutred as on the first day of the blockade.

Meantime there was no lack of spirit in the castle. The storehouse was well supplied for a blockade of many months, and the Geraldine depended much on a letter he had sent beneath the wings of a carrier-pigeon to a distant part of Desmond. The days passed merrily between watching and amusement, and the frequent sounds of mirth and dancing from within showed that the besieged where thinking of something else besides giving up the fortress.

One evening, Margaret, retiring to her chamber, gave orders to her woman to attend her. The latter obeyed, and was employed in assisting her lady to undress, when the following conversation passed between them:

"You have not since discovered by whom the letter was left in the eastern bolt-hole?"

The woman answered in the negative.

"Take this," said Margaret, handing the maid a small wooden tablet, as white as snow, except where it was marked by her own neat characters—"take this, and lay it exactly where the former was deposited. Yet stay! Let me compare the notes again, to be sure that I have worded mine answer aright: 'Sweet Margaret: Be persuaded by one who loves thy welfare. Let thy sweet voice urge the Geraldine to give up the fortress which he must yield perforce ere long, and with sorer loss perchance than that of life and property. Thy friendly enemy, unknown.' Well said, my friendly enemy, not quite, perhaps, so unknown as thou esteemest. Now for mine answer: 'Kind friendly enemy: Thine eloquences will be much better spent on Kildare, in urging him to raise the siege, than my poor accents on the stubborn Geraldine. Wherefore I commend thee to thy task, and warn to beware of my kinsmen's bills, which, how shrewdly they can bite, none ought to know better than the Lord Deputy and his followers. Thy thankful foe."

The tablet was laid on the window, and disappeared in the course of the night. On that which followed, while Margaret and her maid were occupied, as before, in preparing for rest, a noise at the window aroused the attention of the mistress, and struck the woman mute with terror. Dismissing the latter into the sleeping-chamber, which lay adjacent, and carefully shutting the door, the daughter of the Geraldine advanced to the window, and unbarred the curtained lattice. A brilliant moon revealed the lake, in the midst of which the castle rose upon the summit of a rock, the guarded causeway by which it was connected with the shore, the distant camp of Kildare, and the tranquil woods and hills extending far around. Beneath her, on the rock, appeared a figure, the identity of which she could not for an instant mistake; but how it came thither, to what intent, and wherefore undetected, was more than she had skill to penetrate. Perhaps, like a second Leander, he had braved the waves with no other oar than his own vigorous limbs. But the stern of a little currach, peeping from beneath the overhanging rock, gave intimation that Sir Ulick (for he indeed it was) knew a trick worth two of Leander's. Waving his hand to Margaret, he ascended the formidable crag which still separated him from the window of her apartment, and came even within whispering distance. He did but come to be sure that she at least was not in want of food. It so happened that this side of the rock alone was unguarded, being supposed impregnable from the steepness of its ascent, as well as of that of the opposing shore. Sir Ulick, however, gliding under the shadow of the distant cliff, and only venturing to dart for the isle when the sky was darkest, had already visited it for three successive nights, and seemed, at every new venture, more secure of his secret. The alarm of Margaret, however, was excessive. The discovery of an intercourse would be certain death to one or both ; for the Geraldine, in a case of treason, whether real or apparent, would not spare his nearest blood. The same, as Sir Ulick was himself aware, was true of the Lord Deputy. Made bold, however, by impunity, he quieted the lady's fears, and without much difficulty communicated to her mind the security of his own. His visits were continued for a week without interruption; after which period, the fair Geraldine observed with perplexity and uneasiness that they terminated abruptly, nor did she for an equal space of time see or hear anything that could account for this sudden disappearance of her accomplished friend.

One night, as she sat in her window, looking out with the keenest anxiety for the little wicker skiff, she observed, with a thrill of eagerness and delight, some dark object gliding close beneath the cliffs upon the opposite shore. The unclouded brightness of the moon, however, prevented the approach of the boat; and her suspense had reached a painful height, before the sky grew dark. At length a friendly cloud extended its veil beneath the face of the unwelcome satellite; and in a few minutes the plash of oars, scarce louder than the ripple of the wavelets against the rock, gave token to the watchful ear of Margaret of the arrival of the long-expected knight. A figure ascends the rock; the lattice is unbarred; there is sufficient light to peruse the form and features of the stranger. It is not Sir Ulick, but Thomas Butler, the *fidus Achates* and only confidant of the youthful knight.

"What, Thomas, is it thou? Where is thy lord?"

"Ah! lady, it is all over with Sir Ulick!"

"How sayest thou?"

"He is taken, lady, by the Lord Deputy's servants, and stands condemned in the article of treason."

These dreadful tidings, acting on spirits already depressed by a sudden disappointment, proved too much for Margaret's strength, and she fainted away in the window. On reviving, she obtained from Thomas a full detail of the circumstances which had occurred to Sir Ulick since his last appearance at the island, and the cause in which they had their origin.

About a week before, the Lord Deputy was sitting at evening in his tent, when a scout arrived to solicit a private audience. It was granted;

and the man averred that he had discovered the existence of a treasonable communication between the inhabitants of the island and the shore. In his indignation at this announcement, Kildare made a vow that the wretch, whoever he was, should be cast alive into the Raven's Nest; and appointed a party to watch on the following night on the shore beside the cliffs, for the return of the traitor from the rock. Having given the men strict injunctions to bring the villain bound before him the instant he should be apprehended, he ordered a torch to be lighted in his tent, and remained up to await the issue.

Towards morning, footsteps were heard approaching the entrance of the tent. The sentinel challenged, and admitted the party. The astonishment of Kildare may be conceived, when, in the fettered and detected traitor, against whom he had been fostering his liveliest wrath, he beheld his gallant son, the gay and heroic Ulick! The latter did not deny that he had made several nightly visits to the island; but denied with scorn the imputation of treasonable designs, although he refused to give any account of what his real motives were. After long endeavoring, no less by menace than entreaty, to induce him to reveal the truth, the Lord Deputy addressed him with a kindness which affected him more than his severity.

"I believe thee, Ulick," he said; "I am sure thou art no traitor. Nevertheless, thy father must not be thy judge. Go plead thy cause before the Lords of Council, and see if they will yield thee as ready a credit. I fear thou wilt find it otherwise; but thou hast thyself to blame."

A court was formed in the course of a few days consisting of Kildare himself, as resident, and a few of the Council, who were summoned for the purpose. The facts proved before them were those already stated; and Sir Ulick persisted in maintaining the same silence with respect to his designs or motives as he had done before his father. It seemed impossible, under such circumstances, to acquit him; and, having received the verdict of the court, the Lord Deputy gave orders for the fulfilment of his dreadful vow.

On the night after his sentence, his attendant, Thomas Butler, obtained permission to visit him in his dungeon; and received a hint from Kildare, as he granted it, that he would not fare the worse for drawing his master's secret from him. Ulick, however, was inflexible. Fearing the danger to Margaret's life, no less than to her reputation, he maintained his resolution of suffering the sentence to be executed, without further question. "The Lords of Council," he said, "were as well aware of his services to the king's government as he could make them; and, if those services were not sufficient to procure him credit in so slight a matter, he would take no further pains to earn it."

Disappointed and alarmed, on the eve of the morning appointed for the execution, Thomas

Butler, at the hazard of his life, determined to seek the lady Margaret herself, and acquaint her with what had occurred. The daughter of Geraldine did not hesitate long about the course she should pursue. Wrapping a man's cloak around her figure, with the hood (for in those days, fair reader, the gentlemen wore hoods) over her head, she descended from the window, and succeeded in reaching the boat. A few minutes' rapid rowing brought them to the shore. It was already within an hour of dawn, and the sentence was to be completed before sunrise. Having made fast the currach in a secret place, they proceeded amongst crag and copse in the direction of the Raven's Nest. The dismal chasm was screened by a group of alder and brushwood, which concealed it from the view until the passenger approached its very brink. As they came within view of the place, the sight of gleaming spears and yellow uniforms amongst the trees made the heart of Margaret sink with apprehension.

"Run on before, good Thomas!" she exclaimed; "delay their horrid purpose but a moment. Say one approaches who can give information of the whole."

The fetters, designed no more to be unbound, were already fastened on the wrists and ankles of the young soldier when his servant arrived, scarce able to speak for weariness, to stay the execution. He had discovered, he said, the whole conspiracy, and there was a witness coming on who could reveal the object and the motive of the traitors, for there were more than one. At the same instant, Margaret appeared, close wrapt in her cloak, to confirm the statement of Butler. At the request of the latter, the execution was delayed while a courier was despatched to the Lord Deputy with intelligence of the interruption that had taken place. In a few minutes he returned, bringing a summons to the whole party to appear before the Lords of Council. They complied without delay, none being more perplexed than Sir Ulick himself at the meaning of this strange announcement.

On arriving in the camp, the unknown informant entreated to be heard in private by the Council. The request was granted; and Margaret, still closely veiled, was conducted to the hall in which the judge sat. On being commanded to uncover her head, she replied:

"My lords, I trust the tale I have to tell may not require that I should make known the person of the teller. My Lord Deputy, to you the drift of my story must have the nearest concern. When you bade the Geraldine to your court of Dublin, he was accompanied by an only daughter, Margaret, whom your son Ulick saw and loved. He was not without confessing his affection, and I am well assured that it was not unanswered. On the very evening, my Lord Deputy, before that most unhappy affray which led to your disunion, and to the dissolution of our—of Sir Ulick's hopes, a mutual avowal had been made, and a mutual pledge of faith (modestly, my lords) exchanged, always under the favor of our—of the noble parents of the twain. My Lords, I have it under proof that the visits of Sir Ulick were made to the Lady Margaret, that to no other individual of the castle were they known, and that no weightier converse ever passed between them than such silly thoughts of youthful affection as may not be repeated before grave and reverend ears like those to which I speak."

"And what may be thy proof, stranger?" said the Lord Deputy, with a tenderness of voice which showed the anxiety her tale excited in his mind.

"The word of Margaret Fitzgerald," replied the witness, as she dropped the mantle from her shoulders.

The apparition of the Geraldine's daughter in the council-chamber gave a wonderful turn to the proceedings. Kildare was the first to speak. He arose from his seat, and, approaching the spot where the spirited young maiden stood, took her hand with kindness and affection.

"In truth, sweet kinswoman," he said, "thou hast staked a sufficient testimony. And to be sure that it be so with all, as it be with Kildare, I promise thee to back it with my sword; and it shall go hard but thy honest-hearted speech shall save the Geraldine, his lands and towers to boot. My lords, I think I see by your countenances, that you deem the lady's tale a truth. Then summon Ulick hither, and let a flag of truce be sent to the Geraldine, to let him know that his child is in safekeeping. The Raven's Nest has taught me what he feels."

The chroniclers of New Auburn conclude their story by relating that the promise of the Lord Deputy was fulfilled; that the affection of the heroic pair received the sanction of their parents; and that, whenever afterwards in their wedded life a cloud seemed gathering at their castle hearth, the recollection of the Raven's Nest was certain to bring sunshine to the hearts of both.

SIR DOWLING O'HARTIGAN.

"Lochiel, Lochiel, beware of the day
When the lowlands shall meet thee in battle array,
For the field of the dead rushes red on my sight,
And the clans of Culloden are scattered in flight."
Lochiel's Warning.

AMONG the bravest of the followers of the celebrated Prince Murrough O'Brien, whose valor and devotion are not forgotten on his native soil, was a knight named Sir Dowling O'Hartigan, whose character, like that of all the brighter ornaments of Irish chivalry, was a mixture of northern honor, of oriental fervor and devotion, and of the deepest and sincerest religious feeling. In reading the accounts of other days, the pride of modern times takes umbrage at the profound humility which is traced out amid the glorious workings of old heroic zeal, and the sordid levity of our commercial temperament is ready to scoff at the deeply seated and unselfish devotion which gave to the chivalry of the middle ages more than half its grandeur. In those days, the heart of mankind was still profoundly impressed with those great truths which, by keeping continually before the mind the transitory nature of all earthly things, are best calculated to detach it from the baser interests, to elevate its desires, and enlarge its views. But what, gentlemen, has a character of the middle ages to do with my story? And I feel conscious indeed of a somewhat ponderous commencement for a mere fairy tale; for such, after all, is the legend of Sir Dowling O'Hartigan.

Everybody who knows anything of Irish history must have heard of Brian Boru. This we assume as a postulate, without which we can proceed no further. It is equally notorious that in the course of his reign he met with no little annoyance from those unruly neighbors called the Danes, who had now for more than three centuries exercised a barbarous tyranny over the original inhabitants of the isle; sometimes carrying it with a high hand, and sometimes suffering severely in the efforts made by the latter to rid themselves of their unfeeling assailants. Amongst the most distinguished of those native warriors who endeavored to aid the Ard-Righ, or Archking Brian in his battles against the lawless Scandinavian, was the knight whose name I have adopted as the title of my legend. None wielded the *lann* or the battle-axe with a more fatal skill; none stood more firm in the fight; and none appeared so indifferent to the reputation which his deeds had won him, as Sir Dowling O'Hartigan. He fought not for fame, nor power, nor wealth, nor for any selfish end, but purely for his duty—duty to his prince, to his country, and to heaven! Thus despising death, not from animal temperament alone, or the greediness of ambition, but on the principles of right reason, his valor was as constant and steadfast as it was heroic.

It was a few days before the famous battle of Clontarf, in which the venerable monarch gave his enemies a final overthrow, and lost his own life, that Prince Murrough received the orders of the Ard-Righ to be present, with all the force he could muster, at the royal camp within a stated time. At the moment when the royal order arrived, Sir Dowling O'Hartigan was seated at the table of the prince. He immediately rose, and requested permission to return to his own home, in order to muster all the force he could command, and to bid adieu to his wife and family; for it was foreseen that many a warrior would leave home for the approaching contest who might never return. The prince gave him permission to depart, after requesting him to be punctual as to the day of joining them with his force.

Night had fallen before Sir Dowling reached the dreary wilds of Burrin, in which his house was situated. The sky was dark and stormy, and the knight commanded his footboy, or daltin (whose duty it ordinarily was to run by his master's side, holding the stirrup), to mount on his crupper, and to keep his seat as well as he might behind him. Thus doubly freighted, it was matter of wonder to master and squire with how much life and vigor the little hobby continued its journey.

It was interrupted, however, in rather a singular manner. At a gloomy turn in the road the hobby stopped with so much suddenness, that the two riders, were it not for Sir Dowling's superior horsemanship, would, by the impetus of their own motion, have continued their journey homeward in the air for at least a yard or two beyond the hobby's head. Still as a stone statue stood the animal, seeming neither to hear the voice of the knight, nor to feel the still more cogent remonstrances which were applied with profusion both to rib and flank.

"You might as well let him alone, Sir Dowling," said the daltin.

"Why do you think so, Duach?"

"Because Ireland wouldn't make her stir now. There's something near us, masther, that's not good."

"Foolish being!" said the knight; "descend and see what is the matter."

"Me! me get down!" exclaimed Duach; "I had rather face a whole *cath* of the Loch-Lannoch.* Masther, asthore, get down yourself, since you ar'n't in dread of them."

Sir Dowling complied, compassionating the weakness of his attendant, and giving the reins to the awe-struck daltin. Advancing a few paces, he beheld, by the faint light which the stormy sky afforded, the figure of a woman in a sitting posture on the right-hand side of the road, with the hood

* A name given to the Northern pirates

of her cloak turned over her head, and her arms clasped in an attitude of profound affliction.

"Who's there?" exclaimed Sir Dowling in a peremptory tone.

There was no reply.

"Speak!" said the knight. "If you be in sorrow, tell your sorrow; if not, retire and let my hobby pass the road."

Still neither sound nor motion on the part of the hooded figure gave sign of attention or of compliance, and it was not until the knight added menace to his words that he was able to procure an answer.

"You're like the rest of the world," said the woman, slowly revealing in the faint light her worn and wrinkled features, "that never knows its friends."

"Is that Nora?" asked Sir Dowling, in astonishment.

"It is. Ah! Sir Dowling, a'ra gal, I'm in trouble."

"Upon what account, Nora?" asked the knight.

"I'll tell you, then. Do you know that lake you used to be so fond of fishing in when you used to go to visit your relations in the county Galway?"

"Do you mean Lough Ennel?"

"The very same."

"I do, indeed," replied the knight. "Many a pleasant day and moonlight night I spent upon the banks or on its waters. It was a fine lake for fish."

"Well, a'ra gal, you'll never spend another there, except you go to the county Westmeath for it."

"To the county Westmeath!" exclaimed Sir Dowling, in astonishment.

"To the county Westmeath, achree. 'Tis there Lough Ennel is now, and there it will remain, I'm very much in dread."

"Nonsense!" said the knight; "did I not see it with my own eyes the last time I was in Galway, and didn't I send the prince a basket of the finest trout he ever tasted, that I took in the very middle of it with my own hands? What nonsense!" said the knight. "How could it be in the county Westmeath?"

"Oh! then, through nothing in the world, only my folly," said the old woman, "that couldn't but go lend it to an old neighbor of mine, a decent woman, as I thought her, that lives in those parts, and now she won't return it."

"Well, Nora," said Sir Dowling, "I'm surprised at you. Is it possible? A woman of your sense to go lend such a lake as that! And sure you ought to know them Leinster people before now, how hard it is to get anything from them. There's hardly an Ard-Righ we had this length of time but was heart-broken with them, trying to get their tribute. I thought you'd have had more sense, Nora."

"Oh! then," said the old woman, "who'd ever think that she'd serve me such a trick? Last summer twelvemonth, she sent over to me her compliments, and she'd be obliged to me for the loan of a lake for a little while—Westmeath being an inland place, where it was very hard to get fish, and she knew that I couldn't miss it much, as Connaught was bordering upon the sea-coast—and that she'd return it faithfully on the first Monday of the month. Well, I didn't like to refuse her, for she has greater power than I have, and might do me some mischief; so I took Lough Ennel, and rolled it up in an apron, and sent it off to her, with my compliments, and that I was happy to have it in my power to accommdate her. She kept the lake; and the first Monday of the month came, and the first Monday after, and she never sent it home, and little thanks she gave me when I sent for it, neither. I waited as long as I had patience to wait, but not a sight of Lough Ennel did I see from that day to this."

"And you are going to look after it now?" said Sir Dowling.

"I'm going now to look after it," replied the witch; "but indeed I'm afraid it is little good for me. This is my thanks for being obliging."

I may remark that old Nora was right in her apprehensions, as may be ascertained by reference to Shaw Mason's Topography, or the Collectanea; for there lies Lough Ennel to this day in the middle of the county Westmeath, whose inhabitants continue to enjoy the fruits, or rather the fishes, of the old woman's dishonesty, while the poor Galway mountaineer stands often supperless upon the heights of Farmoyle, and overlooks the wide and barren flat where once Lough Ennel basked and tumbled in the sun. It is true that the time of possession specified in the Statute of Limitations has long since expired: but there are points in this case which render it a peculiar one, and I have no doubt that a Chancery injunction might readily be obtained to prevent any intermeddling with the fish until the case should have been fairly argued in equity, and finally adjudged.

"But this," continued old Nora, "is not the only nor the principal cause of my trouble. I had rather all the lakes in Galway were in Westmeath than to hear what I heard to-night, and to know what I know."

"What did you hear?" enquired Sir Dowling.

"I heard thousands of Irish wives and mothers lamenting over the slain and wounded in the battle of Clontarf."

"You heard them lamenting," said the knight, "for a calamity which did not yet take place."

"But it is certain," said the woman. "When the oak shall be levelled by the storm, what will become of the underwood? You know not what this means now, but you will if you should live another week."

"Explain yourself plainly," said Sir Dowling. "Whatever be the issue, it is better I should be prepared for it. I am to join the standard of Prince Murrough at the battle, and I am now returning to take leave of my family and friends."

The woman remained silent for some moments, and then suddenly said:

"Return and collect your force, and meet me here to-morrow evening an hour before midnight —alone—and be sure you do not fail."

With these words she disappeared, and Sir Dowling O'Hartigan, in much perplexity, continued his journey. He arrived at his castle, arranged his temporal affairs, and made the necessary preparation becoming one who was about to encounter imminent danger. On the following day, having bid adieu to those amongst his friends who were to remain behind, he set forward at the head of a strong party, horse and foot, with whom he encamped after nightfall within a short distance of the place of meeting.

About an hour before midnight, Sir Dowling, throwing his war-cloak around him, advanced to the rendezvous, where he found old Nora already expecting him, with an air of deeper anxiety and apprehension than she had shown the night before.

"Are you resolved, Sir Dowling," she said, "to join the standard of O'Brien at Clontarf?"

"Is my prince to be there," said Sir Dowling, "and shall I not be there?'

" Beware !"

" Of what?"

"I passed the field last evening, and the color of death was upon the sod."

" The Men of the Cold Hills, mother, shall make that vision good."

"Beware!" said the old woman again, elevating her finger with a warning look. "Death reaps his harvest without regard to the equality of the grain—the weed and the wheat-ear together fall beneath his sickle. He is a blast that blows its poison indiscriminately upon all that is fair and all that is hideous on the earth—the tender flowcret of the spring that faints, and shrinks, and fades beneath a wind too chill; and the marble rock that accumulates its bulk for ages, and, when its date is reached, rots atom after atom into the embrace of the grim destroyer, are both alike his victims. The ape that gibbers on the bough, and the sage that meditates beneath the shade—the coward that skulks behind a fence, and the warrior that braves him in the daylight—the eagle in the plains of air, and the wren upon the summer spray—the lion in the bosom of the woods, and the hare that glides in the moonlight—the leviathan with the caves of the ocean, and the starfish spangling the wave upon its surface; nay, even the very elements that feed those million shades and rich varieties of life, are all subjected to, and must at some time feel, his power. In the deepest shades, in the heart of the densest substances, there is no escaping that pervading principle of ruin. His wings overshadow the universe, and his breath penetrates to the centre. The tears of the forlorn and the bereaved, the sigh of the widow and orphan, move him not, he has no capability of relenting; to him the Loch

Lannoch and the children of the Dal Gais are alike."

"Whatever be my fate," said Sir Dowling, "I will never leave a tarnished reputation after me. The war-cry of the Strong Hand * shall never find Sir Dowling slow to second it. But tell me if those fatal indications which look on you from the future point directly at my life, or at that of my prince?"

"I can only answer for your own," said the hag; "and I cannot even guess at your fate without your own assistance. Go to the top of yonder hill, and tell me what you see."

Sir Dowling O'Hartigan obeyed, and in a short time returned to the place where he had left the old woman.

"I have seen," said he, "a woman clothed in saffron, and with golden ornaments upon her neck and shoulders."

"The sign is fatal," said the old woman, shaking her head; "go again, and go to the other side of the hill."

Again he went, and again he came.

"I have seen," said he, "a woman clothed in white, and wearing silver ornaments."

"More fatal yet," exclaimed the hag, with a still more ominous shake of the head; "go yet once more, and take the western side of the ascent."

* He alludes to the motto of the O'Briens—"*Lamh Laidler a bo*," or, "The Strong Hand for ever!"

A third time Sir Dowling went, and a third time did Sir Dowling O'Hartigan return.

"I have seen," said he, "a woman clothed in black, and wearing no ornament whatever."

"It is completed then," said the woman; "and your fate, if you should join the fight at Clontarf, is fixed beyond all doubt. You die upon the field."

"I know not how that may be," answered the knight, "but I am sure I shall be with my prince, wherever he is."

"Abstain from the field, Sir Dowling," said the woman, looking on him with much earnestness. "I was present when you received in your boyhood the order of knighthood. The wicker shield was hung up in the centre of the field, and you were provided with your lance. I saw you shiver shaft after shaft from blade to hilt, while the plains rang with acclamations, and the ancient warriors tossed their beards in wonder at the vigor of so young an arm. From that day to this I ever loved your welfare, and I pray you now consult it by remaining from the field of Clontarf."

Sir Dowling, however, would by no means listen to her dishonorable though friendly solicitations. He became so impatient of those unworthy suggestions that he turned his back at length, and was about to depart in considerable wrath.

"Stay, Sir Dowling!" exclaimed the witch; "although I cannot change the nature of the prophecy, I will do my utmost to prolong your life. Take this cloak—it has the power of rendering those who wear it invisible to the eyes of others. If it cannot avert the fate that threatens you, it may at least retard the term of its approach. But above all things, I warn you let nothing ever induce you to resign the cloak until the fight is at an end; if you do, you are lost."

So saying, and flinging the filead upon him, she hobbled off, without waiting for thanks, and took the way towards Westmeath to recover her lost lake, and to harangue the borrower about her want of punctuality.

"It might be pardoned," she muttered to herself, as she moved along, "if there were no other lake in the county Westmeath but the one, although even then the best that could be said of them is that they came by it shabbily enough; but when they have Lough Iron, and Lough Owhel, and Lough Deveragh, and Lough Lane, and a good piece of Lough Ree!—it is scandalous and unneighborly, and I will not submit to it. I'm sure it is we that ought to be borrowing lakes out of Westmeath, and not they out of Galway."

Sir Dowling, in the meantime, returned. Desirous to ascertain whether old Nora's cloak did in reality possess the wonderful virtue which she ascribed to it, he paused at a little distance from the first sentinels, and fastened it about his neck. To his astonishment, he passed all the guards successively, without receiving a single challenge, and reached his own quarters unobserved. Here he found Duach lying half asleep by the watch-fire, which had been lighted for Sir Dowling's use. Knowing his daltin to be one of those persons who are sensible of scarcely any fear, except that which is referred to a supernatural object, he determined to put the power of the cloak to a still surer test.

"Duach!" exclaimed Sir Dowling—"Duach, awake!"

The daltin started up, and gazed around.

"Duach!" continued the knight, "here, take my cloak and *lann*, and watch while I lie down and take a few hours' sleep."

"Mercy on me!" exclaimed the daltin, trembling.

"Do you hear me, sirrah? Have you lost your wits?"

"'Tis the master's voice!" said Duach, rubbing his eyes, and looking around on all sides; "but where in the earthly universe is he?"

"Where am I, rogue? Do you not see me standing close to you?"

"Well," cried Duach, "I never was in trouble till now!"

At these words, Sir Dowling struck him pretty smartly over the shoulders with his sheathed sword.

"If you do not see me, you shall feel me, sirrah," said the knight.

At this unexpected assault, Duach, with a yell

that might have been heard across the Shannon, turned short, and would have fled the camp, had not Sir Dowling seized him by the skirt of his saffron coat, and held him firm. At the same time he undid the tie which made the mantle fast about his own neck, and stood visibly before the astonished daltin.

"Well!" exclaimed the latter, " I often heard of wonders, but if this doesn't flog all Munster, it's no matter. Where in Europe were you, master? Or where do you come from? Or is it to drop out of the sky you did, or to rise out of the ground, or what?"

Nothing could exceed the amazement with which Duach heard his master relate the interview which he had with the old woman, and the extraordinary virtue of the cloak which she had lent him.

"I'll tell you what it is, Sir Dowling," said the daltin, " I don't count it sufficient trial that the guards and myself couldn't see you, for people have often thick sight, and especially at night, that way; but wait till morning, and the first sheiling we pass where we'll see any pigs, you can put it on. They say pigs can see the very wind itself, so, if they don't see you, you may depend your life upon the cloak."

Sir Dowling did not appear to think this test essential to his purpose, and, on the following morning, he set forward, accompanied by his force, to join the standard of the Ard-Righ. That monarch and his son, to whom he had deputed the command of the royal army on this occasion, were already on the field of battle when Sir Dowling O'Hartigan arrived. Many circumstances combine to give a strong and lasting interest to this brilliant day in Ireland's clouded story. King Brian, who was seventy-six years of age when he ascended the throne, had, in the course of twelve years ensuing, raised the condition of the island to a state of almost unexampled prosperity, and acquired for himself the character of a saint, a hero, and a sage. His reign bears a closer resemblance to that of the French St. Louis, or the English Alfred, than that of any other Irish monarch whom we can call to mind. Devoted himself to the cultivation of letters and the practice of religion, he encouraged both by every means which the prerogative of his station could afford. He founded many churches, and added his influence to that of the clergy in promoting a love of piety and virtue. He conciliated the friendship of the independent princes throughout the island by confirming their ancient privileges, and aiding them in the enforcement of their authority. The success with which his efforts to establish national peace and harmony were attended has been celebrated in a legend with which all are familiar who have read the Irish melodies; and, whatever be the truth of the story, it bears testimony at least to the reputation of the monarch with his subjects and their prosperity. At the close of his reign, however, he had the affliction to combat with internal treachery and foreign invasion. The annalists tell us that Malmorda, the Righ, or inferior monarch of Leinster, aided by twelve thousand Danes, whom he had called in to aid him in his rebellious enterprise, arose in arms against his sovereign. The aged monarch was prompt in taking the field against the traitor and his foreign allies, nor were his subjects slow to second him. The field, when Sir Dowling entered it, presented a striking and animated spectacle. The Irish archers and slingers, with their small Scythian bows and krantabals; the gallow-glach heavily armed, with genu and battle-axe; and the shoals of kerne, distinguished by the hanging-cap, the ready skene at the girdle, and javelin in the hand, were arrayed between the royal tents and the rebel force. Amongst these last the island costume was shamefully mingled with the chain armor of the invaders, and the Irish poll-axe advanced in the same cause with the ponderous Northern sparthe, which had so often drunk the blood of the helpless and unresisting in their towns and villages. Mindful of old Nora's warning, Sir Dowling O'Hartigan committed his men to the care of an inferior officer, and, fastening the cloak around his neck, passed, unobserved, to that part of the field where Prince Murrough O'Brien was in the act of persuading his age-stricken parent, the venerable Priam of the day, to retire from a scene in which he could no longer afford assistance, and to await in his tent the issue of the combat. The monarch at length complied, and, bidding an affectionate farewell to his children of two generations, who were about to risk all for his crown and people, slowly retired from the field; and at the same instant Sir Dowling had the mortification to hear the prince give utterance to an exclamation of disappointment and surprise at his non-appearance.

"It is the first time," said Prince Murrough, "that I ever knew Sir Dowling O'Hartigan untrue to his engagement."

The knight had much difficulty in restraining himself from flinging away the cloak, and removing the uneasiness of his prince, but the warning of Nora, and the fear that in the eagerness to manifest his loyalty he might lose the power of manifesting it in a more effectual way, enabled him to control his inclinations.

The battle commenced, and Sir Dowling, taking his position near the prince, wrought prodigies of valor in his defence. The prince and his immediate attendants beheld with astonishment Dane after Dane, and traitor after traitor, fall mortally wounded to the ground, and yet none could say by whose weapon the blow was struck. More than once, the prince, as if his own strength were so gigantic that the mere intention of a blow on his part were more destructive than the practical exertions of another, saw his enemies fall prostrate at his feet when he had but lifted his sword into the air above them. At length a Nordman of prodigious size came bearing down upon the prince, hewing all to pieces before him, and breaking the royal ranks with the strength of a rhinoceros. At the very instant when he had arrived within a sword's length of Murrough O'Brien, and while the latter was in the act of lifting his shield in order to resist his onset, to the astonishment of all, and doubtless to his own, the head of the gigantic Nordman rolled upon the grass. The prince started back amazed.

"These must be Sir Dowling's blows," he exclaimed, "and yet I do not see the man!"

"And what hand," cried Sir Dowling, flinging aside the cloak in a transport of death-defying zeal—"whose hand has a better right than Sir Dowling's to do the utmost for a son of Brian?"

He had scarcely given utterance to his words, when the sparthe of a Loch Lannoch, who stood at some distance, came whistling through the air, and transfixed him on the spot, the victim of his own enthusiasm. The rest is known. The aged monarch, the prince, and many of their house, and four thousand of their followers shared the fate of Sir Dowling O'Hartigan; but their country was redeemed in their destruction, for Clontarf did more than "scotch" the Danish hydra. It was never seen to raise one of its heads again in Ireland.

STORY-TELLER AT FAULT.

A TALE OF MAGIC.

AT the time when the Tuatha Danans held the sovereignty of Ireland, there reigned in Leinster a king who was remarkably fond of hearing stories. Like all the princes and chieftains of the island at this early date, he had a favorite Story-teller, according to the custom of those times, who held a large estate from his majesty, on condition of his telling him a new story every night of his life, before he went to sleep, and sometimes with the laudable purpose of lulling him into that blissful condition. So inexhaustible was the genius of the King of Leinster's Story-teller that he had already reached a good old age without failing even for a single night to have a new story for the king; and such was the skill and tact which he displayed in their construction that, whatever cares of state or other annoyances might prey upon the monarch's mind, one of his Story-teller's narratives was sure to make him fall asleep.

In the course of his career, the Story-teller had

married a wealthy and high-born lady, daughter of a neighboring lord of that country, with whom he lived in peace and prosperity during many years. There is nothing, however, in this world which is not subject to decay or change, and even the human mind, which, from its spiritual nature, might well be supposed incorruptible, is doomed to share the infirmities of the frame with which it is so mysteriously united. The progress of old age began to produce a sensible influence on the imagination of the Story-teller. His fancy grew less brisk and active, and the king observed that he began to diversify his incidents with a greater number of moral and philosophical reflections than he conceived to be necessary to the progress of the narrative. However, he made no complaints, as the Story-teller's reflections evinced a great deal of judgment, and the grand object in view, that of setting the king to sleep, was as perfectly accomplished by his philosophy as by his wit or invention.

Matters thus proceeded, the Story-teller growing older and older, and more and more philosophical, and less and less fanciful, but he was yet true to his engagement, and never failed to have a new story at nightfall for the king's amusement. Every day, however, brought increasing indications of an intellectual crisis, which would not be very distant.

One morning, the Story-teller arose early, and, as his custom was, strolled out into his garden, and through the adjacent fields, in order to turn over in his mind some incidents which he might weave into a story for the king at night. But this morning he found himself quite at fault; after pacing his whole demesne, he returned to his house, without being able to think of anything new or strange. In vain he sent his fancy abroad, it returned as empty as it left him. He found no difficulty in proceeding as far as "There was once a king who had three sons," or "There lived in the reign of Ollav Folla," or "One day the king of all Ireland," but further than that he found it impossible to proceed. At length a servant came to announce to him that breakfast was ready, and his mistress waiting for him in the house. He went in, and found his wife seated at the table, and looking much perplexed at his delay. She was not long observing the air of chagrin that overspread his countenance.

"Why do you not come to breakfast, my dear?" said his wife.

"I have no mind to eat anything," replied the Story-teller. "As long as I have been in the service of the King of Leinster, I never yet sat down to breakfast without having a new story to tell him in the evening; but this morning my mind is quite shut up, and I don't know what to do. I might as well lie down and die at once. I'll be disgraced for ever this evening, when the king calls for his Story-teller."

"That's strange," said the wife. "Can't you think of anything new at all?"

"Nothing whatever; the door of my mind is locked against it."

"Nonsense!" said his wife. "Can't you invent something about a giant, or a dwarf, or a Bean Mhor (huge woman), or a baoch (champion) from foreign parts?"

"Oh! it is easy enough to find heroes," replied the Story-teller; "but what am I to do with them when I have them?"

"And can't you invent anything at all?"

"I cannot our estate is gone from us for ever; besides the open show that will be made of me to-night at the palace."

When the Story-teller's wife heard this dreadful news, she broke into a fit of crying and weeping, as if all her friends and relations were dead. At length her husband prevailed on her to be composed.

"Well," said she, "let us sit down to breakfast, at any rate; the day is long yet, and may be you'd think of something or another in the course of it."

The Story-teller shook his head as if to intimate his distrust of its contents, but sat down to breakfast as his wife desired. When all was removed, and they had sat for awhile in silence:

"Well," she asked, "do you think of anything yet?"

"Not a pin's worth," said the Story-teller. "I might as well lie down and die at once."

"Well, my dear," said the lady, "I'll tell you

what you'll do. Order your horses and chariot, and let us take a good long drive, and may be something might come into your head."

The Story-teller complied, and the chariot was prepared. Two of his finest horses were harnessed in the carriage, and three favorite hounds followed them. After driving a long distance, they took the road homeward once more, and toward evening, when they came within sight of their own demesne, the lady again asked her husband if he had yet thought of anything to tell the king.

"There is no use in my attempting it," he replied, "I can think of nothing. I'm as far from having anything new as I was when we left home."

At this moment, it happened that the lady saw something dark at the end of a field at a little distance from the road.

"My dear," said the wife, "do you see something black at the end of that field?"

"I do," replied her husband.

"Let us drive towards it," said the wife, "and perhaps it might be the means of putting something into your head which it would answer to tell the king."

"I'll do as you desire," replied the Story-teller, "though I am sure it is no use for me."

They turned the horses' heads and drove in the direction pointed out by the lady. When they drew nigh, they saw a miserable-looking old man lying on the ground with a wooden leg placed beside him.

"Who are you, my good man?" asked the Story-teller.

"Oh! then, 'tis little matter who I am. I'm a poor old lame, decrepit, miserable creature, sitting down here to rest awhile."

"And what are you doing with that box and dice I see in your hand?"

"I am waiting here to see whether any one would play a game with me," replied the old *bococh* (beggar-man).

"Play with *you?*" exclaimed the Story-teller. "Why, what has a poor old man like you to play for?"

"I have one hundred pieces of gold here in this leathern purse," replied the old man.

"Do you go down and play with him," said the Story-teller's wife, "and perhaps you might have something to tell the king about it in the evening."

He descended, and a smooth stone was placed between them as a gaming-table. They had not cast many throws, when the Story-teller lost all the money he had about him.

"Much good may it do you, friend," said the Story-teller. "I could not expect better hap in so foolish an undertaking."

"Will you play again?" asked the old man.

"Don't be talking, man; you have all my money."

"Haven't you a chariot, and horses, and hounds?"

"Well, what of them?"

"I'll stake all the money I have against them."

"Nonsense, man!" exclaimed the Story-teller. "Do you think for all the gold in Ireland, I'd run the risk of seeing my lady obliged to go home on foot?"

"May be you'd win," said the bococh.

"May be I wouldn't," said the Story-teller.

"Do play with him, husband," said the lady. "It is the second time, and, as he won before, you might win now. Besides, I don't mind walking."

"I never refused you a request in my life that it was possible to comply with," said the Story-teller, "and I won't do so now."

He sat down accordingly, and in one throw lost horses, hounds, and chariot.

"Will you play again?" asked the bococh.

"Are you making game of me, man?" said the Story-teller. "What else have I to stake?"

"I'll stake the whole money and all against your lady," said the old man.

Now, although these were pagan times, the Story-teller could not help thinking the bococh had a great deal of impudence to make him such a proposition. However, he only looked at him with an expression of great surprise, and was turning away in silence, when his wife spoke to him again.

"Do, my dear," said she, "accept his offer.

This is the third time, and how do you know what luck you may have? Besides, if you lose your estate to-night, as you are afraid, sure I'd be only a bother to you all our life."

"Is that the way you talk," said the Story-teller—"you that I never refused a request to since first I saw you?"

"Well," said she, "if you never refused me a request before, don't refuse me this one now, and may be it would be better for us both. You'll surely win the third time."

They played again, and the Story-teller lost. No sooner had he done so, than, to his great astonishment and indignation, he beheld his lady walk over and sit down near the ugly old bococh.

"Is that the way you're leaving me?" said the Story-teller.

"Sure I was won, my dear," said the lady; "you would not cheat the poor man, would you?"

"Have you any more to stake?" asked the old man.

"You know very well I have not," replied the Story-teller.

"I'll stake the whole, now, your lady and all, against yourself," said the old man.

"Nonsense, man!" said the Story-teller. "What in the world business would you have of an old fellow like me?"

"That's my own affair," said the bococh. "I know myself what use I could make of you; it is enough for you if I am willing to consider you a sufficient stake against all I have."

"Do, my dear," said the lady; "surely you do not mean to leave me here after you?"

The Story-teller complied once more, and lost.

"Well," said he, with a desolate look, "here I am for you now, and what do you want with me? You have the whole of us, now, horses and carriage, and mistress and master, and what business have you of us?"

"I'll soon let you know what business I have of you, at any rate," said the old man, taking out of his pocket a long cord and a wand. "Now," he continued, "as I have possession of your property, I do not choose to be annoyed by you any longer, so I propose transforming you into some kind of an animal, and I give you a free choice to be a hare, or a deer, or a fox, whichever of the three best hits your fancy."

The Story-teller in dismay looked over towards his wife.

"My dear," said she, "do not choose to be a deer, for, if you do, your horns will be caught in the branches, and you will be starved with hunger; neither choose to be a fox, for you will have the curse of everybody down upon you; but choose to be an honest little hare, and every one will love you, and you will be praised by high and low."

"And is that all the compassion you have for

me?" said the Story-teller. "Well, as I suppose it is the last word I have to say to you, it shall not be to contradict you, at any rate."

So he made choice of a hare, and the old man immediately threw the cord around him, and struck him with the wand, when the transformation was effected. Scarcely had the poor hare taken a skip or two, in order to divert himself, when the lady called the hounds, and set them after him. The hare ran, the dogs followed. The field in which they happened to be was enclosed by a high wall, so that the course continued a long time in the sight of the old man and the lady, to the great diversion of both. At length the hare, panting and weary, ran to the feet of the latter for protection. But then was witnessed a singular instance of the caprice and mutability of the sex, for the Story-teller's wife, forgetful of all his kindness experienced during a long course of years, unfeelingly kicked him back again towards the dogs, from whence arose the proverb long current in after-times, *Caith se a glab no con* (She threw him into the hound's mouth), as applied to all who act with similar ingratitude. They coursed him a second and a third time, and at the end of each the lady acted with the same heartlessness, until at length the old man struck the hounds, and took the hare into his lap, where he held him for some time, until he had sufficiently recovered his strength. He then placed him on the ground, and, putting the cord around him, struck him with the wand, on which he immediately reassumed his own form.

"Well," said the old man, "will you tell me how you liked that sport?"

"It might be sport to others," replied the Story-teller, looking at his wife, "but I declare I don't find it so enticing but I could put up with the loss of it. You're a droll man, whoever you are. Would it be asking an impertinent question to know from you who you are at all, or where you came from, or what is your trade, that you should take a pleasure in plaguing a poor old man of my kind in that manner?"

"Oh!" replied the stranger. "I'm a very odd kind of man—a sort of a walking good-for-little fellow—one day in poverty, another day in plenty —and so on—but if you wish to know anything more about me or my habits, come with me in some of my rambles, and perhaps I might show you more then you would be apt to make out if you were to go alone."

"I'm not my own master to go or stay," replied the Story-teller, with a resigned look.

When the stranger heard this, he put one hand into the wallet which he carried at his side, and drew out of it before their eyes a well-looking middle-aged man, to whom he spoke as follows:

"I command you by all you heard and saw since I put you into my wallet to take charge of this lady, together with the carriage, and horses, and all, and have them ready for me at a call whenever I shall require them."

He had scarcely said these words when all vanished from the Story-teller's sight, and he found himself on a sudden transported, he knew not how, to a place which he recognized as the Fox's Ford, well known as the residence of Red Hugh O'Donnell. On looking around, he saw the old man standing near him in a dress still more grotesque than before. His figure was now erect, though tall and lank, his hair gray, and his ears sticking up through his old hat. The greater part of his sword was exposed behind his hip; he wore a pair of tattered brogues, which, at every prodigious stride he made over the marshy ground, sent the water in jets up to his knees; and in his hand he carried three green boughs. It happened on this very day that O'Donnell and his followers and kinsmen were partaking of a splendid banquet in his house. They were very merry, feasting and drinking together, and, as the Story-teller and his companion drew near, they heard one of the guests exclaim in a loud and commanding tone:

"Who will say he ever heard finer music than that? Is it possible that twenty-two musicians could be found from this to the shores of Greece better skilled in their art than the twenty-two who are here to-day—I mean Darby McGillagan, Cormad O'Cregan, Timothy O'Cunningham, and many more whom I do not mention now by name?"

"We do not suppose," said several of his hearers, "that any such thing is possible."

At this moment, the Caol Riava (thin gray man) and the Story-teller entered the house.

"Save all here!" said the Caol Riava.

"And you likewise," replied O'Donnell. "Where do you come from now?"

"I slept last night," replied the stranger, "in the palace of the King of Scotland."

"Call the door-keeper before me," said O'Donnell.

He was summoned accordingly.

"Was it you let in this man?" asked O'Donnell.

"I give you free lave to whip the head from my two shoulders," replied the door-keeper, "if ever I laid eyes upon him before this present moment."

"Let it pass," said the Caol Riava, "for it would come just as easy to me to go out as to come in, whether the door was open or shut."

Then turning to the musicians:

"Play something for us," said he, "that I may judge whether all that I have heard in your praise be merited or otherwise."

They began to play, first successively, and then in full concert, all kinds of airs and elaborate pieces of music, both on wind and stringed instruments; and, when they had concluded, all looked to the new-comer to learn his opinion of their performance.

"I assure you," said the Caol Riava, "that since I first heard of Beelzebub, and Moloch, and Satan, and the rest of their infernal compeers, and of the hideous noise and uproar compounded of rage and lamentation which prevails in the dreary region of the demons and in the court of the sable princes of hell, I never could imagine worse music than what you are just after playing."

"Play something for us yourself, then," said O'Donnell.

"May be I will, and may be I won't," replied the Caol Riava; "for you may be certain I will do exactly what I like myself, and nothing else."

"I don't doubt you," said O'Donnell.

The Caol Riava then took a harp, and began to play in such a manner that the dead might have come out of their graves to hear him without occasioning any astonishment to those who knew the cause they had for so doing. As to the company who were present, sometimes he would make them weep, sometimes laugh, and at other times he could lull them asleep with the power of his enchanting strains.

"You are a sweet man, whoever you are," said O'Donnell.

"Some days sweet, and some days bitter," replied the Caol Riava.

"Go higher up, and sit in company with O'Donnell, and eat along with him," said one of the attendants.

"I will do no such thing," replied the Caol

Riava, "for a pleasing accomplishment in an ugly fellow like me is like honey in the body of a man who is going to be hanged; so I will go no higher up than where I am; but let me see his goodness here, if he has a mind to show it at all."

He kept his place, and O'Donnell sent him by the hands of an attendant a suit of attire, consisting of a cloak of many colors, a fine tunic, and other garments to match.

"Here," said the attendant, "is a full suit that O'Donnell sends you."

"I will not accept it," replied the Caol Riava, "for a good man shall never have to say that he lost so much by me."

"He is either an enemy or something more than mortal," said O'Donnell, when he heard that the stranger had refused his gifts. "Let twenty horsemen in full armor keep guard outside of the house, and as many foot-soldiers be stationed inside to watch his movements."

"What are you going to do with me?" asked the long gray man, when he saw the soldiers gathering round him.

"We mean to have a sharp eye on you, that you may not give us the slip till dinner is over," said O'Donnell.

"You are very hospitable," replied the Caol Riava, "but I give you my word, if you were as good again, it is not with you I'll dine to-day."

"Where else will you dine?" asked O'Donnell.

"Far enough from you, you may be satisfied," replied the Caol Riava.

"I pledge you my word," said one of the galloglasses on guard, "if I find you attempting to stir against O'Donnell's wish, I'll make pound pieces of you with my battle-axe."

The Caol Riava made no reply, but took an instrument, and began to play as before, in such a manner that all within hearing were enchanted with his music. He then laid aside the harp, and stood up in his place.

"Now," he said, "look to yourselves, you who are minding me, for I am off!"

The instant he uttered these words, the soldier who before had menaced him raised his battle-axe, but, instead of wounding the stranger as he intended, he struck a heavy blow on the harness of the man who stood next him. The latter returned the stroke with the best of his will, and in a few moments the whole score of foot-guards were hewing at each other's heads and shoulders with their battle-axes, until the floor was strewed with their disabled bodies. In the midst of this confusion the Caol Riava came to the door-keeper, and said to him:

"Go to O'Donnell, and tell him that, for a reward of twenty cows and a large farm rent free, you will undertake to bring his people to life again. When he accepts your proposal (as I know he will be glad to do), take this herb, and rub a little of it to the roof of each man's mouth, and he will be presently in perfect health again."

The door-keeper did as he directed, and succeeded perfectly, but, when he returned to thank his benefactor, to his great astonishment he could discover no trace of either him or the Story-teller.

It happened at this very time that a worthy man named MacEocha, of Leinster, a doctor in poetry, had been laid up with a broken leg more than eighteen weeks without receiving the least relief, although he had sixteen of the ablest surgeons in Leinster in consultation upon it. Happening to lift up his eyes as he sat before his door, he saw the Caol Riava and the Story-teller approaching, the former having only one large garment around him, and an Irish book in his hand, out of which he read aloud in one monotonous humming tone.

"Save you, MacEocha," said the Caol Riava.

"And you likewise!" replied MacEocha. "May I ask you what is your profession?"

"Why," replied the Caol Riava, "I am what you may call the makings of a physician from Ulster."

"And what is your name?"

"Call me Cathal ō Gein, and I will answer to it," replied the stranger. "I understand you are of a very churlish and inhospitable disposition, and, if you changed your conduct, I would be apt to cure your leg for you."

"I acknowledge my failing," said MacEocha.

'I am as niggardly as any miser until I take my third cup, but from that out I am easy as to what others may do. But I promise you if you cure me that I will not be guilty of that fault again."

While he was speaking, the sixteen doctors who were in attendance on him came up to enquire how he was getting on, upon which he told them of the offer made by the Caol Riava.

The doctors looked at the stranger and at the Story-teller, and then laughed immoderately.

"'Tis very well," said the Caol Riava, "but wait a little. Rise up, now," said he to MacEocha, "and let me see which can, you or your sixteen physicians, run fastest."

Up started MacEocha, and away went the sixteen doctors after their patient, but he left them far behind, and came back in great spirits to his house, while they remained panting and puffing at a distance.

"Now, you MacEocha," said the stranger, "do not be guilty of inhospitality or churlishness from this time forward, or, if you do, I'll come to you again, and break your leg worse than it was before, and not only that, but the other leg also I'll break in such a manner that all the surgeons in the Fenian hosts will not be able to cure it for you. As for these sixteen impostors that pretended to treat it for you, not one of them shall ever walk without a limp from this time forward."

"I promise you I will remember what you say," replied MacEocha; "and, to make a beginning, come in now and partake of a magnificent banquet which shall be prepared on the instant for you and your companion."

They entered the house, and were followed by the sixteen physicians, who shortly after came limping across the threshold. However, while MacEocha was ordering the banquet, an attendant ran to tell him that the Ulster doctor was running down the hill which sloped away from the door, faster than a greyhound with a hare in his eye. MacEocha was so much surprised at his abrupt departure that he made these lines, which were often repeated after him:

> Though my trust in his skill and his learning is high,
> I'd have liked him the better for bidding good-by:
> If the doctors of Ulster have all the same breeding,
> 'Twere fitter they stuck to their cupping and bleeding.

Meanwhile, the Story-teller and his strange master found themselves in a wild heath in Sligo, where they beheld O'Connor of Connaught, at the head of a powerful army, with a vast herd of cattle and other spoils which he had driven from the bondsmen of Munster. The Caol Riava went up and saluted him.

"Save you, O'Connor," he said boldly.

"And you likewise," replied the monarch. "What is your name?"

"Call me Giolla De," said the Caol Riava. "What is the cause of the confusion which I observe amongst your forces?"

"We are expecting an attack from the Munster

men," replied the king, "and are at a loss how to drive the spoils and repel the enemy at the same time."

"What made you drive them at all?" said the Caol Riava.

"You know," replied the king, "that a monarch ought always to be ready to redress the slightest grievance of his subjects. Now, it happened that a Connaught woman lent a basket to a woman of her acquaintance in Munster, who refused to return it at the appointed time. I heard of the injury, and immediately raised an army to avenge it. I am now returning with the spoils, a portion of which I intend to bestow on the poor woman who lost her basket."

"And what will you do with the rest?" enquired the Giolla De.

"I will keep them myself," said the king, "to signalize my victory, and enhance the national glory, after the way of all great kings."

"I'm afraid it will give you enough to do," replied the Caol Riava, "for, before you leave this heath, you will have more Munster men to meet you than there are purple bells all over it."

"That's what I fear," said the king.

"What will you give me if I help you?" said the Caol Riava.

"You!" cried one of O'Connor's men, with a burst of laughter. "It cannot make much difference to O'Connor whether you go or stay."

"What reward would you require?" asked O'Connor.

"A share, little or much, of anything you may get while I am with you," replied the Giolla De.

"Agreed," exclaimed the king.

"Very well," said the Giolla De; "do you hold on your journey, driving your spoils, while I coax the Munster men home again."

The king proceeded, and saw nothing of the men of Munster until he reached his own domain, where he arrived before any of his retinue. As he did so, he perceived the Giolla De and the Story-teller again by his side. Wearied from the fatigue of the expedition, after welcoming them, he entered a sheiling by the wayside, and called for a drink. It was brought, and he drank it off without even thinking of the Giolla De.

"I am sorry to see you forget your agreement," said the latter.

"Do you call that trifle a breach of my agreement?" said the king.

"Ah!" replied the Giolla De, "it is trifles that show the mind. You went to war for a basket, and you call a cup of wine a trifle." And he immediately spoke these lines:

> The wrong a king doth, were it huge as a mountain,
> He weighs it no more than a drop from the fountain;
> The wrong a king suffers, though light as a bubble,
> Sends fools to the slaughter, and kingdoms to trouble.
> Thenceforth I'll not swear by the weight of a feather,
> Nor the firmness of ice in the sunny spring weather;

> But I'll swear by a lighter, more slippery thing,
> And my troth shall be plight, by the word of a king.

The instant he had uttered these lines, the Caol Riava and the Story-teller vanished from the eyes of O'Connor, who looked around for them in vain in all directions. But what astonished him still more was that not a particle of all the spoils he had driven from Munster remained with his host, nor could anything be found throughout the whole army but an old basket, which the Connaught woman already spoken of recognized as the one she had lent to the Munster woman. While all were wondering at those strange events, the Caol Riava and the astonished Story-teller approached the house of a man named Thady O'Kelly, who at that moment happened to be sitting at his own door, in the midst of his friends and dependents. The Caol Riava drew near, dressed in the same tattered garments as usual, and bearing a white crooked wand in his hand.

"Save you, Thady O'Kelly," said the Caol Riava.

"And you likewise," replied Thady. "From whence do you come?"

"From the house of O'Connor, Sligo," answered the Caol Riava.

"What is your occupation?" asked Thady.

"I am a travelling juggler," replied the stranger, "and if you promise to give me five pieces of silver, I will perform a trick for you."

"I do promise you," said Thady.

The Caol Riava then took three small *siveens* or leeks, and placed them lengthwise on his hand, and said he would blow out the middle one and leave the two others in their places. All present said that such a feat was perfectly impossible, for the three *siveens* were so light and lay so close together that the breath which carried away one must necessarily take the two others also. However, the Caol Riava put his two fingers on the two outside leeks, and then blew away that which was in the middle.

"There's a trick for you, Thady O'Kelly," said the Caol Riava.

"I declare to my heart," said Thady, "'tis a good one." And he paid him the five pieces of silver.

"Why, then, that he may get good of your money, himself, and his trick," said one of O'Kelly's men, "if you gave me half what you gave him, I'll engage I'd perform the same trick as well as he did it."

"Oh! 'tis easy enough to do it," said Thady.

"Take him at his word," said the Caol Riava. "I'd wager anything he fails, for I never saw a boaster succeed in anything he attempted."

Thady commanded him to proceed, and the fellow placed three *siveens* on his hand, and, laying his two fingers on the outside ones, was about to blow away that in the centre. However, he had scarcely done so much, when his two fingers went down through the palm of his hand in such a manner that the tips appeared at the back, and would have remained so in all likelihood to the day of his death, if the *Cleasaiye*, or juggler, had not rubbed an herb upon the place and healed it.

"Well," said he, "you perceive that everything is not easy that looks so. But if you Thady O'Kelly, will give me five pieces more, I'll do another trick for you as good as the last."

"You shall have them," answered Thady, "if you let us hear what it is to be."

"Do you see my two ears?" said the juggler, thrusting his head forward.

"What a show they are!" said Thady. "To be sure we do."

"Well, will you give me five pieces if I stir one of my ears without stirring the other?"

"Indeed I will," said Thady; "that is impossible, at all events, for you can only move the ears by moving the whole scalp of your head, and then both must move together."

The juggler put up his hand, and, catching hold of one ear, stirred it.

"Upon my word," said Thady; "you have won my five pieces again, and that is a very good trick.

"He's welcome home to us with his tricks," said the same man who spoke before, "if he calls that a trick. Only I was so hasty and so awkward awhile ago, I could have done the trick well enough, but there's no great art required for this at all events."

So saying, he put up his hand and stirred his ear, but, to his astonishment and terror, it came away between his fingers! However, the juggler rubbed an herb once more to the place, and healed it as before.

"Well, Thady O'Kelly," said the juggler, "I will now show you a more curious trick than either of those if you give me the same money."

"You have my word for it," said Thady.

The juggler then took out of his bag a large ball of thread, and, folding the end around his finger, flung it slantwise up into the air. Up it flew, unrolling as it proceeded, while all gazed after it, lost in wonder, until it disappeared amongst the clouds. He next took out of his bag a fine hare, which he placed on the thread, when, to the increasing astonishment of the beholders, the animal ran up the line with as much dexterity as if she had been all her life at Astley's or Vauxhall. He next took out a greyhound, which he placed on the thread in like manner, when the animal stretched away after the hare with as much zest and security as if both were on the Curragh of Kildare on a March morning.

"Now," said the Caol Riava, "has any one a mind to run up after the dog, and see the course?"

"I will," said the man who had spoken twice before.

"You are always ready," said the juggler, "but I fear you are lazy, for you are almost as broad as you are long, and I'm afraid you'll fall asleep on the way and let the hound eat the hare."

"There is not a more active man in the known world than the very individual who is talking to you now," said the fat man.

"Up with you, then," said the juggler, "but I warn you, if you let my hare be killed, I'll cut off your head when you come down."

The fat fellow ran up the thread, and all three soon disappeared. After looking up for a long time, the Caol Riava said:

"I'm afraid the hound is eating the hare, and that our fat friend has fallen asleep."

Saying this, he began to wind the thread, and found the case as he had suspected it to be—the fat man fast asleep, and the greyhound with the last morsel of the hare between his teeth. He immediately drew his sword, and cut off the young man's head at a blow.

At this Thady O'Kelly stood up, and said he did not relish such conduct, and that it was not a thing he could ever sanction to see a young man murdered in that manner under his roof.

"If it grieves you," said the juggler, "I think as little of curing him now as I did before; but I must leave him some mark to make him remember his rashness."

So saying, he placed the head upon the shoulders again, and healed them, but in such a manner that the countenance looked the wrong way, after which he spoke these lines:

> What I take at my ease, at my ease I restore;
> It becomes him much better, I'm sure, than before:
> If any man says I have wronged him thereby,
> Tell that man from me that I give him the lie;
> For an insolent braggart is odder to see
> Than a fool with his face where his poll ought to be.

The Caol Riava had scarcely uttered those lines, when he and the Story-teller disappeared, nor could any person present tell whether they had flown into the air, or whether the earth had swallowed them. The next place the Story-teller found himself with his whimsical master was in the palace of the King of Leinster, where the customary evening banquet was on the point of being prepared. The Story-teller was grieved and perplexed to hear the king continually asking for his favorite Story-teller, while no one present was able to give any account of him.

"Now," said the Caol Riava, turning to him, "I have rendered you invisible in order that you may witness all that is about to take place here, without being recognized by any of your daily acquaintances."

So saying, he sat down close to the musicians, who were playing in concert at the time. Observing the attention which he paid, the chief musician said, when they concluded:

"Well, my good man, I hope you like our performance?"

"I'll tell you that," replied the Caol Riava. "Were you ever listening to a cat purring over a bowl of broth?"

"I often heard it," replied the chief musician.

"Or did you ever hear a parcel of beetles buzzing about in the dusk on a summer evening?"

"I did," said the chief musician.

"Or a bitter-faced old woman scolding in a passion?"

"I did often," said the chief musician, who was a married man.

"Well, then," said the Caol Riava, "I'd rather be listening to any one of them than to your music."

"You insolent ragamuffin," said the chief musician, "it well becomes you to express yourself in that manner."

"You are the last that ought to say so," replied the Caol Riava, "for though bad is the best of the whole of you, yet, if I were to look out for the worst, I should never stop till I lighted on yourself."

At these words, the chief musician arose, and, drawing his sword, made a blow at the Caol Riava, but, instead of striking him, he wounded one of his own party, who returned the blow forthwith, and in a little time the whole band of musicians were engaged in mortal conflict one with another. While all this confusion prevailed, an attendant came and awoke the king, who had been taking a nap while the music played.

"What's the matter?" said the king.

"The harpers that are murthering one another, please your majesty."

"lease me!" cried the King of Leinster, "it does not please me. They ought to be satisfied with murdering all the music in my kingdom, without murdering the musicians too. Who began it?" says his majesty.

"A stranger that thought proper to find fault with their music," replied the attendant.

"Let him be hanged," said the king, "and do not disturb me again about him."

Accordingly, some of the king's guards took the Caol Riava, and carried him out to a place where they erected a gallows, and hanged him without loss of time. However, on returning to the palace, they found the Caol Riava within sitting among the guests, without having the least appearances of having been ever hanged in his life.

"Never welcome you in!" cried the captain of the guard. "Didn't we hang you this minute, and what brings you here?"

"Is it me myself you mean?" said the Caol Riava.

"Who else?" said the captain.

"That the hand may turn into a pig's foot with you when you think of tying the rope," said the Caol Riava, "why should you speak of hanging me."

They went out in alarm, and, to their horror, found the king's favorite brother hanging in the place of the Caol Riava. One of them went to the king, and woke him up.

"What's the matter now?" cried the king, yawning and stretching himself.

"Please your majesty, we hanged that vagabond according to your majesty's orders, and he's as well as ever again now in spite of us." He was afraid of telling him about his brother.

"Take him and hang him again, then, and don't be disturbing me about such trifles," said the King of Leinster, and he went off to sleep again.

They did as he recommended, and the same scene was repeated three times over, and at each time some near friend or favorite kinsman of the king was hanged instead of the Caol Riava. By this time the captain of the guard was fairly at his wit's end.

"Well," said the Caol Riava, "do you wish to hang me any more?"

"We'll have no more to say to you," said the captain; "you may go wherever you like, and the sooner the better. We got trouble enough by you already. May be 'tis the king himself we'd find hanging the next time we tried it."

"Since you are growing so reasonable," said the Caol Riava, "you may go out now, and take your three friends down again. They will not be so much the worse for their experience but they can thank you for finding them more comfortable quarters; and I give you a parting advice, never while you live again to interpose between a critic and a poet, a man and his wife, or a mother and an only child." After which he spoke these lines:

He who censures a strain which a minstrel composes
Must lie upon something less grateful than roses;
He who takes up a quarrel begun by a poet
May at bottom have wit, but lacks wisdom to show it;
For than him a worse ninny will rarely be found
Who would peril his nose for a dealer in sound.

Immediately after he had uttered these verses, he disappeared, and the Story-teller found himself in company with him on the spot where they had first met, and where his wife with the carriage and horses were awaiting them, under the care of the man to whom the Caol Riava had entrusted them.

"Now," said the latter, "I will not be tormenting you any longer. There are your carriage, and horses, and your dogs, and your money, and your lady, and you may take them with you as soon as you please, for I have no business in life with any of them at all."

The Story-teller paused for some moments to collect his thoughts before he made any reply.

"For my carriage, and horses, and hounds," he said at length, "I thank you, but my lady and my money you may keep."

"No," replied the bococh, "I have told you that I do not want either; and do not harbor any ill-will against your lady on account of what she has done, for she could not help it."

"Not help it!" exclaimed the Story-teller. "Not help kicking me into the mouth of my own hounds! Not help casting me off, after all my kindness to her, in favor of a beggarly old—I beg pardon," he said, correcting himself, "I ought not to speak in that way, but a woman's ingratitude will make a man forget his good manners."

"No offence in life," said the bococh, "for these terms are very just, and apply not to my own real form, but to that which I have assumed for the purpose of befriending you. I am Aongus of Bruff, for whom you obtained many a favor from the King of Leinster. This morning I discovered by my skill in things hidden that you were in a difficulty, and immediately determined to free you from it. As to your lady, do not blame her for what has passed, for, by the same power which enabled me to change the form of your body, I changed the affections of her mind. Go home, therefore, as man and wife should do; and now you have a story to tell the King of Leinster when he calls for it."

Saying this, he disappeared, and the lady, bursting in tears, begged her husband's forgiveness, and assured him that she would sooner die a thousand deaths than act in such a manner, if some extraordinary influence had not possessed her.

This explanation proving entirely satisfactory to the Story-teller, they procceded homeward happily together. Notwithstanding all the speed they could make, it was so late when the Story-teller arrived at the king's palace that his majesty had already retired to his sleeping-chamber.

When the Story-teller entered, the king enquired the cause of his delay.

"Please your majesty," said the Story-teller, "there is nothing like the plain truth, and I will tell it to you if you desire it."

The king commanded him by all means to do so. Accordingly, the Story-teller began, and gave a detailed account of the adventures of the day, his difficulty in trying to invent a story, the benevolence of the friendly Draoidhe (or Druid), and the ingratitude of his wife, remarkable in itself, and still more so in the singular manner in which it was explained. When it was ended, the king laughed so heartily, and was so diverted with his narrative, that he commanded him to commence the whole again, and relate it from beginning to end, before he went to sleep. The Story-teller obeyed, and, when he had concluded, the king commanded him never again to go to the trouble of inventing a new story, but to tell him that one every night, for he never would listen to another story again as long as he lived.

SAMUEL LOVER.

Samuel Lover.

BARNY O'REIRDON.

CHAPTER I.

OUTWARD-BOUND.

"Well, he went further and further than I can tell."—*Nursery Tale.*

A VERY striking characteristic of an Irishman is his unwillingness to be outdone. Some have asserted that this arises from vanity, but I have ever been unwilling to attribute an unamiable motive to my countrymen where a better may be found, and one equally tending to produce a similar result, and I consider a deep-seated spirit of emulation to originate this peculiarity. Phrenologists might resolve it by supposing the organ of love of approbation to predominate in our Irish craniums, and it may be so; but, as I am not in the least a metaphysician, and very little of a phrenologist, I leave those who choose to settle the point in question, quite content with the knowledge of the fact with which I started, viz., the unwillingness of an Irishman to be outdone. This spirit, it is likely, may sometimes lead men into ridiculous positions; but it is equally probable that the desire of surpassing one another has given birth to many of the noblest actions and some of the most valuable inventions; let us therefore not fall out with it.

Now, having vindicated the *motive* of my countrymen, I will prove the total abstinence of national prejudice in so doing by giving an illustration of the ridiculous consequences attendant upon this Hibernian peculiarity.

Barny O'Reirdon was a fisherman of Kinsale, and a heartier fellow never hauled a net nor cast a line into deep water; indeed, Barny, independently of being a merry boy among his companions, a lover of good fun and good whiskey, was looked up to rather by his brother fishermen as an intelligent fellow, and few boats brought more fish to market than Barny O'Reirdon's; his opinion on certain points in the craft was considered law, and, in short, in his own little community, Barny was what is commonly called a leading man. Now, your leading man is always jealous in an inverse ratio to the sphere of his influence, and the leader of a nation is less incensed at a rival's triumph than the great man of a village. If we pursue this descending scale, what a desperately jealous person the oracle of oyster-dredges and cockle-women must be! Such was Barny O'Reirdon.

Seated one night at a public-house, the common resort of Barny and other marine curiosities, our hero got entangled in debate with what he called a strange sail; that is to say, a man he had never met before, and whom he was inclined to treat rather magisterially upon nautical subjects; at the same time, the stranger was equally inclined to assume the high hand over him, till at last the new-comer made a regular outbreak by exclaiming, "Ah! tare-and-ouns, lave aff your balderdash, Mr. O'Reirdon; by the powdhers o' war it's enough, so it is, to make a dog bate his father, to hear you goin' an as if you war Curlumberus or Sir Crustyphiz Wran, when every one knows the divil a farthur you iver war nor ketchen crabs or drudgen oysters."

"Who towld you that, my Watherford Wondher?" rejoined Barny. "What the dickens do you know about sayfarin' farther nor fishin' for sprats in a bowl wid your grandmother?"

"Oh! baithershin," says the stranger.

"And who made you so bowld with my name?" demanded O'Reirdon.

"No matther for that," said the stranger; "but if you'd like for to know, shure it's your own cousin Molly Mullins knows me well, and may be I don't know you and yours as well as the mother that bore you, aye, in troth; and sure I know the very thoughts o' you as well as if I was inside o' you, Barny O'Reirdon."

"By my sowl thin, you know betther thoughts than your own, Mr. Whipper-snapper, if that's the name you go by."

"No, it's not the name I go by; I've as good a

name as your own, Mr. O'Reirdon, for want of a betther, and that's O'Sullivan."

"Throth there's more than there's good o' them," said Barny.

"Good or bad, I'm a cousin o' your own twice removed by the mother's side."

"And is it the Widda O'Sullivan's boy you'd be that left this come Candlemas four years?"

"The same."

"Throth, thin, you might know better manners to your eldhers, though I'm glad to see you, any-how, agin; but a little thravellin' puts us beyant ourselves sometimes," said Barny rather contemptuously.

"Throth I nivir bragged out o' myself yit, and it's what I say that a man that's only fishin' aff the land all his life has no business to compare in the regard o' thracthericks wid a man that has sailed to Fingal."

This silenced any further argument on Barny's part. Where Fingal lay was all Greek to him; but, unwilling to admit his ignorance, he covered his retreat with the usual address of his countrymen, and turned the bitterness of debate into the cordial flow of congratulation at seeing his cousin again.

The liquor was frequently circulated, and the conversation began to take a different turn, in order to lead from that which had very nearly ended in a quarrel between O'Reirdon and his relation. The state of the crops, county cess, road jobs, etc., became topics, and various strictures as to the utility of the latter were indulged in, while the merits of the neighboring farmers were canvassed.

"Why, thin," said one, "that field o' whate o' Michael Coghlan is the finest field o' whate mortial eyes was ever set upon—divil the likes iv it myself ever seen far or near."

"Throth, thin, sure enough," said another, "it promises to be a fine crap anyhow, and myself can't help thinkin' it quare that Mikee Coghlan, that's a plain-spoken, quite (quiet) man, and simple like, should have finer craps than Pether Kelly o' the big farm beyant, that knows all about the great saycrets o' the airth, and is knowledgable to a degree, and has all the hard words that ivir was coined, at his fingers' ends."

"Faith, he has a power o' *blasthogue* about him, sure enough," said the former speaker, "if that could do him any good, but he isn't fit to hould a candle to Michael Coghlan in the regard o' farmin'."

"Why, blur-and-agers," rejoined the upholder of science, "sure he met the Scotch steward that the lord beyant has, one day, that I hear is a wondherful edicated man, and was brought over here to show us all a patthern; well, Pether Kelly met him one day, and, by gor, he discoorsed him to a degree that the Scotch chap hadn't a word left in his jaw."

"Well, and what was he the better o' having more prate than a Scotchman?" asked the other.

"Why,' answered Kelly's friend, "I think it stands to rayson that the man that done out the Scotch steward ought to know somethin' more about farmin' than Mickee Coghlan."

"Augh! don't talk to me about knowing," said the other rather contemptuously. "Sure I gev in to you that he has a power o' prate, and the gift o' the gab, and all to that. I own to you that he has *the-o-ry* and *che-mis-thery*, but he hasn't the *craps*. Now, the man that has the craps is the man for my money.

"You're right, my boy," said O'Reirdon, with an approving thump of his brawny fist upon the table, "it's a little talk goes far—*doin'* is the thing."

"Ah, yiz may run down larnin' if yiz like," said the undismayed stickler for theory versus practice, "but larnin' is a fine thing, and sure where would the world be at all only for it; sure where would the staymers (steamboat) be, only for larnin'?"

"Well," said O'Reirdon, "and the divil may care if we never seen them; I'd rather depind an wind and canvas any day than the likes o' them! What are they good for, but to turn good sailors into kitchen-maids, bilin' a big pot o' wather and oilin' their fire-irons, and throwin' coals an the fire? Augh! thim staymers is a disgrace to the say; they're for all the world like old fogies, smokin' from mornin' till night and doin' no good."

"Do you call it doin' no good to go fasther nor ships iver wint before?"

"Pooh; sure Solomon, queen o' Sheba, said there was time enough for all things."

"Thrue for you," said O'Sullivan, "*'fair and aisy goes far in a day,'* is a good ould sayin'."

"Well, may be you'll own to the improvement they re makin' in the harbor o' Howth beyant, in Dublin, is some good."

"We'll see whether it'll be an improvement first," said the obdurate O'Reirdon.

"Why, man alive, sure you'll own it's the greatest o' good it is, taken' up the big rocks out o' the bottom o' the harbor."

"Well, an' where's the wondher o' that? Sure we done the same here."

"Oh! yis, but it was whin the tide was out and the rocks was bare; but up at Howth, they cut away the big rocks from undher the say intirely."

"Oh! be aisy; why, how could they do that?"

"Ay, there's the matther, that's what larnin' can do; and wondherful it is intirely! and the way it is, is this, as I hear it, for I never seen it, but heerd it described by the lord to some gintlemin and ladies one day in his garden where I was helpin' the gardener to land some salary (celery). You see the ingineer goes down undher the wather intirely, and can stay there as long as he plazes."

"Whoo! and what o' that? Sure I heerd the long sailor say that come from the Aystern

Ingees that the ingineers there can a'most live under wather, and goes down looking for diamonds, and has a sledge-hammer in their hand, brakin' the diamonds when they're too big to take them up whole, all as one as men brakin' stones an the road."

"Well, I don't want to go beyant that; but the way the lord's ingineer goes down is he has a little bell wid him, and, while he has that little bell to ring, hurt nor harm can't come to him."

"Arrah be aisy."

"Divil a lie in it."

"May be it's a blissed bell," said O'Reirdon, crossing himself.*

"No, it is not a blissed bell."

"Why thin, now, do you think me sitch a born nathral as to give in to that? As if the ringin' iv the bell, barrin it was a blissed bell, could do the like. I tell you it's unpossible."

"Ah! nothin's unpossible to God."

"Sure I wasn't denyin' that; but I say the bell is unpossible."

"Why," said O'Sullivan, "you see he's not altogether complete in the demonstheration o' the mashine; it is not by the ringin' o' the bell it is done, but—"

"But what?" broke in O'Reirdon impatiently.

---

* There is a relic in the possession of the MacNamara family, in the county Clare, called the "blessed bell of the MacNamaras," sometimes used to swear upon in cases of extreme urgency, in preference to the Testament; for a violation of truth, when sworn upon the blessed bell, is looked upon by the peasantry as a sacrilege, placing the offender beyond the pale of salvation.

"Do you mane for to say there is a bell in it at all at all?"

"Yes, I do," said O'Sullivan.

"I towld you so," said the promulgator of the story.

"Ay," said O'Sullivan, "but it is not by the ringin' iv the bell it is done."

"Well, how is it done, then?" said the other, with a half offended, half supercilious air.

"It is done," said O'Sullivan, as he returned the look with interest—"it is done entirely by jommethry."

"Oh! I understan' it now," said O'Reirdon, with an inimitable affectation of comprehension in the " Oh!"—" but to talk of the ringin' iv a bell doin' the like is beyant the beyants intirely, barrin', as I said before, it was a blissed bell, glory be to God!"

"And so you tell me, sir, it is jommethry," said the twice discomfited man of science.

"Yis, sir," said O'Sullivan with an air of triumph, which rose in proportion as he carried the listeners along with him—"jommethry."

"Well, have it your own way. There's them that won't hear rayson sometimes, nor have belief in larnin'; and you may say it's jommethry if you plaze; but I heerd them that knows betther than iver you knew, say—"

"Whisht, whisht! and bad cess to you both," said O'Reirdon; "what the dickens are yiz goin' to fight about now, and sitch good liquor before yiz? Hillo! there, Mrs. Quigley, bring uz another quart i' you plaze; ay, that's the chat, another quart. Augh! yiz may talk till yo're black in the face about your invintions, and your staymers, and bell ringin', and gash, and railroads; but here's long life and success to the man that invinted the impairil (imperial) quart*; that was the rail beautiful invintion." And he took a long pull at the replenished vessel, which strongly indicated that the increase of its dimensions was a very agreeable *measure* to such as Barny.

After the introduction of this and *other* quarts, it would not be an easy matter to pursue the conversation that followed. Let us therefore transfer our story to the succeeding morning, when Barny O'Reirdon strolled forth from his cottage, rather later than usual, with his eyes bearing *eye-*witness to the carouse of the preceding night. He had not a headache, however; whether it was that Barny was too experienced a campaigner under the banners of Bacchus, or that Mrs. Quigley's boast was a just one, namely, "that, of all the drink in her house, there was't a headache in a hogshead of it," is hard to determine, but I rather incline to the strength of Barny's head.

The above-quoted declaration of Mrs. Quigley is the favorite inducement held out by every

---

* Until the assimilation of currency, weights, and measures between England and Ireland, the Irish quart was a much smaller measure than the English. This part of the assimilation pleased Pat exceedingly, and he has no anxiety to have that repealed.

boon companion in Ireland at the head of his own table. "Don't be afraid of it, my boys, it's the right sort. There's not a headache in a hogshead of it."

This sentiment has been very seductively rendered by More, with the most perfect unconsciousness on his part of the likeness he was instituting. Who does not remember—

> "Friend of my soul, this goblet sip,
>   'Twill chase the pensive tear;
>   'Tis not so sweet as woman's lip
>   But, oh! 'tis more sincere:
> Like her delusive beam,
>   'Twill steal away the mind;
> But, like affection's dream,
>   It leaves no sting behind."

Is not this very elegantly saying "there's not a headache in a hogshead of it"? But I am forgetting my story all this time.

Barny sauntered about in the sun, at which he often looked up, under the shelter of compressed bushy brows, and long-lashed eyelids, and a shadowing hand across his forehead, to see "what o' day" it was; and, from the frequency of this action, it was evident the day was hanging heavily with Barny. He retired at last to a sunny nook in a neighboring field, and, stretching himself at full length, basked in the sun, and began "to chew the cud of sweet and bitter thought." He first reflected on his own undoubted weight in his little community, but still he could not get over the annoyance of the preceding night, arising from his being silenced by O'Sullivan; "a chap," as he said himself, "that lift the place four years agon a brat iv a boy, and to think iv his comin' back and outdoin' his elders, that saw him runnin' about the place a gassoon that one could tache a few months before"; 'twas too bad. Barny saw his reputation was in a ticklish position, and began to consider how his disgrace could be retrieved. The very name of Fingal was hateful to him; it was a plague spot on his peace that festered there incurably. He first thought of leaving Kinsale altogether; but flight implied so much of defeat that he did not long indulge in that notion. No, he *would* stay, "in spite of all the O'Sullivans, kith and kin, breed, seed, and generation." But, at the same time, he knew he should never hear the end of that hateful place, Fingal; and, if Barny had had the power, he would have enacted a penal statute making it death to name the accursed spot, wherever it was; but, not being gifted with such legislative authority, he felt Kinsale was no place for him, if he would not submit to be flouted every hour out of the four-and-twenty by man, woman, and child that wished to annoy him. What was to be done? He was in the perplexing situation, to use his own words, "of the cat in the thripe shop"—he didn't know which way to choose. At last, after turning himself over in the sun several times, a new idea struck him. Couldn't he go to Fingal himself? And then he'd be equal to that upstart O'Sullivan. No sooner was the thought engendered than Barny sprang to his feet a new man; his eye brightened, his step became once more elastic, he walked erect, and felt himself to be all over Barny O'Reirdon once more—" Richard was himself again."

But where was Fingal?—there was the rub. That was a profound mystery to Barny, which, until discovered, must hold him in the vile bondage of inferiority. The plain-dealing reader would say, " Couldn't he ask?" No, no; that would never do for Barny; that would be an open admission of ignorance his soul was above; and, consequently, Barny set his brains to work to devise measures of coming at the hidden knowledge by some circuitous route that would not betray the end he was working for. To this purpose, fifty stratagems were raised and demolished in half as many minutes in the fertile brain of Barny as he strided along the shore, and, as he was working hard at the fifty-first, it was knocked all to pieces by his jostling against some one whom he never perceived he was approaching, so immersed was he in his speculations; and, on looking up, who should it prove to be but his friend, " the long sailor from the Aystern Injees." This was quite a godsend to Barny, and much beyond what he could have hoped for. Of all men under the sun, the long sailor was the man in a million for Barny's net at that minute, and accordingly he made a haul of him, and thought it the greatest catch he ever made in his life.

Barny and the long sailor were in close companionship for the remainder of the day, which was closed, as the preceding one, in a carouse; but, on this occasion, there was only a duet performance in honor of the jolly god, and the treat was at Barny's expense. What the nature of their conversation during the period was I will not dilate on, but keep it as profound a secret as Barny himself did, and content myself with saying that Barny looked a much happier man the next day. Instead of wearing his hat slouched, and casting his eyes on the ground, he walked about with his usual unconcern, and gave his nod, the passing word of "*civilitude*," to every friend he met; he rolled his quid of tobacco about in his jaw with an air of superior enjoyment, and, if disturbed in his narcotic amusement by a question, he took his own time to eject "the leperous distilment" before he answered the querist, a happy composure that bespoke a man quite at ease with himself. It was in this agreeable spirit that Barny bent his course to the house of Peter Kelly, the owner of the "big farm beyant" before alluded to, in order to put in practice a plan he had formed for the fulfilment of his determination of rivalling O'Sullivan.

He thought it probable that Peter Kelly, being one of the "snuggest men in the neighborhood, would be a likely person to join him in a spec," as he called it (a favorite abbreviation of his for the word speculation), and accordingly, when he reached the "big farm house," he accosted the owner with his usual "Good save you!" "God save you kindly, Barny," returned Peter Kelly. "An' what is it brings you here, Barny," asked Peter, "this fine day, instead o' being out in the boat?"—"Oh! I'll be out in the boat soon enough, and it's far enough, too, I'll be in her; an' indeed it's partly that same is bringin' me here to yourself."

"Why, do you want me to go along wid you, Barny?"

"Troth an' I don't, Mr. Kelly. You're a knowledgable man an land, but I'm afeard it's a bad bargain you'd be at say."

"And what wor you talking about me and your boat for?"

"Why, you see, sir, it was in the regard of a little bit o' business, an', if you'd come wid me and take a turn in the praty-field, I'll be behouldin' to you, and may be you'll hear somethin' that won't be displazin' to you."

"An' welkim, Barny," said Peter Kelly.

When Barny and Peter were in the "praty-field," Barny opened the trenches (I don't mean the potato trenches), but, in military parlance, he opened the trenches, and laid siege to Peter Kelly, setting forth the extensive profits that had been realized at various "specs" that had been made by his neighbors in exporting potatoes. "And sure," said Barny, " why shouldn't *you* do the same, and they are ready to your hand? As much as to say, *Why don't you profit by me, Peter Kelly?* And the boat is below there in the harbor, and I'll say this much, the devil a betther boat is betune this and herself."

" Indeed, I b'lieve so, Barny," said Peter, " for, considhering where we stand at this present, there's no boat at all at all betune us." And Peter laughed with infinite pleasure at his own hit.

"Oh! well, you know what I mane, any how; an', as I said before, the boat is a darlint boat, and as for him that commands her—I b'lieve I need say nothin' about that." And Barny gave a toss of his head and a sweep of his open hand, more than doubling the laudatory nature of his comment on himself.

But, as the Irish saying is, "to make a long story short," Barny prevailed on Peter Kelly to make an export; but in the nature of the venture they did not agree. Barny had proposed potatoes; Peter said there were enough of them already where he was going; and Barny rejoined that " praties were so good in themselves there never could be too much o' thim anywhere." But Peter, being a knowledgable man, and up to all "saycrets o' the airth, and understanding the the-o-ry and the che-mis-thery," overruled Barny's proposition, and determined upon a cargo of *scalpeens* (which name they gave to pickled mackerel) as a preferable merchandise, quite forgetting that Dublin Bay herrings were a much better and as cheap a commodity, at the command of the Fingalians. But in many similar mistakes the ingenious Mr. Kelly has been paralleled by other speculators. But that is neither here nor there, and it was all one to Barny whether his boat was freighted with potatoes or *scalpeens*, so long as he had the honor and glory of becoming a navigator, and being as good as O'Sullivan.

Accordingly the boat was laden and all got in readiness for putting to sea, and nothing was now wanting but Barny's orders to haul up the gaff and shake out the jib of his hooker.

But this order Barny refrained to give, and, for the first time in his life, exhibited a disinclination to leave the shore. One of his fellow-boatmen at last said to him: " Why, thin, Barny O'Reirdon, what the divil is come over you, at all at all? What's the maynin' of your loitherin' about here, and the boat ready, and a lovely fine breeze aff o' the land?"

"Oh! never you mind; I b'lieve I know my own business anyhow, an' it's hard, so it is, if a man can't ordher his own boat to sail when he plazes."

"Oh! I was only thinking it quare—and a pity more betoken, as I said before, to lose the beautiful breeze, and—"

"Well, just keep your thoughts to yourself, i' you plaze, and stay in the boat as I bid you, and don't be out of her on your apperl, by no manner o' manes, for one minit, for you see I don't know when it may be plazin' to me to go aboord an' set sail."

"Well, all I can say is I never seen you afeard to go to say before."

"Who says I'm afeard?" said O'Reirdon; "you'd betther not say that agin, or in troth I'll give you a leatherin' that won't be for the good o' your health—troth, for three straws this minit I'd lave you that your own mother wouldn't know you with the lickin' I'd give you; but I scorn your dirty insinuation; no man ever seen Barny O'Reirdon afeard yet, anyhow. Howld your prate, I tell you, and look up to your betthers. What do you know iv navigation? May be you think it's as aisy for to sail on a voyage as to go start a-fishin'." And Barny turned on his heel, and left the shore.

The next day passed without the hooker sailing, and Barny gave a most sufficient reason for the delay, by declaring that he had a warnin' givin' him in a dhrame (Glory be to God!), and that it was given to him to understand (under Heaven) that it wouldn't be lucky that day.

Well, the next day was Friday, and Barny of course would not sail any more than any other sailor who could help it on this unpropitious day. On Saturday, however, he came running in a great hurry down to the shore, and, jumped aboard, he gave orders to make all sail, and, taking the helm of the hooker, he turned her head to the sea, and soon the boat was cleaving the blue waters with a velocity seldom witnessed in so small a craft, and scarcely conceivable to those who have not seen the speed of a Kinsale hooker.

"Why, thin, you tuk the notion mighty suddint, Barny," said the fisherman next in authority to O'Reirdon, as soon as the bustle of getting the boat under way had subsided.

"Well, I hope it's plazin' to you at last," said Barny; "troth, one 'ud think you were never at say before, you wor in such a hurry to be off; as new-fangled a'most as the child with a play-toy."

"Well," said the other of Barny's companions, for there were but two with him in the boat, "I was thinkin' myself, as well as Jemmy, that we lost two fine days for nothin', and we'd be there a'most, may be, now, if we sailed three days agon."

"Don't b'lieve it," said Barny emphatically. "Now, don't you know yourself that there is some days that the fish won't come near the lines at all, and that we might as well be castin' our nets on the dhry land as in the say, for all we'll catch if we start on an unlooky day? And sure I towld you I was waitin' only till I had it given to me to undherstan' that it was looky to sail, and I go bail we'll be there sooner than if we started three days agon, for, if you don't start with good look before you, faix may be it's never at all to the end o' your trip you'll come."

"Well, there's no use in talkin' aboot it now, anyhow; but when do you expec' to be there?"

"Why, you see we must wait antil I can tell how the wind is like to howld on, before I can make up my mind to that."

"But you're sure now, Barny, that you're up to the coorse you have to run?"

"See now, lave me alone and don't be cross crass-questionin' me—tare-an-ouns, do you think me sitch a bladdherang as for to go to shuperinscribe a thing I wasn't aiquil to?"

"No; I was only goin' to ax you what coorse you wor goin' to steer."

"You'll find out soon enough when we get there, and so I bid you agin' lay me alone—just keep your toe in your pump. Shure I'm here at the helm, and a weight on my mind, and it's fitther for you, Jim, to mind your own business, and lay me to mind mine; away wid you there, and be handy; haul taut that foresheet there, we must run close on the wind; be handy, boys, make everything dhraw."

These orders were obeyed, and the hooker soon passed to windward of a ship that left the harbor before her, but could not hold on a wind with the same tenacity as the hooker, whose qualities in this particular render it peculiarly suitable for the purposes to which it is applied, namely, pilot and fishing boats.

We have said a ship left the harbor before the hooker had set sail, and it is now fitting to inform the reader that Barny had contrived, in the course of his last meeting with the "long sailor," to ascertain that this ship, then lying in the harbor, was going to the very place Barny wanted to reach. Barny's plan of action was decided upon in a moment; he had now nothing to do but to watch the sailing of the ship, and follow in her course. Here was at once a new mode of navigation discovered.

The stars, twinkling in mysterious brightness through the silent gloom of night, were the first encouraging, because visible, guides to the adventurous mariners of antiquity. Since then, the sailor, encouraged by a bolder science, relies on the *unseen* agency of nature, depending on the fidelity of an atom of iron to the mystic law that claims its homage in the north. This is one refinement of science upon another. But the beautiful simplicity of Barny O'Reirdon's philosophy cannot be too much admired, to follow the ship that is going to the same place. Is not this navigation made easy?

But Barny, like many a great man before him, seemed not to be aware of how much credit he was entitled to for his invention, for he did not divulge to his companions the originality of his proceeding; he wished them to believe he was only proceeding in the commonplace manner, and had no ambition to be distinguished as the happy projector of so simple a practice.

For this purpose, he went to windward of the ship, and then fell off again, allowing her to pass him, as he did not wish even those on board the ship to suppose he was following in their wake; for Barny like all people that are full of one scheme, and fancy everybody is watching them, dreaded lest any one should fathom his motives. All that day, Barny held on the same course as his leader, keeping at a respectful distance, however, "for fear 'twould look like dodging her," as he said to himself; but, as night closed in, so closed in Barny with the ship, and kept a sharp lookout that she would not give him the slip. The next morning dawned, and found the hooker and ship companions still; and thus matters proceeded for four days, during the entire of which time they had not seen land since their first losing sight of it, although the weather was clear.

"By my sowl," thought Barny, "the channel must be mighty wide in these parts, and for the last day or so we've been goin' purty free with a flowing sheet, and I wondher we aren't closin' in wid the shore by this time; or may be it's farther off than I thought it was." His companions, too, began to question Barny on the subject, but to their queries he presented an impenetrable front of composure, and said, "It was always the best plan to keep a good bowld offin'." In two days more, however, the weather began to be sensibly warmer, and Barny and his companions remarked that it was "goin' to be the finest sayson—God bless it!—that ever kem out o' the skies for many a long year, and may be it's the whate would not be beautiful, and a great dale of it." It was at the end of a week that the ship which Barny had hitherto kept ahead of him showed symptoms of bearing down upon him, as he thought; and, sure enough, she did, and Barny began to conjecture what the deuce the ship could want with him, and commenced inventing answers to the questions he thought it possible might be put to him in case the ship spoke him. He was soon put out of suspense by being hailed and ordered to run under her lee, and the captain, looking over the quarter, asked Barny where he was going.

"Faith, then, I'm goin' an my business,' said Barny.

" But where?" said the captain.

" Why, sure, an it's no matther where a poor man like me id be goin'," said Barny.

" Only I'm curious to know what the deuce you've been following my ship for the last week?"

" Follyin' your ship! Why, thin, blur-an-agers, do you think it's follyin' yiz I am?"

" It's very like it," said the captain.

" Why, did two people niver thravel the same road before?"

" I don't say they didn't; but there's a great difference between a ship of seven hundred tons and a hooker."

" Oh! as for that matther," said Barny, " the same highroad sarves a coach and four, and a lowback car; the thravellin' tinker an' horseback."

" That's very true," said the captain, " but the

cases are not the same, Paddy, and I can't conceive what the devil brings *you* here."

"And who ax'd you to consayve anything about it?" asked Barny somewhat sturdily.

"D—n me if I can imagine what you're about, my fine fellow," said the captain; "and my own notion is that you don't know where the d—l you're going yourself."

"O *baithershin!*" said Barny, with a laugh of derision.

"Why, then, do you object to tell?" said the captain.

"Arrah sure, captain, an' don't you know that sometimes vessels is bound to sail under *saycret ordhers?*" said Barny, endeavoring to foil the question by badinage.

There was a universal laugh from the deck of the ship, at the idea of a fishing-boat sailing under secret orders; for, by this time, the whole broadside of the vessel was crowded with grinning mouths and wondering eyes at Barny and his boat.

"Oh! it's a thrifle makes fools laugh," said Barny.

"Take care, my fine fellow, that you don't be laughing at the wrong side of your mouth before long, for I've a notion that you're cursedly in the wrong box, as cunning a fellow as you think yourself. D—n your stupid head, can't you tell what brings you here?"

"Why, thin, by gor, one id think the whole say belonged to you, you're so mighty bowld in axin questions an it. Why, tare-an-ouns, sure I've as much right to be here as you, though I haven't as big a ship nor as fine a coat; but may be I can take as good a sailin' out o' the one, and has as bowld a heart under th' other."

"Very well," said the captain, "I see there's no use in talking to you, so go to the d—l your own way." And away bore the ship, leaving Barny in indignation and his companions in wonder.

"An' why wouldn't you tell him?" said they to Barny.

"Why, don't you see," said Barny, whose object was now to blind them—"don't you see, how do I know but may be he might be goin' to the same place himself, and may be he has a cargo of *scalpeens* as well as uz, and wants to get before us there?"

"True for you, Barny," said they. "By dad, you're right." And their enquiries being satisfied, the day passed, as former ones had done, in pursuing the course of the ship.

In four days more, however, the provisions in the hooker began to fail, and they were obliged to have recourse to the *scalpeens* for sustenance, and Barny then got seriously uneasy at the length of the voyage and the likely greater length, for any thing he could see to the contrary; and, urged at last by his own alarms and those of his companions, he was enabled, as the wind was light, to gain on the ship, and, when he found himself alongside, he demanded a parley with the captain.

The captain, on hearing that the "hardy hooker," as she got christened, was under his lee, came on deck, and, as soon as he appeared, Barny cried out—

"Why, thin, blur-an-agers, captain dear, do you expec' to be there soon?"

"Where?" said the captain.

"Oh! you know yourself," said Barny.

"It's well for me I do," said the captain.

"Thrue for you, indeed, your honor," said Barny, in his most insinuating tone; "but whin will you be at the ind o' your voyage, captain jewel?"

"I dare say in about three months," said the captain.

"O Holy Mother!" ejaculated Barny; "three months!—arrah, it's jokein' you are, captain dear, and only want to freken me."

"How should I frighten you?" asked the captain.

"Why, thin, your honor, to tell God's truth, I heard you were goin' *there*, an', as I wanted to go there too, I thought I couldn't do better nor to folly a knowledgable gintleman like yourself, and save myself the throuble iv findin' it out."

"And where do you think I *am* going?" said the captain.

"Why, thin," said Barny, "isn't it to Fingal?"

"No," said the captain; "it's to *Bengal*."

"Oh! Gog's blakey!" said Barny, "what'll I do now at all at all?"

CHAPTER II.

HOMEWARD-BOUND.

" 'Tis an ill wind that blows nobody good."—Old Saying.

THE captain ordered Barny on deck, as he wished to have some conversation with him on what he very naturally considered a most extraordinary adventure. Heaven help the captain! he knew little of Irishmen, or he would not have been so astonished. Barny made his appearance. Puzzling question, and more puzzling answer, followed in quick succession between the commander and Barny, who, in the midst of his dilemma, stamped about, thumped his head, squeezed his caubeen into all manner of shapes, and vented his despair anathematically:

"Oh! my heavy hathred to you, you tarnal thief iv a long sailor! It's a purty scrape yiv led me into. By gor, I thought it was *Fingal* he said, and now I hear it is *Bingal*. Oh! the divil sweep you for navigation, why did I meddle or make wid you at all at all? And my curse light on you, Terry O'Sullivan, why did I iver come across you, you onlooky vagabone, to put sitch thoughts in my head? And so its *Bingal*, and not *Fingal*, you're goin' to, captain?"

"Yes, indeed, Paddy."

"An' might I be so bowld to ax, captain, is Bingal much farther nor Fingal?"

"A trifle or so, Paddy."

"Och, thin, millia murther, weirasthru, how 'ill I iver get there at all at all?" roared out poor Barny.

"By turning about, and getting back the road you've come, as fast as you can."

"Is it back? O Queen iv Heaven! an how will I iver get back?" said the bewildered Barny.

"Then you don't know your course, it appears?"

"Oh! faix I know it, iligant, as long as your honor was before me."

"But you don't know your course back?"

"Why, indeed, not to say rightly all out, your honor."

"Can't you steer?" said the captain.

"The devil a betther hand at the tiller in all Kinsale," said Barny, with his usual brag.

"Well, so far so good," said the captain. "And you know the points of the compass—you have a compass, I suppose?"

"A compass! by my sowl an it's not let alone a compass, but a *pair* a compasses I have, that my brother the carpinthir left me for a keepsake whin he wint abroad; but, indeed, as for the points o' thim, I can't say much, for the childer spylt thim intirely, rootin' holes in the flure."

"What the plague are you talking about?" asked the captain.

"Wasn't your honor discoorsin' me about the points o' the compasses?"

"Confound your thick head!" said the captain. "Why, what an ignoramus you must be, not to know what a compass is, and you at sea all your life? Do you even know the cardinal points?"

"The cardinals! faix, an it's a great respect I have for them, your honor. Sure, ar'n't they belongin' to the pope?"

"Confound you, you blockhead!" roared the captain, in a rage; "'twould take the patience of the pope and the cardinals, and the cardinal virtues into the bargain, to keep one's temper with you. Do you know the four points of the wind?"

"By my sowl, I do, and more."

"Well, never mind more, but let us stick to four. You're sure you know the four points of the wind?"

"By dad, it would be a quare thing if a sayfarin' man didn't know somethin' about the wind, anyhow. Why, captain, dear, you must take me for a nath'ral intirely, to suspect me o' the like o' not knowin' all about the wind. By gor, I know as much o' the wind a'most as a pig."

"Indeed, I believe so," laughed out the captain.

"Oh! you may laugh if you plaze, and I see by the same that you don't know about the pig, with all your edication, captain."

"Well, what about the pig?"

"Why, sir, did you never hear a pig can see the wind?"

"I can't say that I did."

"Oh! thin, he does, and, for that reason, who has a right to know more about it?"

"You don't, for one, I dare say, Paddy; and may be you have a pig aboard to give you information."

"Sorra taste, yer honor, not as much as a rasher o' bacon; but it's may be your honor never seen a pig tossing up his snout consaited like, and running like mad afore a storm."

"Well, what if I have?"

"Well, sir, that is when they see the wind a-comin."

"May be so, Paddy, but all this knowledge in piggery won't find you your way home; and, if you take my advice, you will give up all thoughts of endeavoring to find your way back, and come on board. You and your messmates, I dare say, will be useful hands, with some teaching; but, at all events, I cannot leave you here on the open sea, with every chance of being lost."

"Why, thin, indeed, and I'm behowldin' to your honor; and it's the hoighth o' kindness, so it is, you offer; and it's nothin' else but a gintleman you are, every inch o' you; but I hope it's not so bad wid us yet as to do the likes o' that."

"I think it's bad enough," said the captain, "when you are without a compass, and knowing nothing of your course, and nearly a hundred and eighty leagues from land."

"An' how many miles would that be, captain?'

"Three times as many."

"I never larned the rule o' three, captain, and may be your honor id tell me yourself."

"That is rather more than five hundred miles."

"Five hundred miles!" shouted Barny. "Oh! the Lord look down upon us! How 'ill we ever get back?"

"That's what I say," said the captain; "and, therefore, I recommend you to come aboard with me."

"And where 'ud the hooker be all the time?" said Barny.

"Let her go adrift," was the answer.

"Is it the darlint boat? Oh! by dad, I'll never hear o' that, at all."

"Well, then, stay in her and be lost. Decide upon the matter at once—either come on board or cast off."

And the captain was turning away as he spoke, when Barny called after him: "Arrah, thin, your honor, don't go jist for one minit antil I ax you one word more. If I wint wid you, whin would I be home again?"

"In about seven months."

"Oh! thin, that puts the wig an it at wanst. I dar'n't go at all."

"Why, seven months are not long passing."

"Thrue for you, in troth," said Barny, with a shrug of his shoulders. "Faix, it's myself knows, to my sorrow, the half year comes round mighty suddint, and the lord's agint comes for the thrifle o' rent; and, faix, I know by Molly that nine months is not long in comin' over either," added Barny, with a grin.

"Then, what's your objection as to the time?" asked the captain.

"Arrah, sure, sir, what would the woman that owns me do while I was away? And may be it's break her heart the craythur would, thinking I was lost intirely! And who'd be at home to take care o' the childher' and airn thim the bit and the sup, whin I'd be away? And who knows but it's all dead they'd be afore I got back? Och hone! sure the heart id fairly break in my body, if hurt or harm kem to them through me. So say no more, captain, dear, only give me a thrifle o' directions how I'm to make an offer at gettin' home, and it's myself that will pray for you night, noon, and mornin' for that same."

"Well, Paddy," said the captain, "as you are determined to go back, in spite of all I can say, you must attend to me well while I give you as simple instructions as I can. You say you know the four points of the wind, north, south, east, and west?"

"Yes, sir."

"How do you know them? for I must see that you are not likely to make a mistake. How do you know the points?"

"Why, you see, sir, the sun, God bless it, rises in the aist, and sets in the west, which stands to raison; and, whin you stand bechuxt the aist and the west, the north is forninst you."

"And when the north is forninst you, as you say, is the east on your right or your left hand?"

"On the right hand, your honor."

"Well, I see you know that much, however. Now," said the captain, "the moment you leave the ship you must steer a north-east course, and you will make some land near home in about a week, if the wind holds as it is now, and it is likely to do so; but, mind me, if you turn out of the course in the smallest degree, you are a lost man."

"Many thanks to your honor."

"And how are you off for provisions?"

"Why, thin, indeed, in the regard o' that same, we are in the hoighth o' distress; for exceptin' the *scalpeens*, sorra taste passed our lips for these four days."

"Oh! you poor devils!" said the commander, in a tone of sincere commiseration. "I'll order you some provisions on board before you start."

"Long life to your honor! And *I'd like to drink the health* of so noble a gintleman."

"I understand you, Paddy, you shall have grog, too."

"Musha, the heavens shower blessins an you, I pray the Virgin Mary and the twelve apostles, Matthew, Mark, Luke, and John, not forgittin' St. Pathrick!"

"Thank you, Paddy; but keep your prayers for yourself, for you need them all to help you home again."

"Oh! never fear; when the thing is to be done, I'll do it, by dad, wid a heart and a half. And sure, your honor, God is good, an' will mind dessolute craythurs like uz on the wild oceant as well as ashore."

While some of the ship's crew were putting the captain's benevolent intentions to Barny and his companions into practice, by transferring some provisions to the hooker, the commander entertained himself by further conversation with Barny, who was the greatest original he had ever met. In the course of their colloquy, Barny drove many hard queries at the captain respecting the wonders of the nautical profession, and at last put the question to him plump:

"Oh! thin, captain dear, and how is it at all at all that you make your way over the wide says intirely to them furrin parts?"

"You would not understand, Paddy, if I attempted to explain to you."

"Sure enough, indeed, your honor, and I ask your pardon, only I was curious to know, and sure no wondher."

"It requires various branches of knowledge to make a navigator."

"Branches!" said Barny, "by gar, I think it id take *the whole tree o' knowledge* to make it out. And that place you are going to, sir, that *Bin*gal (oh! bad luck to it for a *Bin*gal, it's the sore *Bin*gal to me), is it so far off as you say?"

"Yes, Paddy, half round the world."

"Is it round in airnest, captain dear? Round about?"

"Aye, indeed."

"Oh! thin, ar'n't you afeard that whin you come to the top and that you're obleedged to go down, that you'd go slidderhin away intirely, and never be able to stop may be? It's bad enough, so it is, going downhill by land, but it must be the dickens all out by wather."

"But there is no hill, Paddy; don't you know that water is always level?"

"By dad, it's very *flat*, anyhow, and by the same token it's seldom I throuble it; but sure, your honor, if the wather is level, how do you make out that it is *round* you go?"

"That is a part of the knowledge I was speaking to you about," said the captain.

"Musha, bad luck to you, knowledge, but you're a quare thing! And where is it Bingal, bad cess to it, would be at all at all?"

"In the East Indies."

"Oh! that is where they make the *tay*, isn't it, sir?"

"No; where the tea grows is further still."

"Further! Why, that must be the ind of the world intirely; and they don't make it thin, sir, but it grows, you tell me."

"Yes, Paddy."

"Is it like hay, your honor?"

"Not exactly, Paddy; what puts hay in your head?"

"Oh! only bekase I hear them call it Bo*hay*."

"A most logical deduction, Paddy."

"And is it a great deal farther, your honor, the *tay* country is?"

"Yes, Paddy; China it is called."

"That's, I suppose, what we call Chaynee, sir?"

"Exactly, Paddy."

"By dad, I never could come at it rightly before, why it was nath'ral to drink tay out o' chaynee. I ax your honor's pardon for bein' troublesome, but I hard tell from the long sailor iv a place they call Japan, in them furrin parts; and *is* it there, your honor?"

"Quite true, Paddy."

"And I suppose it's there the blackin' comes from?"

"No, Paddy; you are out there."

"Oh! well, I thought it stood to rayson, as I heerd of Japan blackin', sir, that it would be there it kem from; besides, as the blacks themselves— the naygers, I mane—is in them parts."

"The negroes are in Africa, Paddy, much nearer to us."

"God betune us and harm! I hope I would not be too near them," said Barny.

"Why, what's your objection?"

"Arrah, sure, sir, they're hardly mortials at all, but has the mark o' the bastes an thim."

"How do you make out that, Paddy?"

"Why, sure, sir, and didn't Nature make thim

wid wool on their heads, plainly makin' it undherstood to Chrishthans that they were little more nor cattle?"

"I think your head is a wool-gathering now, Paddy," said the captain, laughing.

"Faix, may be so, indeed," answered Barny good-humoredly; "but it's seldom I ever went out to look for wool and kem home shorn, anyhow," said he, with a look of triumph.

"Well, you won't have that to say for the future, Paddy," said the captain, laughing again.

"My name's not Paddy, your honor," said Barny, returning the laugh, but seizing the opportunity to turn the joke aside that was going against him— "my name isn't Paddy, sir, but Barny."

"Oh! if it was Solomon, you'll be bare enough when you go home this time; you have not gathered much this trip, Barny."

"Sure I've been gathering knowledge, anyhow, your honor," said Barny, with a significant look at the captain, and a complimentary tip of his hand to his caubeen; "and God bless you for being so good to me."

"And what's your name besides Barny?" asked the captain.

"O'Reirdon, your honor—Barny O'Reirdon's my name."

"Well, Barny O'Reirdon, I won't forget your name nor yourself in a hurry, for you are certainly the most original navigator I ever had the honor of being acquainted with."

"Well," said Barny, with a triumphant toss of his head, "I have done Terry O'Sullivan, at any rate; the devil a half so far he ever was, and that's a comfort. I have muzzled his clack for the rest iv his life, and he won't be comin' over us wid the pride iv his *Fingal,* while I'm to the fore, that was a'most at *Bingal.*"

"Terry O'Sullivan—who is he, pray?" said the captain.

"Oh! he's a scut iv a chap that's not worth your axin for—he's not worth your honor's notice—a braggin' poor crathur. Oh! wait till I get home, and the devil a more braggin' they'll hear out of his jaw."

"Indeed, then, Barny, the sooner you turn your face towards home, the better," said the captain; "since you will go, there is no need of your losing more time."

"Thrue for you, your honor; and sure it's well for me I had the luck to meet with the likes o' your honor, that explained the ins and the outs iv it to me, and laid it all down as plain as prent."

"Are you sure you remember my directions?" said the captain.

"Troth an' I'll niver forget them to the day o' my death, and is bound to pray, more betoken, for you and yours."

"Don't mind praying for me till you get home, Barny; but answer me—how are you to steer when you shall leave me?"

"The nor'-aist coorse, your honor, that's the coorse agin the world."

"Remember that! Never alter that course till you see land—let nothing make you turn out of a north-east course."

"Throth an' that would be the dirty turn, seein' that it was yourself that ordhered it. Oh! no, I'll depend my life an the *nor'-aist coorse*, and God help any that comes betune me an' it!—I'd run him down if he was my father."

"Well, good-by, Barny."

"Good-by, and God bless you, your honor, and send you safe!"

"That's a wish you want for yourself, Barny—never fear for me, but mind yourself well."

"Oh! sure I'm as good as at home wanst I know the way, barrin' the wind is conthrary; sure the nor'-aist coorse 'll do the business complate. Good-by, your honor, and long life to you, and more power to your elbow, and a light heart and a heavy purse to you ever more, I pray the Blessed Virgin and all the saints, amin!" And so saying, Barny descended the ship's side, and once more assumed the helm of the "hardy hooker."

The two vessels now separated on their opposite courses. What a contrast their relative situations afforded! Proudly the ship bore away under her lofty and spreading canvas, cleaving the billows before her, manned by an able crew, and under the guidance of experienced officers; the finger of science to point the course of her progress, the faithful chart to warn of the hidden rock and the shoal, the long line and the quadrant to measure her march and prove her position. The poor little hooker cleft not the billows, each wave lifted her on its crest like a sea-bird; but the three inexperienced fishermen to manage her; no certain means to guide them over the vast ocean they had to' traverse; and the holding of the "fickle wind"—the only *chance* of their escape from perishing in the wilderness of waters. By the one, the feeling excited is supremely that of man's power. By the other, of his utter helplessness. To the one, the expanse of ocean could scarcely be considered "trackless"; to the other, it was a waste indeed. Yet the cheer that burst from the ship at parting was answered as gaily from the hooker as though the odds had not been so fearfully against her, and no blither heart beat on board the ship than that of Barny O'Reirdon.

Happy light-heartedness of my countrymen! How kindly have they been fortified by nature against the assaults of adversity; and, if they blindly rush into dangers, they cannot be denied the possession of gallant hearts to fight their way out of them.

But each hurrah became less audible; by degrees the cheers dwindled into faintness, and finally were lost in the eddies of the breeze.

The first feeling of loneliness that poor Barny experienced was when he could no longer hear the exhilarating sound. The plash of the surge as it broke on the bows of his little boat was uninterrupted by the kindred sound of human voice; and, as it fell upon his ear, it smote upon his heart. But he replied, waved his hat, and the silent signal was answered from those on board the ship.

"Well, Barny," said Jemmy, "what was the captain sayin' to you at the time you wor wid him?"

"Lay me alone," said Barny; "I'll talk to you when I see her out o' sight, but not a word till thin. I'll look afther him, the rale gintleman that he is, while there's a top-sail of his ship to be seen; and then I'll send my blessin' afther him, and pray for his good fortune wherever he goes, for he's the right sort, and nothin' else." And Barny kept his word, and, when his straining eye could no longer trace a line of the ship, the captain certainly had the benefit of "a poor man's blessing."

The sense of utter loneliness and desolation had not come upon Barny until now; but he put his trust in the goodness of Providence, and, in a fervent mental outpouring of prayer, resigned himself to the care of his Creator. With an admirable fortitude, too, he assumed a composure to his companions that was a stranger to his heart; and we all know how the burden of anxiety is increased when we have none with whom to sympathize. And this was not all. He had to affect ease and confidence; for Barny not only had no dependence on the firmness of his companions to go through the undertaking before them, but dreaded to betray to them how he had imposed on them in the affair. Barny was equal to all this. He had a stout heart, and was an admirable actor; yet, for the first hour after the ship was out of sight, he could not quite recover himself, and every now and then unconsciously he would look back with a wishful eye to the point where last he saw her. Poor Barny had lost his leader!

The night fell, and Barny stuck to the helm as long as nature could sustain want of rest, and then left it in charge of one of his companions, with particular directions how to steer, and ordered, if any change in the wind occurred, that they should instantly awake him. He could not sleep long, however, the fever of anxiety was upon him, and the morning had not long dawned when he awoke. He had not well rubbed his eyes and looked about him when he thought he saw a ship in the distance approaching them. As the haze cleared away, she showed distinctly bearing down towards the hooker. On board the ship, the hooker, in such a sea, caused surprise as before, and in about an hour she was so close as to hail and order the hooker to run under her lee."

"The devil a taste," said Barny. "I'll not quit my *nor'-aist coorse* for the King of Ingland, nor Bonyparty into the bargain. Bad cess to you, do you think I've nothin' to do but plaze you?"

Again he was hailed.

"Oh! bad luck to the toe I'll go to you."

Another hail.

"Spake loudher, you'd betther," said Barny jeeringly, still holding on his course.

A gun was fired ahead of him.

"By my sowl, you spoke loudher that time, sure enough," said Barny.

"Take care, Barny!" cried Jemmy and Peter together. "Blur-an-agers, man, we'll be kilt, if you don't go to them."

"Well, and we'll be lost if we turn out iv our *nor'-aist coorse*, and that's as broad as it's long. Let them hit iz if they like; sure it ud be a pleasant death nor starvin' at say. I'll tell you agin, I'll turn out o' my *nor'-aist coorse* for no man."

A shotted gun was fired. The shot hopped on the water, as it passed before the hooker.

"Phew! you missed it like your mammy's blessin'," said Barny.

"Oh! murthur!" said Jemmy. "Didn't you see the ball hop aff the wather forninst you? Oh! murthur, what 'ud we ha' done if we wor there at all at all?"

"Why, we'd have taken the ball at the hop," said Barny, laughing, "accordin' to the ould sayin'."

Another shot was ineffectually fired.

"I'm thinking that's a Connaughtman* that's

---

* This is an allusion of Barny's to a prevalent saying in Ireland, addressed to a sportsman who returns home unsuccessful: "So you've killed what the Connaughtman shot at?" Besides, Barny herein indulges a provincial pique for the people of Munster have a profound contempt for Connaughtmen.

shootin'," said Barny, with a sneer. The allusion was so relished by Jemmy and Peter that it excited a smile in the midst of their fears from the cannonade.

Again the report of the gun was followed by no damage.

"Augh! never heed them!" said Barny contemptuously. "It's a barkin' dog that never bites, as the owld sayin' says." And the hooker was soon out of reach of further annoyance.

"Now, what a pity it was, to be sure," said Barny, "that I wouldn't go aboord to plaze them! Now, who's right? Ah! lave me alone, always, Jemmy; did you iver know me wrong yet?"

"Oh! you may hillow now that you are out o' the wood," said Jemmy; "but, accordin' to my idays, it was runnin' a grate risk to be conthrary wid them at all, and they shootin' balls afther us."

"Well, what matther," said Barny, "since they wor only blind gunners, *an' I knew it*. Besides, as I said afore, I won't turn out o' my *nor'-aist coorse* for no man."

"That's a new turn you tuk lately," said Peter. "What's the raison you're runnin' a nor'-aist coorse now, an we never heard iv it afore at all, till afther you quitted the big ship?"

"Why, thin, are you sitch an ignoramus all out," said Barny, "as not for to know that in navigation you must lie in a great many different tacks before you can make the port you steer for?"

"Only I think," said Jemmy, "that it's back intirely we're goin' now, and I can't make out the rights o' that at all."

"Why," said Barny, who saw the necessity of mystifying his companions a little, "you see, the captain towld me that I kum around, an' rekimminded me to go th' other way."

"Faix, it's the first time I ever heard o' goin' round by say," said Jemmy.

"Arrah, sure, that's part o' the saycrets o' navigation and the various branches o' knowledge that is requizit for a navigator; and that's what the captain, God bless him! and myself was discoorsin an aboord ; and, like a rale gintleman as he is, Barny, says he ; Sir, says I ; You've come the round, says he. I know that, says I, bekase I like to keep a good bowld offin', says I, in contrairy places. Spoke like a good sayman, says he. That's my principles, says I. They're the right sort, says he. But says he (no offence), I think you wor wrong, says he, to pass the short turn in the ladi-shoes,* says he. I know, says I, you mane beside the three-spike headlan'. That's the spot, says he, I see you know it. As well as I know my father, says I."

"Why, Barny," said Jemmy, interrupting him, "we seen no head-lan' at all."

"Whisht, whisht!" said Barny, "bad cess to you, don't thwart me! We passed it in the night, and you couldn't see it. Well, as I was saying, I

* Some offer Barny is making at latitudes.

knew it as well as I know my father, says I, but I gev the preference to go the round, says I. You're a good sayman for that same, says he, an' it would be right at any other time than this present, says he, but it's onpossible now, teetotally, on account o' the war, says he. Tare alive, says I, what war? An' didn't you hear o' the war? says he. Divil a word, says I. Why, says he, the Naygurs has made war on the king o' Chaynee, says he, bekase he refused them any more tay; an' with that, what do they do, says he, but they put a lumbago on all the vessels that sails the round, an' that's the rayson, says he, I carry guns, as you may see; and I rekimmind you, says he, to go back, for you're not able for thim, and that's jist the way iv it. An' now, wasn't it looky that I kem acrass him at all? Or may be we might be cotch by the Naygurs, and ate up alive."

"Oh! thin, indeed, and that's thrue," said Jemmy and Peter, "and when will we come to the short turn?"

"Oh! never mind," said Barny, "you'll see it when you get there; but wait till I tell you more about the captain and the big ship. He said, you know, that he carried guns afeard o' the Naygurs; and, in troth, it's the hoight o' care he takes o' them same guns; and small blame to him, sure, they might be the salvation of him. 'Pon my conscience, they're taken betther care of than any poor man's child. I heerd him cautionin' the sailors about them, and givin them ordhers about their clothes."

" Their clothes!" said his two companions at once in much surprise; " is it clothes upon cannons ?"

" It's thruth I'm tellin' you," said Barny. " Bad luck to the lie in it, he was talkin' about their aprons and their breeches."

" Oh! think o' that!" said Jemmy and Peter, in surprise.

" An' 'twas all iv a piece," said Barny, " that an' the rest o' the ship all out. She was as nate as a new pin. Throth I was a'most ashamed to put my fut on the deck, it was so clane, and she painted every color in the rainbow ; and all sorts o' curiosities about her ; and, instead iv a tiller to steer her, like this darlin' craythur iv ours, she goes wid a wheel, like a coach all as one ; and there's the quarest thing you iver seen, to show the way, as the captain gev me to understan',—a little round rowly-powly thing in a bowl, that goes waddlin' about as if it didn't know it's own way, much more nor show anybody theirs. Throth myself thought that if that's the way they're obliged to go, that it's with a great deal of *fear and thrimblin'* they find it out."

Thus it was that Barny continued most marvellous accounts of the ship and captain to his companions, and, by keeping their attention so engaged, prevented their being too inquisitive as to their own immediate concerns ; and **for two days** more Barny and the hooker held on their respective courses undeviatingly.

The third day Barny's fears for the continuity of his *nor'-aist coorse* were excited, as a large brig hove in sight, and the nearer she approached, the more directly the appeared to be coming athwart Barny's course.

"May the divil sweep you!" said Barny. "And will nothin' else sarve you than comin' forninst me that away? Brig ahoy, there!" shouted Barny, giving the tiller to one of his messmates, and standing at the bow of his boat. "Brig ahoy, there!—bad luck to you, go 'long out o' my *nor'-aist coorse!*" The brig, instead of obeying him, hove to, and lay right ahead of the hooker. "Oh! look at this!" shouted Barny, and he stamped on the deck with rage—"look at the blackguards where they're stayin', just a-purpose to ruin an unfortunate man like me. My heavy hathred to you! Quit this minit, or I'll run down an yez, and, if we go to the bottom, we'll haunt you for evermore—go 'long out o' that, I tell you! The curse o' Crummil on you, you stupid vagabones, that won't go out iv a man's nor'-aist coorse!"

From cursing, Barny went to praying as he came closer. "For the tendher marcy o' heaven, an' lave my way. May the Lord reward you, and get out o' my nor'-aist coorse! May angels make your bed in heavin and don't ruinate me this a way." The brig was immovable, and Barny finished with a duet volley of prayers and curses together, apostrophizing the hard case of a man being "*done out o' his nor'-aist coorse.*"

"Ahoy there!" shouted a voice from the brig. "Put down your helm, or you'll be aboard of us. I say, let go your jib and foresheet—what are you about, you lubbers?"

'Twas true that the brig lay so fair in Barny's course that he would have been aboard, but that, instantly the manœuvre above alluded to was put in practice on board the hooker as she swept to destruction towards the heavy hull of the brig, he luffed up into the wind alongside her. A very pale and somewhat emaciated face appeared at the side, and addressed Barny—

"What brings you here?" was the question.

"Throth, thin, and I think I might bether ax what brings *you* here, right in the way o' my *nor'-aist coorse.*"

"Where do you come from?"

"From Kinsale; and you didn't come from a bether place, I go bail."

"Where are you bound to?"

"To Fingal."

"Fingal—where's Fingal?"

"Why, then, ain't you ashamed yourself an' not to know where Fingal is?"

"It is not in these seas."

"Oh! and that's all you know about it," says Barny.

"You're a small craft to be so far at sea. I suppose you have provisions on board?"

"To be sure we have; throth if we hadn't, this id be a bad place to go a beggin'."

"What have you eatable?"

"The finest o' *scalpeens*."

"What are *scalpeens*?"

"Why, you're mighty ignorant intirely," said Barny; "why, *scalpeens* is pickled mackerel."

"Then you must give us some, for we have been out of everything eatable these three days; and even pickled fish is better than nothing."

It chanced that the brig was a West India trader, which unfavorable winds had delayed much beyond the expected period of time on her voyage, and, though her water had not failed, everything eatable had been consumed, and the crew reduced almost to helplessness. In such a strait, the arrival of Barny O'Reirdon and his *scalpeens* was a most providential succor to them, and a lucky chance for Barny, for he got in exchange for his pickled fish a handsome return of rum and sugar, much more than equivalent to their value. Barny lamented much, however, that the brig was not bound for Ireland, that he might practise his own peculiar system of navigation; but, as staying with the brig could do no good, he got himself put into his *nor'-aist coorse* once more, and ploughed away towards home.

The disposal of his cargo was a great godsend to Barny in more ways than one. In the first place, he found the most profitable market he could have had; and, secondly, it enabled him to cover his retreat from the difficulty which still was before him of not getting to Fingal after all his dangers, and consequently being open to discovery and disgrace. All these beneficial results were thrown away upon one of Barny's readiness to avail himself of every point in his favor ; and, accordingly, when they left the brig, Barny said to his companions, " Why, thin, boys, 'pon my conscience, but I'm as proud as a horse wid a wooden leg this minit, that we met them poor unfortinate craythers this blessed day, and was enabled to extind our charity to them. Sure an' it's lost they'd be, only for our comin' acrass them, and we, through the blessin' o' God, enabled to do an act o' marcy, that is, feedin' the hungry ; and sure every good work we do here is before uz in heaven—and that's a comfort anyhow. To be sure, now that the *scalpeens* is sowld, there's no use in goin' to Fingal, and we may as well jist go home."

" Faix, I'm sorry myself," said Jemmy, " for Terry O'Sullivan said it was an iligant place intirely, an' I wanted to see it."

" To the divil wid Terry O'Sullivan!" said Barny ; " How does he know what's an iligant place ? What knowledge has he of iligance ! I'll go bail he never was half as far a navigatin' as we —he wint the short cut, I go bail, and never dar'd for to vinture the round, as I did."

" By dad, we wor a great dale longer anyhow than he towld me he was."

"To be sure we wor," said Barny; "he wint skulkin' in by the short cut, I tell you, and was afeard to keep a bowld offin' like me. But come, boys, let uz take a dhrop o' the bottle o' sper'ts we got out o' the brig. By gor, it's well we got some bottles iv it; for I wouldn't much like to meddle wid that darlint little kag iv it antil we get home." The rum was put on its trial by Barny and his companions, and in their critical judgment was pronounced quite as good as the captain of the ship had bestowed upon them, but that neither of those specimens of spirit was to be compared to whiskey. "By dad," says Barny, "they may rack their brains a long time before they'll make out a purtier invintion than *potteen;* that rum may do very well for thim that has the misforthin not to know betther; but the whiskey is a more nath'ral sper't, accordin' to my idays." In this, as in most other of Barny's opinions, Peter and Jemmy coincided.

Nothing particular occurred for the two succeeding days, during which time Barny most religiously pursued his *nor'-aist coorse*, but the third day produced a new and important event. A sail was discovered on the horizon, and in the direction Barny was steering, and a couple of hours made him tolerably certain that the vessel in sight was an American; for though it is needless to say that he was not very conversant in such matters, yet, from the frequency of his seeing Americans trading to Ireland, his eye had become sufficiently accustomed to their lofty and tapering spars and peculiar smartness of rig to satisfy him that the ship before him was of transatlantic build; nor was he wrong in his conjecture.

Barny now determined on a manœuvre classing him among the first tacticians at securing a good retreat.

Moreau's highest fame rests upon his celebrated retrograde movement through the Black Forest.

Xenophon's greatest glory is derived from the deliverance of his ten thousand Greeks from impending ruin, by his renowned retreat.

Let the ancient and the modern hero "repose under the shadow of their laurels," as the French have it, while Barny O'Reirdon's historian, with a pardonable jealousy for the honor of his country, cuts down a goodly bough of the classic tree, beneath which our Hibernian hero may enjoy his "*otium cum dignitate.*"

Barny calculated the American was bound for Ireland, and, as she lay *almost* as directly in the way of his "*nor'-aist coorse*" as the West Indian brig, he bore up to and spoke her.

He was answered by a shrewd Yankee captain.

"Faix, an' it's glad I am to see your honor again," said Barny.

The Yankee had never been to Ireland, and told Barny so.

"Oh! throth I couldn't forget a gentleman so aisy as that," said Barny.

"You're pretty considerable mistaken now, I guess," said the American.

"Divil a taste," said Barny, with inimitable composure and pertinacity.

"Well, if you know me so tarnation well, tell me what's my name?" The Yankee flattered himself he had nailed Barny now.

"Your name, is it?" said Barny, gaining time by repeating the question. "Why, what a fool you are not to know your own name."

The oddity of the answer posed the American, and Barny took advantage of the diversion in his favor, and changed the conversation.

"By dad, I've been waitin' here these four or five days, expectin' some of you would be wantin' me."

"Some of us!—how do you mean?"

"Sure an' ar'n't you from Amerikay?"

"Yes; and what then?"

"Well, I say I was waitin' for some ship or other from Amerikay that 'ud be wantin' me. It's to Ireland you're goin?'

"Yes."

"Well, I suppose you'll be wanting a pilot," said Barny.

"Yes, when we get in shore, but not yet."

"Oh! I don't want to hurry you," said Barny.

"What port are you a pilot of?"

"Why, indeed, as for the matther o' that," said Barny, "they're all aiquel to me, a'most."

"All!" said the American. "Why, I calculate

you couldn't pilot a ship into all the ports of Ireland."

"Not all at wanst (once)," said Barny, with a laugh, in which the American could not help joining.

"Well, I say, what ports do you know best?"

"Why, thin, indeed," said Barny, "it would be hard for me to tell; but, wherever you want to go, I'm the man that'll do the job for you complate. Where is your honor going?"

"I won't tell you that—but do you tell me the ports you know best."

"Why, there's Watherford, and there's Youghal, an' Fingal."

"Fingal—where's that?"

"So you don't know where Fingal is? Oh! I see your a sthranger, sir—an' then there's Cork."

"You know Cove, then?"

"Is it the Cove o' Cork?"

"Yes."

"I was bred and born there, and pilots as many ships into Cove as any other two min *out* of it."

Barny thus sheltered his falsehood under the idiom of his language.

"But what brought you so far out to sea?" asked the captain.

"We wor lyin' out lookin' for ships that wanted pilots, and there kem an the terriblest gale o' wind aff the land, an' blew us to say out intirely, an' that's the way iv it, your honor."

"I calculate we got a share of the same gale; 'twas from the nor'-east."

"Oh! directly!" said Barny. "Faith you're right enough; 'twas the *nor'-aist coorse* we were an, sure enough; but no matther now that we've met wid you—sure we'll have a job home, anyhow."

"Well, get aboard then," said the American.

"I will in a minit, your honor, whin I jist spake a word to my comrades here."

"Why, sure it's not goin' to turn pilot you are?" said Jemmy, in his simplicity of heart.

"Whist, you omadhaun!" said Barny, "or I'll cut the tongue out o' you. Now mind me, Pether. You don't undherstan' navigashin and the varrious branches o' knowledge, an' so all you have to do is to folly the ship when I get into her, an' I'll show you the way home."

Barny then got aboard the American vessel, and begged of the captain that, as he had been out to sea so long, and had gone through "a power o' hardship intirely," that he would be permitted to go below and turn in to take a sleep; "for, in throth, it's myself and sleep that is sthrayngers for some time," said Barny, "an', if your honor 'll be plazed, I'll be thankful if you won't let them disturb me until I'm wanted, for sure till you see the land there's no use for me in life, an' throth I want a sleep sorely."

Barny's request was granted, and it will not be wondered at that, after so much fatigue of mind and body, he slept profoundly for four-and-twenty hours. He then was called, for land v /.· i·ι ∴ight, and when he came on deck the captain rallied him upon the potency of his somniferous qualities, and "calculated" he had never met any one who could sleep "four-and-twenty hours at a stretch before."

"Oh! sir," said Barny, rubbing his eyes, which were still a little hazy, "whiniver I go to sleep, *I pay attintion to it.*"

The land was soon neared, and Barny put in charge of the ship when he ascertained the first landmark he was acquainted with; but, as soon as the Head of Kinsale hove in sight, Barny gave a "whoo!" and cut a caper that astonished the Yankees, and was quite inexplicable to them, though I flatter myself it is not to those who do Barny the favor of reading his adventures.

"Oh! there you are, my darlint ould head! An' where's the head like o' you? Throth it's little I'd thought I'd ever set eyes an your good-looking faytures agin. But God's good!"

In such half-muttered exclamations did Barny apostrophize each well-known point of his native shore, and, when opposite the harbor of Kinsale, he spoke the hooker that was somewhat astern, and ordered Jemmy and Peter to put in there and tell Molly immediately that he was come back, and would be with her as soon as he could, after piloting the ship into the Cove. "But, on your apperl, don't tell Pether Kelly o' the big farm, nor indeed don't mintion to man or mortial, about the navigation we done antil I come home myself and make them sensible o' it, bekase, Jemmy and Pether, neither o' yiz is equal to it, and doesn't undherstan' the branches o' knowledge requizit for discoorsin' o' navigation."

The hooker put into Kinsale, and Barny sailed the ship into Cove. It was the first ship he ever had acted the pilot for, and his old luck attended him; no accident befell his charge, and, what was still more extraordinary, he made the American believe he was absolutely the most skilful pilot on the station. So Barny pocketed his pilot's fee, swore the Yankee was a gentleman, for which the republican did not thank him, wished him goodby, and then pushed his way home with what Barny swore was the aisiest made money he ever had in his life. So Barny got himself paid for *piloting* the ship that *showed him the way home.*

On reaching home, all were ready to throw their caps at his feet. None but an Irishman, I fearlessly assert, could have executed so splendid a *coup de finesse.*

As some *curious* persons (I *don't* mean the ladies) may wish to know what became of some of the characters who have figured in this tale, I beg to inform them that Molly continued a faithful wife and time-keeper, as already alluded to, for many years; that Peter Kelly was so pleased with his share in the profits arising from the trip, in the ample return of rum and sugar, that he freighted a large brig with *scalpeens* to the West Indies, and went supercargo himself. All he got in return was yellow fever.

Barny profited better by his share; he was enabled to open a public-house which had more custom than any ten within miles of it. Molly managed the bar very efficiently, and Barny " discoorsed" the customers most seductively; in short, Barny, at all times given to the *marvellous*, became a greater romancer than ever, and for years attracted even the gentlemen of the neighborhood who loved fun to his house, for the sake of his magnanimous mendacity.

As for the hitherto triumphant Terry O'Sullivan, from the moment Barny's *Bingal* adventure became known, he was obliged to fly the country, and was never heard of more, while the hero of the hooker became a greater man than before, and never was addressed by any other title afterwards than that of THE COMMODORE.

THE PRIEST'S STORY.

I HAVE already made known unto you that a younger brother and myself were left to the care of my mother. Best and dearest of mothers, said the holy man—sighing deeply, and clasping his hands fervently, while his hands were lifted to heaven, as if love made him conscious that the spirit of her he lamented had found its eternal rest there—thy gentle and affectionate nature sank under the bitter trial that an all-wise Providence was pleased to visit thee with! Well, sir, Frank was my mother's darling; not that you are to understand, by so saying, that she was of that weak and capricious tone of mind which lavished its care upon one at the expense of others—far from it; never was a deep store of maternal love more equally shared than among the four brothers; but when the two seniors went away, and I was some time after sent, for my studies, to St. Omer, Frank became the object upon which all the tenderness of her affectionate heart might exercise the little maternal cares that hitherto had been divided amongst many. Indeed, my dear Frank deserved it all; his was the gentlest of natures, combined with a mind of singular strength and brilliant imagination. In short, as the phrase has it, he was "the flower of the flock," and great things were expected from him.

It was some time after my return from St. Omer, while preparations were making for advancing Frank in the pursuit which had been selected as the business of his life, that every hour which drew nearer to the moment of his departure made him dearer not only to us, but to all who knew him, and each friend claimed a day that Frank should spend with him, which always passed in recalling the happy hours they had already spent together, in assurances given and received, of kindly remembrances that still should be cherished, and in mutual wishes for success, with many a hearty prophecy from my poor Frank's friends that he would one day be a great man.

One night, as my mother and myself were sitting at home beside the fire, expecting Frank's return from one of these parties, my mother said, in an unusually anxious tone:

"I wish Frank was come home."

"What makes you think of his return so soon?" said I.

"I don't know," said she, "but somehow I'm uneasy about him."

"Oh! make yourself quiet," said I, "on that subject; we cannot possibly expect Frank for an hour to come yet."

Still my mother could not become calm, and

she fidgeted about the room, became busy in doing nothing, and now and then would go to the door of the house to listen for the distant tramp of Frank's horse; but Frank came not.

More than the hour I had named as the probable time of his return had elapsed, and my mother's anxiety had amounted to a painful pitch, and I began myself to blame my brother for so long and late an absence. Still, I endeavored to calm her, and had prevailed on her to seat herself again at the fire, and commenced reading a page or two of an amusing book, when suddenly she stopped me, and turned her head to the window in the attitude of listening.

"It is! it is!" said she; "I hear him coming."

And now the sound of a horse's feet in a rapid pace became audible. She rose from her chair, and, with a deeply aspirated "Thank God!" went to open the door for him herself. I heard the horse now pass by the window; in a second or two more, the door was opened, and instantly a fearful scream from my mother brought me hastily to her assistance. I found her lying in the hall in a deep swoon; the servants of the house hastily crowded to the spot and gave her immediate aid. I ran to the door to ascertain the cause of my mother's alarm, and there I saw Frank's horse panting and foaming, and the saddle empty. That my brother had been thrown and badly hurt was the first thought that suggested itself; and a car and horse were immediately ordered to drive in the direction he had been returning; but in a few minutes our fears were excited to the last degree by discovering there was blood on the saddle.

We all experienced inconceivable terror at the discovery; but, not to weary you with details, suffice it to say that we commenced a diligent search, and at length arrived at a small by-way that turned from the main road and led through a bog, which was the nearest course for my brother to have taken homewards, and we accordingly began to explore it. I was mounted on the horse my brother had ridden, and the animal snorted violently, and exhibited evident symptoms of dislike to retrace this by-way, which, I doubted not, he had already travelled that night; and this very fact made me still more apprehensive that some terrible occurrence must have taken place to occasion such excessive repugnance on the part of the animal. However, I urged him onward, and, telling those who accompanied me to follow with what speed they might, I dashed forward, followed by a faithful dog of poor Frank's.

At the termination of about half a mile, the horse became still more impatient of restraint, and started at every ten paces, and the dog began to traverse the little road, giving an occasional yelp, sniffing the air strongly, and lashing his sides with his tail, as if on some scent.

At length he came to a stand, and beat about

within a very circumscribed space, yelping occasionally, as if to draw my attention. I dismounted immediately, but the horse was so extremely restless that the difficulty I had in holding him prevented me from observing the road by the light of the lantern which I carried. I perceived, however, it was very much trampled hereabouts, and bore evidence of having been the scene of a struggle.

I shouted to the party in the rear, who soon came up and lighted some fagots of bog-wood, which they brought with them to assist in our search, and we now more clearly distinguished the marks I have alluded to.

The dog still howled and indicated a particular spot to us; and on one side of the path, upon the stunted grass, we discovered a quantity of fresh blood, and I picked up a pencil-case which I knew had belonged to my murdered brother—for I now was compelled to consider him as such—and an attempt to describe the agonized feelings which at that moment I experienced would be in vain.

We continued our search for the discovery of his body for many hours without success, and the morning was far advanced before we returned home—how changed a home from the preceding day!

My beloved mother could scarcely be roused for a moment from a sort of stupor which seized upon her when the paroxysm of frenzy was over which the awful catastrophe of the fatal night had produced.

If ever heart was broken, hers was. She lingered but a few weeks after the son she adored, and seldom spoke during the period, except to call upon his name.

But I will not dwell on this painful theme. Suffice it to say she died; and her death, under such circumstances, increased the sensation which my brother's mysterious murder had excited. Yet, with all the horror which was universally entertained for the crime, and the execrations poured upon its atrocious perpetrator, still the doer of the deed remained undiscovered; and even I, who of course was the most active in seeking to develop the mystery, not only could catch no clue to lead to the discovery of the murderer, but failed even to ascertain where the mangled remains of my lost brother had been deposited.

It was nearly a year after the fatal event that a penitent knelt to me and confided to the ear of his confessor the misdeeds of an ill-spent life! I say of his whole life, for he had never before knelt at the confessional.

Fearful was the catalogue of crime that was revealed to me—unbounded selfishness, oppression, revenge, and lawless passion had held unbridled influence over the unfortunate sinner, and sensuality in all its shapes, even to the polluted home and betrayed maiden, had plunged him deeply into sin.

I was shocked—I may even say I was disgusted—
and the culprit himself seemed to shrink from the
recapitulation of his crimes, which he found more
extensive and appalling than he had dreamed of,
until the recital of them called them all up in fearful array before him. I was about to commence
an admonition, when he interrupted me—he had
more to communicate. I desired him to proceed
—he writhed before me. I enjoined him in the
name of the God he had offended, and who
knoweth the inmost heart, to make an unreserved
disclosure of his crimes before he dared to seek a
reconciliation with his Maker. At length, after
many a pause and convulsive sob, he told me, in a
voice almost suffocated by terror, that he had been
guilty of bloodshed. I shuddered, but in a short
time I recovered myself, and asked how and
where he had deprived a fellow-creature of life.
Never, to the latest hour of my life, shall I forget
the look which the miserable sinner gave me at
that moment. His eyes were glazed and seemed
starting from their sockets with terror; his face
assumed a deadly paleness; he raised his clasped
hands up to me in the most imploring action, as if
supplicating mercy, and, with livid and quivering
lips, he gasped out, " 'Twas I who killed your
brother!"

O God! how I felt at that instant! Even now,
after the lapse of years, I recollect the sensation—
it was as if the blood were flowing back upon my
heart, until I felt as if it would burst; and then a

few convulsive breathings, and back rushed the blood again through my tingling veins. I thought I was dying; but suddenly I uttered an hysteric laugh, and fell back senseless in my seat.

When I recovered, a cold sweat was pouring down my forehead, and I was weeping copiously. Never before did I feel my manhood annihilated under the influence of an hysterical affection—it was dreadful.

I found the blood-stained sinner supporting me, roused from his own prostration by a sense of terror at my emotion; for, when I could hear anything, his entreaties that I would not discover upon him were poured forth in the most abject strain of supplication. "Fear not for your miserable life," said I; "the seal of confession is upon what you have revealed to me, and so far you are safe; but leave me for the present, and come not to me again until I send for you." He departed.

I knelt and prayed for strength to him who alone could give it to fortify me in this dreadful trial. Here was the author of a brother's murder, and a mother's consequent death, discovered to me in the person of my penitent. It was a fearful position for a frail mortal to be placed in; but as a consequence of the holy calling I professed, I hoped, through the blessing of him whom I served, to acquire fortitude for the trial into which the ministry of his Gospel had led me.

The fortitude I needed came through prayer, and, when I thought myself equal to the task, I sent for the murderer of my brother. I officiated for him as our church has ordained—I appointed penances to him, and, in short, dealt with him merely as any other confessor might have done.

Years thus passed away, and during that time he constantly attended his duty; and it was remarked through the country that he had become a quieter person since Father Roach had become his confessor. But still he was not liked, and, indeed, I fear he was far from a reformed man, though he did not allow his transgressions to be so glaring as they were wont to be; and I began to think that terror and cunning had been his motives in suggesting to him the course he had adopted, as the opportunities which it gave him of being often with me as his confessor were likely to lull every suspicion of his guilt in the eyes of the world; and, in making me the depositary of his fearful secret, he thus placed himself beyond the power of my pursuit, and interposed the strongest barrier to my becoming the avenger of his bloody deed.

Hitherto I have not made you acquainted with the cause of that foul act—it was jealousy. He found himself rivalled by my brother in the good graces of a beautiful girl of moderate circumstances, whom he would have wished to obtain as his wife, but to whom Frank had become an object of greater interest; and I doubt not, had my poor fellow been spared, that marriage would ultimately have drawn closer the ties that were so savagely severed. But the ambuscade and the knife had done their deadly work; for the cowardly villain had lain in wait for him on the lonely bog-road he guessed he would travel on that fatal night, and, springing from his lurking-place, he stabbed my noble Frank in the back.

Well, sir, I fear I am tiring you with a story which you cannot wonder is interesting to me; but I shall hasten to a conclusion.

One gloomy evening in March, I was riding along the very road where my brother had met his fate, in company with his murderer. I know not what brought us together in such a place, except the hand of Providence that sooner or later brings the murderer to justice; for I was not wont to pass the road, and loathed the company of the man who happened to overtake me upon it. I know not whether it was some secret visitation of conscience that influenced him at the time, or that he thought the lapse of years had wrought upon me so far as to obliterate the grief for my brother's death, which had never been till that moment alluded to, however remotely, since he confessed his crime. Judge, then, my surprise, when, directing my attention to a particular point in the bog, he said:

"'Tis close by that place that your brother is buried."

I could not, I think, have been more astonished had my brother appeared before me.

"What brother?" said I.

"Your brother Frank," said he; "'twas there I buried him, poor fellow, after I killed him."

"Merciful God! thy will be done." And, seizing the rein of the culprit's horse, I said, "Wretch that you are! you have owned to the shedding of the innocent blood that has been crying to heaven for vengeance these ten years, and I arrest you here as my prisoner."

He turned ashy pale, as he faltered out a few words to say I had promised not to betray him.

"'Twas under the seal of confession," said I, "that you disclosed the deadly secret, and under that seal my lips must have been for ever closed; but now, even in the very place where your crime was committed, it has pleased God that you should arraign yourself in the face of the world, and the brother of your victim is appointed to be the avenger of his innocent blood."

He was overwhelmed by the awfulness of this truth, and unresistingly he rode beside me to the adjacent town of——, where he was committed for trial.

The report of this singular and providential discovery of a murderer excited a great deal of interest in the country; and, as I was known to be the culprit's confessor, the bishop of the diocese forwarded a statement to a higher quarter, which procured for me a dispensation as regarded the confessions of the criminal; and I was handed this instrument absolving me from further secrecy, a few days before the trial. I was the principal evidence against the prisoner. The body of my brother had, in the interim, been found in the spot his murderer had indicated, and the bog preserved it so far from decay as to render recognition a task of no difficulty. The proof was so satisfactorily adduced to the jury that the murderer was found guilty and executed ten years after he had committed the crime.

The judge pronounced a very feeling comment on the nature of the situation in which I had been placed for so many years, and passed a very flattering eulogium upon what he was pleased to call, " my heroic observance of the obligation of the secrecy by which I had been bound."

Thus, sir, you see how sacred a trust that of a fact revealed under confession is held by our church, when even the avenging of a brother's murder was not sufficient warranty for its being broken.*

---

* This story is a fact, and the comment of the judge upon the priest's fidelity, I am happy to say, is true.

PADDY THE PIPER.

Dogberry.—" Marry, sir, they have committed false reports; moreover, they have spoken untruths; secondarily, they are slanderers; sixthly, and lastly, they have belied a lady; thirdly, they have verified unjust things; and, to conclude, they are lying knaves."—*Much Ado about Nothing.*

THE only introduction I shall attempt to the following *extravaganza*, is to request the reader to suppose it to be delivered by a frolicking Irish peasant, in the richest brogue and most dramatic manner:

I'll tell you, sir, a mighty quare story, and it's as thrue as I'm standin' here, and that's no lie.

It was in the time of the *"ruction,"** when the long summer days, like many a fine fellow's precious life, was cut short by raison of the martial law that wouldn't let a dacent boy be out in the evenin', good or bad; for, whin the day's work was over, divil a one of uz dar to go to meet a frind over a glass, or a girl at the dance, but must go home, and shut ourselves up, and never budge, nor rise latch, nor dhraw boult until the morning kem again. Well, to come to my story. 'Twas afther nightfall, and we wor sittin' round the fire,

* Insurrection.

and the praties were boiling, and the noggins of butthermilk was standin' ready for our suppers, whin a knock kem to the door.

"Whist!" says my father, "here's the sojers come upon us now," says he. "Bad luck to them, the villians, I'm afeerd they seen a glimmer of the fire through the crack in the door," says he.

"No," says my mother; "for I'm afther hangin' an ould sack and my new petticoat agin it, a while ago."

"Well, whistht, anyhow," says my father, "for there's a knock agin." And we all held our tongues till another thump kem to the door.

"Oh! it's a folly to purtind any more," says my father, "they're too cute to be put off that a' way," says he. "Go, Shamus," says he to me, "and see who's in it."

"How can I see who's in it, in the dark?" says I.

"Well," says he, "light the candle, thin, and see who's in it, but don't open the door for your life, barrin' they brake it in," says he, "exceptin' to the sojers, and spake thim fair, if it's thim."

So with that I wint to the door, and there was another knock.

"Who's there?" says I.

"It's me," says he.

"Who are you?" says I.

"A frind," says he.

"*Baithershin!*" says I. "Who are you at all?"

"Arrah! don't you know me?" says he.

"Divil a taste," says I.

"Shure I'm Paddy the Piper," says he.

"Oh! thunder-an'-turf," says I. "Is it you, Paddy, that's in it?"

"Sorra one else," says he.

"And what brought you at this hour?" says I.

"By gar," says he, "I didn't like goin' the roun' by the road," says he, "and so I kem the short cut, and that's what delayed me," says he.

"Oh! bloody wars!" says I, "Paddy, I wouldn't be in your shoes for the king's ransom," says I; "for you know it's a hangin' matther to be cotched out these times," said I.

"Sur, I know that," says he, "God help me! and that's what I kem to you for," says he. "And let me in for ould acquaintance' sake," says poor Paddy.

"Oh! by this and that," says I, "I darn't open the door for the wide world, and sure you know it; and troth, if the Husshians or the Yeos* ketches you," says I, "they'll murthur you, as sure as your name's Paddy."

"Many thanks to you," says he, "for your good intintions; but, plaze the pigs, I hope it's not the likes o' that is in store for me, anyhow."

"Faix, then," says I, "you'd betther lose no time in hidin' yourself," says I; "for, throth, I tell you it's a short thrial and a long rope the Husshians would be afther givin' you, for they've no justice, and less marcy, the villians!"

* Yeomen.

"Faith, thin, more's the raison you should let me in, Shamus," says poor Paddy.

"It's a folly to talk," says I; "I darn't open the door."

"Oh! thin, millia murther!" says Paddy. "What'll become of me at all at all?" says he.

"Go aff into the shed," says I, "behin' the house, where the cow is, and there's an illigant lock o' straw that you may go sleep in," says I; "and a fine bed it ud be for a lord, let alone a piper."

So off Paddy set to hide in the shed, and, troth, it wint to our hearts to refuse him and turn him away from the door, more by token when the praties was ready, for sure the bit and the sup is always welkim to the poor traveller. Well, we all wint to bed, and Paddy hid himself in the cow-house; and now I must tell you how it was with Paddy.

You see, afther sleeping for some time, Paddy wakened up, thinkin' it was mornin', but it wasn't mornin' at all, but only the light o' the moon that desaved him; but, at all events, he wanted to be stirrin' airly, bekase he was going off to the town hard by, it bein' fair-day, to pick up a few ha'pence with his pipes, for the divil a betther piper was in all the counthry round nor Paddy; and every one gave it up to Paddy that he was illigant an the pipes, and played "Jinny bang'd the Weaver" beyant tellin', and the "Hare in the Corn" that you'd think the very dogs was in it, and the horsemen ridin' like mad.

Well, as I was sayin', he set off to go to the fair, and he went meandherin' along through the fields, but he didn't go far, antil, climbin' up through a hedge, when he was comin' out at t'other side, his head kem plump agin somethin' that made the fire flash out iv o' his eyes. So with that he looks up, and what do you think it was, Lord be merciful to uz! but a corpse hangin' out of a branch of a three?

"Oh! the top o' the mornin' to you, sir," says Paddy; "and is that the way with you, my poor fellow? Throth you took a start out o' me," says poor Paddy. And 'twas true for him, for it would make the heart of a stouter man nor Paddy jump to see the like, and to think of a Christian crathur being hanged up all as one as a dog.

Now, 'twas the rebels that hanged this chap; because, you see, the corpse had got clothes an him, and that's the raison that one might know it was the rebels—by raison that the Husshians and the Orangemen never hanged anybody with good clothes an him, but only the poor and definceless crathurs like uz; so, as I said before, Paddy knew well it was the *boys* that done it. "And," says Paddy, eyein' the corpse, "by my sowl, thin, but you have a beautiful pair o' boots an you," says he, "and it's what I am thinkin' you won't have any great use for thim no more; and sure it's a shame to see the likes o' me," says he, "the best piper in the sivin counties, to be trampin' wid a pair of ould brogues not worth three *traneens*, and a corpse with such an iligant pair o' boots that wants some one to wear thim." So, with that, Paddy lays hould of him by the boots, and began a pullin' at thim, but they were mighty stiff; and, whether it was by raison of their bin' so tight, or the branch of the three a-giggin' up and down all as one as a weighdee buckettee, an' not lettin Paddy cotch any right hoult o' thim, he could get no *advantage* o' thim at all; and at last he gev it up, and was goin' away, when, lookin' behind him agin, the sight of the iligant fine boots was too much for him, and he turned back, determined to have the boots anyhow, by fair means or foul. And I'm loath to tell you now how he got them; for, indeed, it was a dirty turn, and throth it was the only dirty turn I ever knew Paddy to be guilty av; and you see it was this a-way: 'pon my sowl, he pulled out a big knife, and, by the same token, it was a knife with a fine buck-handle, and a murtherin' big blade, that an uncle o' mine that was a gardener at the lord's made Paddy a prisint av; and, more by token, it was not the first mischief that knife done; for it cut love between thim that was the best of friends before; and sure 'twas the wondher of every one that two knowledgable men that ought to know better would do the likes, and give and take sharp steel in friendship; but I'm forgettin'—well, he outs with his knife, and what does he do but he cuts off the legs of the corpse. "And," says he, "I can take off the boots at my convaynience." And throth it was, as I said before, a dirty turn.

Well, sir, he tucked the legs under his arms, and at that minit the moon peeped out from behind a cloud. "Oh! is it there you are?" says he to the moon, for he was an impident chap; and thin, seein' that he made a mistake, and that the moonlight deceived him that it was the airly dawn, as he conceived; and bein' friken'd for fear himself might be cotched and trated like the poor corpse he was afther malthreating, if *he* was found walking the counthry at that time—by gar, he turned about, and walked back agin to the cow-house, and hidin' the corpse's legs in the sthraw, Paddy went to sleep agin. But what do you think? The devil a long Paddy was there antil the sojers came in airnest, and, by the powers, they carried off Paddy—and faith it was only sarvin' him right for what he had done to the poor corpse.

Well, whin the mornin' kem, my father says to me, "Go, Shamus," says he, "to the shed, and bid poor Paddy come in, and take share o' the praties; for, I go bail, he's ready for his breakquest by this anyhow."

Well, out I wint to the cow-house, and called out "Paddy!" and, afther callin' three or four times and getting no answer, I wint in, and called agin, and divil an answer I got still. "Blood-an-agers!" says I, "Paddy, where are you at all at all?" And so, castin' my eyes about the shed, I seen two feet

sticking out from undher the hape o' sthraw
"Musha! thin," says I, "bad luck to you, Paddy,
but you're fond of a warm corner, and may be you
haven't made yourself as snug as a flay in a blanket? But I'll disturb your dhrames, I'm thinkin',"
says I. And with that I laid hold of his heels (as I
thought, God help me!), and, givin' a good pull to
waken him, as I intinded, away I wint head over
heels, and my brains was a'most knocked out agin
the wall.

Well, whin I recovered myself, there I was
on the broad o' my back, and two things stickin'
out o' my hands like a pair o' Husshian's horse-pist'ls, and I thought the sight id lave my eyes
whin I seen they were two mortial legs.

My jew'l! I threw them down like a hot pratee, and, jumpin' up, I roared out millia murther.
"Oh! you murtherin' villain," says I, shaking my
fist at the cow. "Oh! you unnath'ral *baste*," says
I, "you've ate poor Paddy, you thievin' cannibal.
You're worse than a naygar," says I; "and, bad
luck to you, how dainty you are, that nothin' 'id
sarve you for your supper but the best piper in
Ireland! *Weirasthru! weirasthru!* What'll the
whole counthry say to such a unnath'ral murther?
And you lookin' as innocent there as a lamb, and
atin' your hay as quiet as if nothin' happened."
With that I run out—for throth I didn't like to be
near her—and, goin' to the house, I tould them
all about it.

"Arrah! be aisy," says my father.

"Bad luck to the lie I tell you," says I.

"Is it ate Paddy?" says they.

"Divil a doubt of it," says I.

"Are you sure, Shamus?" says my mother.

"I wish 1 was as sure of a new pair o' brogues," says I. "Bad luck to the bit she has left iv him but his two legs."

"And do you tell me she ate the pipes, too?" says my father.

"By gor, I b'lieve so," says I.

"Oh! the divil fly away wid her," says he. "What a cruel taste she has for music!"

"Arrah!" says mother, "don't be cursin' the cow that gives milk to the childer."

"Yis, I will," says my father. "Why shouldn't I curse sich an unnath'ral baste?'

"You oughtn't to curse any livin' thing that's under your roof," says my mother.

"By my soul, thin," says my father, "she sha'n't be undher my roof any more; for I'll sind her to the fair this minit," says he, "and sell her for whatever she'll bring. Go aff," says he, "Shamus, the minit you've ate your breakquest, and dhrive her to the fair."

"Throth I don't like to dhrive her," says I.

"Arrah! don't be makin' a gommach of yourself," says he.

"Faith, I don't," says I.

"Well, like or no like," says he, "you must dhrive her,"

"Sure, father," says I, "you could take more care iv her yourself."

"That's mighty good," says he, "to keep a dog and bark myself"—and, faith, I rec'llected the sayin' from that hour—"let me have no more words about it," says he, "but be aff with you."

So aff I wint, and it's no lie I'm tellin' when I say it was sore agin my will I had anything to do with such a villain of a baste. But, howsomever, I cut a brave long whattle, that I might drive the man-ather iv a thief, as she was, without bein' near her at all at all.

Well, away we wint along the road, and mighty throng it was with the boys and the girls—and, in short, all sorts, rich and poor, high and low, crowdin' to the fair.

"God save you!" says one to me.

"God save you, kindly!" says I.

"That's a fine baste you're dhrivin'," says he.

"Throth she is," says I, though God knows it wint agin my heart to say a good word for the likes of her.

"It's to the fair you're goin', I suppose," says he, "with the baste?" (He was a snug-lookin' farmer, ridin' a purty little gray hack.)

"Faith, thin, you're right enough," says I. "It's to the fair I'm goin'."

"What do you expec' for her?" says he.

[1] "Faith, thin, myself doesn't know," says I—and that was thrue enough, you see, bekase I was bewildered like about the baste entirely.

"Och!" says I, not likin' to let him suspict there was any thing wrong wid her—"och!" says I, in a careless sort of a way, "sure no one can tell what a baste'll bring antil they come to the fair," says I, "and see what price is goin'."

"Indeed, that's nath'ral enough," says he. "But if you wor bid a fair price before you come to the fair, sure you might as well take it," says he.

"Oh! I've no objection in life," says I.

"Well, thin, what'll you ax for her?" says he.

"Why, thin, I wouldn't like to be onraysonable," says I (for the thruth was, you know, I wanted to get rid iv her), "and so I'll take four pounds for her," says I, "and *no less*.'

"No less!" says he.

"Why, sure, that's chape enough," says I.

"Troth it is," says he; "and I'm thinkin it's *too* chape it is," says he; "for, if there wasn't somethin' the matter, it's not for that you'd be sellin' the fine milch cow as she is to all appearance."

"Indeed, thin," says I, "upon my conscience, she *is* a fine milch cow."

"May be," says he, "she's gone off her milk, in regard that she doesn't feed well?"

"Och! by this and that," says I, "in regard of feedin' there's not the likes of her in Ireland; so make your mind aisy, and, if you like her for the money, you may have her."

"Why, indeed, I'm not in a hurry," says he, "and I'll wait to see how they'll go in the fair."

"With all my heart," says I, purtending to be no ways consarned; but, in throth, I began to be afeerd that the people was seein' somethin' unnath'ral about her, and that we'd never get rid of her at all at all. At last we kem to the fair, and a great sight o' people was in it; throth you'd think the whole world was there, let alone the standin's o' gingerbread, and iligant ribbins, and makin's o' beautiful gownds, and pitch-and-toss, and merry-go-rouns, and tints with the best av drink in them, and the fiddles playin' up t' encourage the boys and girls; but I never minded them at all, but determint to sell the thieven' rogue av a cow afore I'd mind any divarshin in life; so an I dhriv her, into the thick av the fair, when all of a suddint, as I kem to the door av a tint, up struck the pipes to the tune av " Tatterin' Jack Welsh," and, my jew'l! in a minit, the cow cocked her ears, and was makin' a dart at the tint.

"O murther!" says I to the boys standin' by, "hould her!" says I, "hould her! She ate one piper already, the vagabone, and, bad luck to her, she wants another now."

" Is it a cow for to ate a piper?" says one of them.

" Divil a word o' lie in it, for I seen his corpse myself, and nothin' left but the two legs," says I. " And it's folly to be strivin' to hide it, for I see she'll never lave it aff, as poor Paddy Grogan knows to his cost, the Lord be merciful to him!"

" Who's that takin' my name in vain?" says a

voice in the crowd; and, with that, shovin' the throng a one side, who the devil should I see but Paddy Grogan to all appearance.

"Oh! hould him, too!" says I; "keep him aff me, for it's not himself at all, but his ghost," says I; "for he was kilt last night to my sartin knowledge, every inch of him, all to his legs."

Well, sir, with that, Paddy, for it was Paddy, as it kem out after, fell a-laughin' that you'd think his sides ud split, and, when he kem to himself, he ups and he tould us how it was, as I tould you already; and the likes av the fun they made av me was beyant tellin' for wrongfully misdoubtin' the poor cow, and layin' the blame iv atin a piper an her. So we all wint into the tint to have it explained, and, by gor, it took a full gallon o' sper'ts to explain it, and we dhrank health and long life to Paddy and the cow, and Paddy played that day beyant all tellin', and many a one said the likes was never heerd before nor sence, even from Paddy himself; and av coorse the poor slandered cow was dhruv home agin, and many a quiet day she had wid us afther that; and, whin she died, throth, my father had sitch a regard for the poor thing, that he had her skinned, and an iligant pair of breeches made out iv her hide, and it's in the family to this day; and isn't it mighty remarkable it is, what I'm goin' to tell you now, but it's as thrue as I'm here, that, from that out, any one that has them breeches on, the minit a pair o' pipes sthrikes up they can't rest, but goes jiggin' and jiggin' in their sate, and never stops as long as the pipes is playin'; and there," said he, slapping the garment in question that covered his sinewy limb, with a spank of his brawny hand that might have startled nerves more tender than mine—"there is the very breeches that's an me now, and a fine pair they are this minit."

THE WHITE TROUT.

A LEGEND OF CONG.

> Oh! I would ask no happier bed
> Than the chill wave my love lies under;
> Sweeter to rest together, dead,
> Far sweeter than to live asunder.
> —*Lalla Rookh.*

THE next morning I proceeded alone to the cave, to witness the natural curiosity of its subterranean river, my interest in the visit being somewhat increased by the foregoing tale. Leaving my horse at the little village of Cong, I bent my way on foot through the fields, if you may venture to give that name to the surface of this immediate district of the county Mayo, which, presenting large flat masses of limestone, intersected by patches of verdure, gives one the idea much more of a burial-ground covered with monumental slabs, than a formation of nature. Yet (I must make the remark *en passant*) such is the richness of the pasture in these little verdant interstices that cattle are fattened upon it in a much shorter time than on a meadow of the most cultured aspect; and though to the native of Leinster this *land* (if we may be pardoned a premeditated *bull*) would appear all *stones*, the Mayo farmer knows it from experience to be a profitable tenure. Sometimes deep clefts occur between these laminæ of limestone rock, which, closely overgrown with verdure, have not unfrequently occasioned serious accidents to man and beast; and one of these chasms, of larger dimensions than usual, forms the entrance to the celebrated cave in question. Very rude steps of unequal height, partly natural and partly artificial, lead the explorer of its quiet beauty, by an abrupt descent, to the bottom of the cave, which contains an enlightened area of some thirty or forty feet, whence a naturally vaulted passage opens, of the deepest gloom. The depth of the cave may be about equal to its width at the bottom; the mouth is not more than twelve or fifteen feet across; and pendent from its margin clusters of ivy and other parasite plants hang and cling in all the fantastic variety of natural festooning and tracery. It is a truly beautiful and poetical little spot, and particularly interesting to the stranger, from being unlike anything else one has ever seen, and having none of the noisy and vulgar pretence of regular *show places*, which calls upon you every moment to exclaim " Prodigious!"

An elderly and decent-looking woman had just filled her pitcher with the deliciously cold and clear water of the subterranean river that flowed along its bed of small, smooth, and many-colored pebbles, as I arrived at the bottom; and, perceiving at once that I was a stranger, she paused, partly, perhaps, with the pardonable pride of displaying her local knowledge, but more from the native peasant politeness of her country to become the temporary *cicerone* of the cave. She spoke some words of Irish, and hurried forth on her errand a very handsome and active boy, of whom she informed me she was the great-grandmother.

"Great-grandmother!" I repeated, in unfeigned astonishment.

"Yes, your honor," she answered, with evident pleasure sparkling in her eyes, which time had not yet deprived of their brightness, or the soul-subduing influence of this selfish world bereft of their kind-hearted expression.

"You are the youngest woman I have ever seen," said I, "to be a great-grandmother."

"Troth I don't doubt you, sir," she answered.

"And you seem still in good health, and likely to live many a year yet," said I.

"With the help of God, sir," said she reverently.

"But," I added, "I perceive a great number of persons about here of extreme age. Now, how long generally do the people in this country live?"

"Troth, sir," said she, with the figurative drollery of her country, "we live here as long as we like."

"Well, that is no inconsiderable privilege," said I; "but you nevertheless must have married very young?"

"I was not much over sixteen, your honor, when I had my first child at my breast."

"That was beginning early," said I.

"Thrue for you, sir; and, faith, Noreen (that's my daughter, sir)—Noreen herself lost no time either; I suppose she thought she had as good a right as the mother before her—she was married at seventeen, and a likely couple herself and her husband was. So you see, sir, it was not long before I was a granny. Well, to make the saying good, 'As the ould cock crows, the young bird chirrups,' and, faiks, the whole breed, seed, and generation tuk after the ould woman (that's myself, sir); and so, in coorse of time, I was not only a granny, but a *grate*-granny; and, by the same token, here comes my darling Paudeen Bawn* with what I sent him for."

Here the fine fellow I have spoken of, with his long, fair hair curling about his shoulders, descended into the cave, bearing some fagots of bogwood, a wisp of straw, and a lighted sod of turf.

"Now, your honor, it's what you'll see the pigeon-hole to advantage."

"What pigeon-hole?" said I.

"Here, where we are," she replied.

"Why is it so called?" I inquired.

"Because, sir, the wild pigeons often builds in the bushes and the ivy that's round the mouth of the cave, and in here, too," said she, pointing into the gloomy depth of the interior.

* Fair little Paddy.

"Blow that turf, Paudeen." And Paudeen, with distended cheeks and compressed lips, forthwith poured a few vigorous blasts on the sod of turf, which soon flickered and blazed, while the kind old woman lighted her fagots of bogwood at the flame.

"Now, sir, follow me," said my conductress.

"I am sorry you have had so much trouble on my account," said I.

"Oh! no throuble in life, your honor, but the greatest of pleasure." And so saying, she proceeded into the cave, and I followed, carefully choosing my steps, by the help of her torch-light, along the slippery path of rock that overhung the river. When she had reached a point of some little elevation, she held up her lighted pine branches, and, waving them to and fro, asked me could I see the top of the cave.

The effect of her figure was very fine, illumined as it was, in the midst of utter darkness, by the red glare of the blazing fagots; and, as she wound them round her head, and shook their flickering sparks about, it required no extraordinary sketch of imagination to suppose her, with her ample cloak of drapery and a few straggling tresses of gray hair escaping from the folds of a rather Eastern head-dress, some sibyl about to commence an awful rite, and evoke her ministering spirits fron the dark void, or call some waterdemon from the river which rushed unseen along, telling of its wild course by the turbulent dash of its waters, which the reverberation of the cave rendered still more hollow.

She shouted aloud, and the cavern-echoes answered to her summons. "Look!" said she; and she lighted the wisp of straw, and flung it on the stream; it floated rapidly away, blazing in wild undulations over the protruded surface of the river, and at length suddenly disappeared altogether. The effect was most picturesque and startling; it was even awful—I might almost say sublime.

Her light being nearly expired, we retrace our steps, and, emerging from the gloom, stood beside the river, in the enlightened area I have described.

"Now, sir," said my old woman, "we must thry and see the white throut; and you never seen a throut o' that color yet, I warrant."

I assented to the truth of this.

"They say it's a fairy throut, your honor, and tells mighty quare stories about it."

"What are they?" I inquired.

"Throth it's myself doesn't know the half o' them—only partly; but sthrive and see it before you go, sir, for there's thim that says it isn't lucky to come to the cave, and lave it without seeing the white throut; and, if you're a bachelor, and didn't get a peep at it, throth you'd never get married; and sure that i'd be a marther."*

"Oh!" said I, "I hope the fairies would not be so spiteful—"

* A great pity.

"Whist—whist!" said she looking fearfully around; then knitting her brows, she gave me an admonitory look, and put her finger on her lip, in token of silence, and then, coming sufficiently near me to make herself audible in a whisper, she said, "Never speak ill, your honor, of the good people, beyant all in sich a place as this; for it's in the likes they always keep; and one doesn't know who may be listenin'. God keep uz! But look, sir, look!"—and she pointed to the stream—"there she is."

"Who? What?" said I.

"The throut, sir."

I immediately perceived the fish in question, perfectly a trout in shape, but in color a creamy white, heading up the stream, and seeming to keep constantly within the region of the enlightened part of it.

"There it is, in that very spot evermore," continued my guide, "and never anywhere else."

"The poor fish, I suppose, likes to swim in the light," said I.

"Oh! no, sir," said she, shaking her head significantly, "the people here has a mighty owld story about that throut."

"Let me hear it, and you will oblige me."

"Och! it's only laughin' at me you'd be, and call me an owld fool, as the misthiss beyant in the big house often did afore when she first kem among us; but she knows the differ now."

"Indeed, I shall not laugh at your story," said I,

"but, on the contrary, shall thank you very much for your tale."

"Then sit down a minit, sir," said she, throwing her apron upon the rock, and pointing to the seat, "and I'll tell you to the best of my knowledge." And, seating herself on an adjacent patch of verdure, she began her legend.

"There was wanst upon a time long ago a beautiful young lady that lived in a castle up by the lake beyant, and they say she was promised to the king's son, and they wor to be married; when, all of a suddint, he was murthered, the crathur, (Lord help us!), and threwn into the lake abow,* and so, of coorse, he couldn't keep his promise to the fair lady—and more's the pity.

"Well, the story goes that she went out iv her mind bekase av loosin' the king's son—for she was tinder-hearted, God help her! like the rest iv us —and pined away afther him, until at last no one about seen her, good or bad; and the story wint that the fairies took her away.

"Well, sir, in coorse o' time, the white throut, God bless it! was seen in the sthrame beyont; and sure the people didn't know what to think av the crathur, seein' as how a *white* throut was never heerd av afore nor sence: and years upon years the throut was there, just where you seen it this blessed minit, longer nor I can tell—ay, throth, and beyant the memory o' th' ouldest in the village.

"At last the people began to think it must be a

*Above.

fairy—for what else could it be?—and no hurt nor harm was iver put on the white throut, antil some wicked sinners of sojers kem to these parts, and laughed at all the people, and gibed and jeered them for thinkin' o' the likes; and one o' them in partic'lar (bad luck to him!—God forgi' me for sayin' it!) swore he'd catch the throut, and ate it for his dinner—the blackguard!

"Well, what would you think o' the villany of the sojer? Sure enough he cotch the throut, and away wid him home, and puts an the fryin'-pan, and into it he pitches the purty little thing. The throut squeeled all as one as a Christian crather, and, my dear, you'd think the sojer id split his sides laughin'—for he was a harden'd villain—and, when he thought one side was done, he turns it over to fry the other; and what would you think, but the divil a taste of a burn was an it at all at all, and sure the sojer thought it was a *quare* throut that couldn't be briled; 'but,' says he, 'I'll give it another turn by-and-by, little thinkin' what was in store for him, the haythen.

"Well, when he thought that side was done, he turns it again, and, lo and behould you, the divil a taste more done that side was nor the other. 'Bad luck to me,' says the sojer, 'but that bates the world,' says he; 'but I'll thry you agin, my darlint,' says he, 'as cunnin' as you think yourself.' And so, with that, he turns it over and over; but the divil a sign av the fire was an the purty throut.

"'Well,' says the desperate villain—(for sure, sir,

he was a desperate villain *entirely;* he might know he was doing a wrong thing, seein' that all his endayvors was no good)—'well,' says he, 'my jolly little throut, may be you're fried enough, though you don't seem over well dressed; but you may be better than you look, like a singed cat, and a titbit, afther all,' says he. And, with that, he ups with his knife and fork to taste a piece o' the throut; but, my jew'l! the minit he put his knife into the fish there was a murtherin' screech, that you'd think the life id lave you if you heerd it, and away jumps the throut out av the fryin'-pan into the middle o' the flure; and an the spot where it fell up riz a lovely lady—the beautifullest young crathur that eyes ever seen, dressed in white, with a band o' goold in her hair, and a sthrame o' blood runnin' down her arm.

" ' Look where you cut me, you villain,' says she, and she held out her arm to him; and, my dear, he thought the sight id lave his eyes.

" ' Couldn't you lave me cool and comfortable in the river where you snared me, and not disturb me in my duty?' says she.

" Well, he thrimbled like a dog in a wet sack, and at last he stammered out somethin', and begged for his life, and ax'd her ladyship's pardin, and said he didn't know she was an duty, or he was too good a soger not to know betther nor to meddle wid her.

" ' I *was* on duty, then,' says the lady; ' I was watchin' for my thrue love that is comin' by wather to me,' says she; 'an' if he comes while I am away, an' that I miss iv him, I'll turn you into a pinkeen,* and I'll hunt you up and down for evermore, while grass grows or wather runs.'

"Well, the sojer thought the life id lave him at the thoughts iv his bein' turned into a pinkeen, and begged for marcy; and with that says the lady, 'Renounce your evil coorses,' says she, 'you villain, or you'll repint it too late; be a good man for the futher, and go to your duty† reg'lar. And now,' says she, 'take me back, and put me into the river agin where you found me."

"'Oh! my lady,' says the sojer, 'how could I have the heart to drownd a beautiful lady like you?'

"But before he could say another word, the lady was vanished, and there he saw the little throut an the ground. Well, he put it an a clane plate, and away he run for the bare life, for fear her lover would come while she was away; and he run and he run ever till he came to the cave agin, and threw the throut into the river. The minit he did, the wather was as red as blood for a little while, by rayson av the cut, I suppose, until the sthrame washed the stain away; and to this day there's a little red mark an the throut's side, where it was cut.‡

"Well, sir, from that day out the sojer was an

---

* Stickleback.

† The Irish peasant calls his attendance at the confessional "going to his duty."

‡ The fish has really a red spot on its side.

althered man, and reformed his ways, and wint to his duty reg'lar and fasted three times a week—though it was never fish he tuk an fastin' days, for, afther the fright he got, fish id never rest an his stomach, God bless us! savin' your presence. But, anyhow, he was an althered man, as I said before; and in coorse o' time he left the army, and turned hermit at last; and they say he *used to pray evermore for the sowl of the white throut.*"

WILLIAM CARLETON.

THE DONAGH.*

CARNMORE, one of those small villages that are to be found in the outskirts of many parishes in Ireland, whose distinct boundaries are lost in the contiguous mountain-wastes, was situated at the foot of a deep gorge or pass, overhung by two bleak hills, from the naked sides of which the storm swept over it, without discomposing the peaceful little nook of cabins that stood below.

* In reference to the precious reliquary mentioned in the following true tale, the learned George Petrie wrote in the 18th vol. of the *Transactions of the Royal Irish Academy:*

"On these evidences—and more might probably be procured if time had allowed—we may, I think, with tolerable certainty, rest the following conclusions:

"1. That the Domnach is the identical reliquary given by St. Patrick to MacCarthen.

"2. As the form of the cumdach indicates that it was intended to receive a book, and as the relics are all attached to the outer and the least ancient cover, it is manifest that the use of the box as a reliquary was not its original intention. The natural inference, therefore, is that it contained a manuscript which had belonged to St. Patrick; and, as a manuscript copy of the Gospels, apparently of that early age, is found within it, there is every reason to believe it to be that identical one for which the box was originally made, and which the Irish apostle probably brought with him on his mission into this country. It is, indeed, not merely possible, but even probable, that the existence of this manuscript was unknown to the monkish biographers of St. Patrick and St. MacCarthen, who speak of the box as a *scrinium*, or reliquary, only. The outer cover was evidently not made to open; and some, at least, of the relics attached to it were not introduced into Ireland before the twelfth century. It will be remembered, also, that no superstition was and is more common in connection with the ancient cumdachs, than the dread of their being opened."

About a furlong further down were two or three farm-houses, inhabited by a family named Cassidy, men of simple, inoffensive manners and considerable wealth. They were, however, acute and wise in their generation; intelligent cattle-dealers, on whom it would have been a matter of some difficulty to impose an unsound horse, or a cow older than it was intimated by her horn-rings, even when conscientiously dressed up for sale by the ingenious aid of the file or burning-iron. Between their houses and the hamlet rose a conical pile of rocks, loosely heaped together, from which the place took it's name of Carnmore.

About three years before the time of this story, there came two men with their families to reside in the upper village, and the house which they chose as a residence was one at some distance from those which composed the little group we have just been describing. They said their name was Meehan, although the general report went that this was not true, that their name was an assumed one, and that some dark mystery which none could penetrate shrouded their history and character. They were certainly remarkable men. The elder, named Anthony, was a dark, black-browed person, stern in his manner, and atrociously cruel in his disposition. His form was herculean, his bones strong and hard as iron, and his sinews stood out in undeniable evidence of a life hitherto spent in severe toil and exertion, to bear which he appeared to an amazing degree capable. His brother Denis was a small man, less savage and daring in his character, and consequently more vacillating and cautious than Anthony; for the points in which he resembled him were superinduced upon his natural disposition by the close connection that subsisted between them, and by the identity of their former pursuits in life, which, beyond doubt, had been such as could not bear investigation.

The old proverb of " Birds of a feather flock together" is certainly a true one, and in this case it was once more verified. Before the arrival of these men in the village, there had been two or three bad characters in the neighborhood, whose delinquencies were pretty well known. With these persons, the strangers, by that sympathy which assimilates with congenial good or evil, soon became acquainted; and although their intimacy was as secret and cautious as possible, still it had been observed, and was known; for they had frequently been seen skulking together at daybreak or in the dusk of evening.

It is unnecessary to say that Meehan and his brother did not mingle much in the society of Carnmore. In fact, the villagers and they mutually avoided each other. A mere return of the common phrases of salutation was generally the most that passed between them; they never entered into that familiarity which leads to mutual intercourse, and justifies one neighbor in freely entering the cabin of another, to spend a winter's night or a summer's evening in amusing conversation. Few had ever been in the house of the Meehans since it became theirs; nor were the means of their subsistence known. They led an idle life, had no scarcity of food, were decently clothed, and never wanted money—circumstances which occasioned no small degree of conjecture in Carnmore and its vicinity.

Some said they lived by theft; others that they were coiners; and there were many who imagined, from the diabolical countenance of the elder brother, that he had sold himself to the devil, who, they affirmed, set his mark upon him, and was his paymaster. Upon this hypothesis, several were ready to prove that he had neither breath nor shadow; they had seen him, they said, standing under a hedge-row of *elder*, that unholy tree which furnished wood for the cross, and on which Judas hanged himself; yet, although it was noonday in the month of July, his person threw out no shadow. Worthy souls! because the man stood in the shade at the time. But with these simple explanations superstition had nothing to do, although we are bound in justice to the reverend old lady to affirm that she was kept exceedingly busy in Carnmore. If a man had a sick cow, she was elf-shot; if his child became consumptive, it had been overlooked, or received *a blast* from the fairies; if the whooping-cough was rife, all the afflicted children were put three times under an ass; or, when they happened to have the "mumps," were led, before sunrise, to a south-running stream, with a halter hanging about their necks, under an obligation of silence during the ceremony. In short, there could not possibly be a more superstitious spot than that which these men of mystery had selected for their residence. Another circumstance which caused the people to look upon them with additional dread was their neglect of Mass on Sundays and holidays, though they avowed themselves Roman Catholics. They did not, it is true, join in the dances, drinking-matches, foot-ball, and other sports with which the Carnmore folk celebrated the Lord's day ; but they scrupled not, on the other hand, to mend their garden ditch, or mould a row of cabbages on the Sabbath—a circumstance for which two or three of the Carnmore boys were one Sunday evening, when tipsy, well-nigh chastising them. Their usual manner, however, of spending that day was by sauntering lazily about the fields, or stretching themselves supinely on the sunny side of the hedges, their arms folded on their bosoms, and their hats lying over their faces to keep off the sun.

In the meantime, loss of property was becoming quite common in the neighborhood. Sheep were stolen from the farmers, and cows and horses from the more extensive graziers in the parish. The complaints against the authors of these depredations were loud and incessant; watches were set, combinations for mutual security formed, and subscriptions to a considerable amount entered into, with a hope of being able, by the temptation of a large reward, to work upon the weakness or cupidity of some accomplice to betray the gang of villains who infested the neighborhood. All, however, was in vain; every week brought some new act of plunder to light, perpetrated upon such unsuspecting persons as had hitherto escaped the notice of the robbers; but no trace could be discovered of the perpetrators. Although theft had from time to time been committed upon a small scale before the arrival of the Mechans in the village, yet it was undeniable that since that period the instances not only multiplied, but became of a more daring and extensive description. They arose in a gradual scale, from the hen-roost to the stable; and with such ability were they planned and executed that the people, who in every instance identified Meehan and his brother with them, began to believe and hint that, in consequence of their compact with the devil, they had power to render themselves invisible. Common fame, who can best treat such subjects, took up this, and never laid it aside until, by narrating several exploits which Meehan the elder is said to have performed in other parts of the kingdom, she wound it up by roundly informing the Carnmorians that, having been once taken prisoner for murder, he was caught by the leg when half through a hedge, but that, being most wickedly determined to save his neck, he left the leg with the officer who took him, shouting out that it was a new species of leg-bail; and yet he moved away with surprising speed, upon two of as good legs as any man in his majesty's dominions might wish to walk off upon, from the insinuating advances of a bailiff or a constable.

The family of the Meehans consisted of their wives and three children, two boys and a girl; the former were the offspring of the younger brother, and the latter of Anthony. It has been observed, with truth and justice, that there is no man, how hardened and diabolical soever in his natural temper, who does not exhibit to some particular object a peculiar species of affection. Such a man was Anthony Meehan. That sullen hatred which he bore to human society, and that inherent depravity of heart which left the trail of vice and crime upon his footsteps, were flung off his character when he addressed his daughter Annie. To him her voice was like music; to her he was not the reckless villain, treacherous and cruel, which the helpless and unsuspecting found him, but a parent kind and indulgent as ever pressed an only and beloved daughter to his bosom. Annie was handsome; had she been born and educated in an elevated rank in society, she would have been softened by the polish and luxury of life into perfect beauty; she was, however, utterly without education. As Annie experienced from her father no unnatural cruelty, no harshness, nor even indifference, she consequently loved him in return; for she knew that tenderness from *such* a man was a proof of parental love rarely to be found in life. Perhaps she loved not her father the less on perceiving that he was proscribed by the world—a circumstance which might also have enhanced in his eyes the affection she bore him. When Meehan came to Carnmore, she was sixteen; and, as that was three years before the incident occurred on which we have founded this narrative, the reader may now suppose her to be about nineteen; an interesting country girl as to person, but with a mind completely neglected, yet remarkable for an uncommon stock of good-nature and credulity.

About the hour of eleven o'clock one winter's night in the beginning of December, Meehan and his brother sat moodily at their hearth. The fire was of peat which had recently been put down, and from between the turf the ruddy blaze was shooting out in those little tongues and gusts of sober light which throw around the rural hearth one of those charms which make up the felicity of domestic life. The night was stormy, and the wind moaned and howled along the dark hills beneath which the cottage stood. Every object in the house was shrouded in a mellow shade which afforded to the eye no clear outline, except around the hearth alone, where the light brightened into a golden hue, giving the idea of calmness and peace. Anthony Meehan sat on one side of it, and his daughter opposite him knitting; before the fire sat Denis, drawing shapes in the ashes for his own amusement.

" Bless me ! " said he, " how sthrange it is ! "

" What is ? " inquired Anthony, in his deep and grating tones.

" Why, thin, it *is* sthrange ! " continued the other, who, despite of the severity of his brother, was remarkably superstitious. " A coffin I made in the ashes three times runnin' ! Isn't it very quare, Annie ? " he added, addressing the niece.

" Sthrange enough, of a sartinty," she replied, being unwilling to express before her father the alarm which the incident, slight as it was, created in her mind; for she, like her uncle, was subject to such ridiculous influences. " How did it happen, uncle ? "

" Why, thin, no way in life, Anne; only, as I was thryin' to make a shoe, it turned out a coffin on my hands. I thin smoothed the ashes, and began agin, an' sorra bit of it but was a coffin still. Well, says I, I'll give you another chance—here goes once more—an', as sure as gun's iron, it was a coffin the third time. Heaven be about us, it's odd enough ! "

" It would be little matther you were nailed down in a coffin," replied Anthony fiercely ; " the world would have little loss. What a pitiful, cowardly rascal you are ! Afraid o' your own shadow afther the sun goes down, except *I'm* at your elbow ! Can't you dhrive all them palavers out o' your head? Didn't the sargint tell us an' prove to us the time we broke the guard-house an' took Frinch lave o' the ridgment for good that the whole o' that, an' more along wid it, is all priestcraft?"

"I remimber he did, sure enough. I dunna where the same sargint is now, Tony. About no good, anyway, I'll be bail. Howsomever, in regard o' that, why doesn't yourself give up fastin' from the mate of a Friday?"

"Do you want me to sthretch you on the hearth?" replied the savage, whilst his eyes kindled into fury, and his grim visage darkened into a satanic expression. "I'll tache you to be puttin' me through my catechiz about atin' mate. I may manage that as I plase; it comes at first-cost, anyhow; but no cross-questions to me about it, if you regard your health!'

"I must say for you," replied Denis reproachfully, "that you're a good warrant to put the health astray upon us of an odd start; we're not come to this time o' day widout carryin' somethin' to remimber you by. For my own part, Tony, I don't like such tokens; an', moreover, I wish you had resaved a thrifle o' larnin', espishily in the writin' line; for, whenever we have any difference, you're so ready to prove your opinion by settin' your mark upon me that I'd rather, fifty times over, you could write it with pen an' ink."

"My father will give that up, uncle," said the nicce; "it's bad for anybody to be fightin', but worst of all for brothers that ought to live in peace and kindness. Won't you, father?"

"May be I will, dear, some o' these days, on your account, Anne; but you must get this creature of an uncle of yours to let me alone, an' not be aggravatin' me with his folly. As for your mother, she's worse; her tongue's sharp enough to skin a flint, and a batin' a day has little effect on her."

Anne sighed, for she knew how low an irreligious life, and the infamous society with which, as her father's wife, her mother was compelled to mingle, had degraded her.

"Well, but, father, you don't set her a good example yourself," said Anne; "and, if she scoulds and drinks *now*, you know she was a different woman when you got her. You allow this yourself; and the crathur, the dhrunkest time she is, doesn't she cry bittherly, remimberin what she *has* been? Instead of *one* batin' a day, father, thry no batin' a day, an' may be it 'ill turn out betther than thumpin' an' smashin' her as you do."

"Why, thin, there's truth an' sinse in what the girl says, Tony," observed Denis.

"Come," replied Anthony, "whatever *she* may say, I'll suffer none of *your* interference. Go an' get us the black bottle from the *place;* it'll soon be time to move. I hope *they* won't stay too long."

Denis obeyed this command with great readi

ness, for whiskey in some degree blunted the fierce passions of his brother, and deadened his cruelty; or rather diverted it from minor objects to those which occurred in the lawless perpetration of his villany.

The bottle was got, and in the meantime the fire blazed up brightly; the storm without, however, did not abate, nor did Meehan and his brother wish that it should. As the elder of them took the glass from the hands of the other, an air of savage pleasure blazed in his eyes, on reflecting that the tempest of the night was favorable to the execution of the villanous deed on which they were bent.

"More power to you!" said Anthony, impiously personifying the storm. "Sure that's *one* proof that God doesn't throuble his head about what we do, or we would not get such a murdherin' fine night as is in it, anyhow. That's it! blow an' tundher away, an' keep yourself an' us as black as hell, sooner than we should fail in what we intend! Anne, your health, acushla. Yours, Dinny! If you keep your tongue off o' me, I'll neither make nor meddle in regard o' the batin' o' you."

"I hope you'll stick to that, anyhow," replied Denis; "for my part I'm sick and sore o' you every day in the year. Many another man would put salt wather between himself and yourself, sooner nor become a battin'-stone for you, as I have been. Few would bear it when they could mend themselves."

"What's that you say?" replied Anthony, suddenly laying down his glass, catching his brother by the collar, and looking him with a murderous scowl in the face. "Is it thrachery you hint at, eh? Sarpent, is it thrachery you mane?" And, as he spoke, he compressed Denis's neck between his powerful hands until the other was black in the face.

Anne flew to her uncle's assistance, and with much difficulty succeeded in rescuing him from the deadly grip of her father, who exclaimed, as he loosed his hold, "You may thank the girl, or you'd not spake nor dare to spake about crossin' the salt wather or lavin' me in a desateful way agin. If I ever suspect that a thought of thrachery comes into your heart, I'll *do* for you; and you may carry your story to the world I'll send you to."

"Father, dear, why are you so suspicious of my uncle?" said Anne; "sure he's a long time livin' with you, an' goin' step for step in all the danger you meet with. If he had a mind to turn out a Judas agin you, he might a done it long agone; not to mintion the throuble it would bring on his own head, seen' he's as deep in everything as you are."

"If that's all that's throubling you," replied Denis, trembling, "you may make yourself asy on the head of it; but well I know 'tisn't *that* that's on your mind; 'tis your own conscience; but sure it's not fair nor rasonable for you to vent your evil thoughts on me!"

"Well, he won't," said Anne; "he'll quit it; his mind's throubled; an', dear knows, it's no wondher it should. Och! I'd give the world wide that his conscience was lightened of the load that's upon it! My mother's lameness is nothin'; but the child, poor thing! An' it was only widin three days of her lyin'-in. Och! it was a cruel sthroke, father! An' when I seen its little innocent face dead, an' me widout a brother, I thought my heart would break, thinkin' upon who did it!" The tears fell in showers from her eyes, as she added, "Father, I don't want to vex you; but I wish you to feel sorrow for *that*, at laste. Oh! if you'd bring the priest, an' give up sich coorses, father dear, how happy we'd be, an' how happy yourself 'ud be!"

Conscience for a moment started from her sleep, and uttered a cry of guilt in his spirit; his face became ghastly; and his eyes full of horror; his lips quivered, and he was about to upbraid his daughter with more harshness than usual, when a low whistle, resembling that of a curlew, was heard at a chink of the door. In a moment he gulped down another glass of spirits, and was on his feet. "Go, Denis, an' get the arms," said he to his brother, "while I let them in."

On opening the door, three men entered, having their great-coats muffled about them, and their hats slouched. One of them named Kenny was a short villain, but of a thick-set, hairy frame. The other was known as the "Big Mower," in con sequence of his following that employment every season, and of his great skill in performing it. He had a deep-rooted objection against permitting the palm of his hand to be seen—a reluctance which common fame attributed to the fact of his having received on that part the impress of a hot iron, in the shape of the letter T, not forgetting to add that T was the hieroglyphic for Thief. The villain himself affirmed it was simply the mark of a cross, burned into it by a blessed friar, as a charm against St. Vitus's dance, to which he had once been subject. The people, however, were rather sceptical, not of the friar's power to cure that malady, but of the fact of his ever having moved a limb under it; and they concluded with telling him, good-humoredly enough, that, notwithstanding the charm, he was destined to die "wid the threble of it in his toe." The third was a noted pedlar called Martin, who, under pretence of selling tape, pins, scissors, etc., was very useful in *setting* such premises as this virtuous fraternity might, without much risk, make a descent upon.

"I thought yez would outstay your time," said the elder Meehan, relapsing into his determined hardihood of character. "We're ready hours a-gone. Dick Rice gave me two curlew an' two patrich calls to-day. Now pass the glass among yez, while Denny brings the arms. I know there's danger in this business, in regard of the Cassidys livin' so near us. If I see anybody afut, I'll use the *curlew* call; an', if not, I'll whistle twice on the *patrich** one, an' ye may come an. The horse is worth eighty guineas, if he's worth a shillin'; an' we'll make sixty of him ourselves."

For some time they chatted about the plan in contemplation, and drank freely of the spirits, until at length the impatience of the elder Meehan at the delay of his brother became ungovernable. His voice deepened into tones of savage passion as he uttered a series of blasphemous curses against this unfortunate butt of his indignation and malignity. At length he rushed out furiously to know why he did not return; but, on reaching a secret excavation in the mound against which the house was built, he found, to his utter dismay, that Denis had made his escape by an artificial passage scooped out of it to secure themselves a retreat in case of surprise or detection. It opened behind the house among a clump of blackthorn and brushwood, and was covered with green turf in such a manner as to escape the notice of all who were not acquainted with the secret. Meehan's face on his return was worked up into an expression truly awful.

"We're sould!" said he. "But stop, I'll tache the thraithur what revinge is!"

In a moment he awoke his brother's two sons, and dragged them by the neck, one in each hand, to the hearth.

"Your villain of a father's off," said he, "to betray us; go an' folly him; bring him back, an'

---

* Partridge.

he'll be safe from me; but let him become a *stag* agin us, and, if I should hunt you both into the bowels of the airth, I'll send yez to a short account. I don't care that"—and he snapped his fingers—"ha! ha!—no, I don't care that for the law; I know how to dale with it when it comes! An' what's the stuff about the *other* world but priestcraft and lies?"

"May be," said the Big Mower, "Denis is gone to get the foreway of us, an' to take the horse himself. Our best plan is to lose no time, at all events; so let us hurry, for fraid the night might happen to clear up."

"He!" said Meehan, "he go alone! No; the miserable wretch is afeard of his own shadow. I only wondher he stuck to me so long; but sure he wouldn't, only I bate the courage in and the fear out of him. You're right, Brian," said he, upon reflection, "let us lose no time, but be off. Do ye mind?" he added to his nephews. "Did ye hear me? If you see him, let him come back, an' all will be berrid; but, if he doesn't, you know your fate!" saying which, he and his accomplices departed amid the howling of the storm.

The next morning, Carnmore, and indeed the whole parish, was in an uproar; a horse worth eighty guineas had been stolen in the most daring manner from the Cassidys, and the hue-and-cry was up after the thief or thieves who took him. For several days the search was closely maintained, but without success; not the slightest trace could be found of him or them. The Cassidys could very well bear to lose him; but there were many struggling farmers, on whose property serious depradations had been committed, who could not sustain their loss so easily. It was natural under these circumstances that suspicion should attach to many persons, some of whom had but indifferent characters before, as well as to several who certainly had never deserved suspicion. When a fortnight or so had elapsed, and no circumstances transpired that might lead to discovery, the neighbors, including those who had principally suffered by the robberies, determined to assemble on a certain day at Cassidy's house, for the purpose of clearing themselves, on oath, of the imputations thrown out against some of them, as accomplices in the thefts. In order, however, that the ceremony should be performed as solemnly as possible, they determined to send for Father Farrell and Mr. Nicholson, a magistrate, both of whom they requested to undertake the task of jointly presiding upon this occasion; and, that the circumstance should have every publicity, it was announced from the altar by the priest, on the preceding Sabbath, and published on the church-gate in large legible characters, ingeniously printed with a pen by the village schoolmaster.

In fact, the intended meeting, and the object of it, were already notorious; and much conversation was held upon its probable result and the measures which might be taken against those who refused to swear. Of the latter description there was but one opinion, which was that their refusal in such a case would be tantamount to guilt. The innocent were anxious to vindicate themselves from suspicion; and, as the suspected did not amount to more than a dozen, of course the whole body of the people, including the thieves themselves, who applauded it as loudly as the others, all expressed their satisfaction at the measures about to be adopted. A day was therefore appointed, on which the inhabitants of the neighborhood, particularly the suspected persons, should come to assemble at Cassidy's house in order to have the characters of the innocent cleared up, and the guilty, if possible, made known.

On the evening before this took place were assembled in Meehan's cottage the elder Meehan and the rest of the gang, including Denis, who had absconded on the night of the theft.

" Well, well, Denny," said Anthony, who forced his rugged nature into an appearance of better temper, that he might strengthen the timid spirit of his brother against the scrutiny about to take place on the morrow—perhaps too, he dreaded him—" Well, well, Denny, I thought sure enough that it was some new piece of cowardice came over you. Just think of him," he added, "shabbin' off, only because he made with a bit of a rod three strokes in the ashes that he thought resembled a coffin!—ha! ha! ha!"

This produced a peal of derision at Denis's pusillanimous terror.

"Ay," said the Big Mower, "he was makin' a coffin, was he? I wondher it wasn't a rope you drew, Denny. If any one dies in the coil, it will be the greatest coward, an' that's yourself."

"You may all laugh," replied Denis, "but I know such things to have a manin'. When my mother died, didn't my father—the heaven's be his bed!—see a black coach about a week before it? An' sure from the first day she tuck ill the dead-watch was heard in the house every night; and what was more nor that, she kept *warm* until she went into her grave;* an', accordingly, didn't my sister Shibby die within a year afther?"

"It's no matther about thim things," replied Anthony; "it's thruth about the dead-watch, my mother keepin' warm, an' Shibby's death, anyway. But on the night we tuk Cassidy's horse, I thought you were goin' to betray us; I was surely in a murdherin' passion, an' would have done harm, only things turned out as they did."

"Why," said Denis, "the thruth is I was afeard *some* of us would be shot, an' that the lot would fall on myself; for the coffin, thinks I, was sent as a warnin'. How-and-ever, I spied about Cassidy's stable till I seen that the coast was clear; so, when I heard the low cry of the

---

* It is supposed in Ireland when a corpse retains, for a longer space of time than usual, anything like animal heat, that some person belonging to the family of the deceased will die within a year.

patrich that Anthony and I agreed on, I joined yez."

" Well, about to-morrow," observed Kenny— "ha! ha! ha!—there'll be lots o' swearin'. Why, the whole parish is to switch the primer; many a thumb and coat-cuff will be kissed in spite of priest or magistrate. I remimber once, when I was swearin' an *alibi* for long Paddy Murray, that suffered for the M'Gee's, I kissed my thumb, I thought, so smoothly that no one would notice it; but I had a keen one to dale with; so says he, ' You know, for the matther o' that, my good fellow, that you have your *thumb* to kiss every day in the week,' says he, ' but you might salute the *book* out o' dacency and good manners ; not,' says he, ' that you an' it are strangers, aither; for, if I don't mistake, you're an ould hand at swearin' alibis.'

" At all evints, I had to smack the book itself, and it's I, and Barney Green, and Tim Casserly that did swear stiffly for Paddy, but the thing was too clear agin him. So he suffered, poor fellow, an' died right game, for he said over his *dhrop*—ha! ha! ha!—that he was as innocent o' the murder as a child unborn; an' so he was in *one* sinse, bein' afther gettin' absolution."

" As to thumb-kissin'," observed the elder Meehan, " let there be none of it among us to-morrow; if we're caught at it, 'twould be as bad as stayin' away altogether; for my part, I'll give it a smack like a pistol shot—ha! ha! ha!"

"I hope they won't bring the priest's book," said Denis. "I haven't the laste objection agin payin' my respects to the *magistrate's* paper, but somehow I don't like tastin' the *priest's* in a falsity."

"Don't you know," said the Big Mower, "that, whin a magistrate's present, it's ever an' always only the Tistament *by law* that's used? I myself wouldn't kiss the Mass-book in a falsity."

"There's none of us sayin' we'd do it in a lie," said the elder Meehan; "an' it's well for thousands that the law doesn't use the priest's book; though, afther all, aren't there books that say religion's all a sham? I think myself it is; for, if what they talk about justice an' Providence is thrue, would Tom Dillon be transported for the robbery *we* committed at Bantry? Tom, it's true, was an ould offender; but he was innocent of *that*, anyway. The world's all chance, boys, as Sargint Eustace used to say, and whin we die there's no more about us; so that I don't see why a man mightn't as well *switch* the priest's book as any other, only that somehow a body can't shake the terror of it off o' them."

"I dunna, Anthony, but you an' I ought to curse that sargint; only for him we mightn't be as we are, sore in our conscience, and afeard of every fut we hear passin'," observed Denis.

"Spake for your own cowardly heart, man alive!" replied Anthony; "for my part, I'm afeard o' nothin'. Put round the glass, and don't be nursin' it there all night. Sure we're not so bad as the rot among the sheep, nor the blackleg among the bullocks, nor the staggers among the horses, anyhow; an' yet they'd hang us up only for bein' fond o' a bit o' mate—ha! ha! ha!"

"Thrue enough," said the Big Mower, philosophizing; "God made the beef and the mutton, and the grass to feed it; but it was man made the ditches; now we're only bringin' things back to the right way that Providence made them in when ould times were in it, manin' before ditches war invinted—ha! ha! ha!"

"'Tis a good argument," observed Kenny, "only that judge and jury would be a little delicate in actin' up to it; an' the more's the pity. Howsomever, as Providence made the mutton, sure it's not harm for us to take what he sends."

"Ay, but," said Denis—

> 'God made man, an' man made money;
> God made bees, and bees made honey;
> God made Satan, an' Satan made sin;
> An' God made a hell to put Satan in.'

Let nobody say there's not a hell; isn't there it plain from Scripthur?"

"I wish you had the Scripthur tied about your neck!" replied Anthony. "How fond o' it one o' the greatest thieves that ever missed the rope is! Why, the fellow could plan a roguery with any man that ever danced the hangman's hornpipe, and yet he be's repatin' bits an' scraps of ould prayers, an' charms, an stuff. Ay, indeed!

Shure he has a varse out o' the Bible that he thinks can prevent a man from bein' hung up any day!"

While Denny, the Big Mower, and the two Mechans were thus engaged in giving expression to their peculiar opinions, the pedlar held a conversation of a different kind with Anne.

With the secrets of the family in his keeping, he commenced a rather penitent review of his own life, and expressed his intention of abandoning so dangerous a mode of accumulating wealth. He said that he thanked Heaven he had already laid up sufficient for the wants of a reasonable man; that he understood farming and the management of *sheep* particularly well; that it was his intention to remove to a different part of the kingdom, and take a farm; and that nothing prevented him from having done this before, but the want of a helpmate to take care of his establishment; he added that his present wife was of an intolerable temper, and a greater villain by fifty degrees than himself. He concluded by saying that his conscience twitched him night and day for living with her, and that by abandoning her immediately, becoming truly religious, and taking Anne in her place, he hoped, he said, to atone in some measure for his former errors.

Anthony, however, having noticed the earnestness which marked the pedlar's manner, suspected him of attempting to corrupt the principles of his daughter, having forgotten the influence which his own opinions were calculated to produce upon her heart.

"Martin," said he, "'twould be as well you ped attention to what we're sayin' in regard o' the thrial to-morrow, as to be palaverin' talk into the girl's ear that can't be good comin' from *your* lips. Quit it, I say, quit it! *Corp an duowol**—I won't allow such proceedin's!"

"Swear till you blister your lips, Anthony," replied Martin; "as for me, bein' no residenthur, I'm not bound to it; an' what's more, I'm not suspected. 'Tis settin' some other bit o' work for yez I'll be, while you're all clearin' yourselves from stealin' honest Cassidy's horse. I wish we had him safely disposed of in the mane time, an' the money for him an' the other beasts in our pockets."

Much more conversation of a similar kind passed between them upon various topics connected with their profligacy and crimes. At length they separated for the night, after having concerted their plan of action for the ensuing scrutiny.

The next morning, before the hour appointed arrived, the parish, particularly the neighborhood of Carnmore, was struck with deep consternation. Labor became suspended, mirth disappeared, and every face was marked with paleness, anxiety, and apprehension. If two men met, one shook his head mysteriously, and inquired from the other, "Did you hear the news?"

* My body to Satan.

"Ay! ay! the Lord be about us all, I did! an' I pray God that it may lave the counthry as it came to it."

"Oh! an' that it may, I humbly make supplication this day!"

If two women met, it was with similar mystery and fear. "*Vread*,* do you know what's at the Cassidy's?"

"Whisht, a-hagur, I do; but let what will happen sure, it's best for us to say nothin'."

"Say! the blessed Virgin forbid! I'd cut my hand off o' me, afore I'd spake a word about it; only that—"

"Whisht! woman—for mercy's sake—don't—"

And so they would separate, each crossing herself devoutly.

The meeting at Cassidy's was to take place that day at twelve o'clock; but, about two hours before the appointed time, Anne, who had been in some of the other houses, came into her father's, quite pale, breathless, and trembling.

"Oh!" she exclaimed, with clasped hands, while the tears fell fast from her eyes, "we'll be lost, ruined! Did yez hear what's in the neighborhood wid the Cassidys?"

"Girl," said the father, with more severity than he had ever manifested to her before, "I never yet *ris* my hand to you, but *ma corp an duowol*, if you open your lips, I'll *fell* you where you stand. Do you want that cowardly uncle o' yours to be

---

* Vread—*Anglicè*, Margaret.

the manes o' hanging your father? May be that was one o' the lessons Martin gave you last night?" And as he spoke he knit his brows at her with that murderous scowl which was habitual to him. The girl trembled, and began to think that, since her father's temper deepened in domestic outrage and violence as his crimes multiplied, the sooner she left the family the better. Every day, indeed, diminished that species of instinctive affection which she had entertained towards him; and this, in proportion as her reason ripened into a capacity for comprehending the dark materials of which his character was composed. Whether he himself began to consider detection at hand or not, we cannot say; but it is certain that his conduct was marked with a callous recklessness of spirit, which increased in atrocity to such a degree that even his daughter could only *not* look on him with *disgust*.

"What's the matter now?" inquired Denis, with alarm. "Is it anything about us, Anthony?"

"No, 'tisn't," replied the other, "anything about us! What 'ud it be about us for? 'Tis a lyin' report that some cunnin' knave spread, hopin' to find out the guilty. But hear me, Denis, once for all; we're goin' to clear ourselves—now listen—an' let my words sink deep into your heart; if you refuse to swear this day—no matther *what's* put into your hand—you'll do harm—that's all; have courage, man; but should you *cow*, your coorse will be short ; an' mark, even if *you* escape me, your sons won't ; I have it all planned; an' *corp an duowol!* thim you won't know from Adam will revenge me, if I am taken up through your unmanliness."

" 'Twould be betther for us to lave the counthry," said Anne ; "we might slip away as it is."

"Ay," said the father, "an' be taken by the neck afore we get two mile from the place ! No, no, girl; it's the safest way to brazen thim out. Did you hear me, Denis?"

Denis started, for he had been evidently pondering on the mysterious words of Anne, to which his brother's anxiety to conceal them gave additional mystery. The coffin, too, recurred to him, and he feared that the death shadowed out by it would in some manner or other occur in the family. He was, in fact, one of those miserable villains with but half a conscience;—that is to say, as much as makes them the slaves of the fear which results from crime, without being the slightest impediment to their committing it. It was no wonder he started at the deep pervading tones of his brother's voice, for the question was put with ferocious energy.

On starting, he looked with vague terror on his brother, fearing, but not comprehending, his question.

"What is it, Anthony?" he inquired.

"Oh! for that matter," replied the other, "nothin' at all; think of what I said to you, anyhow ; swear through thick and thin, if you have a regard for your own health, or for your childher. May be I had betther repate it agin for you?" he continued, eyeing him with mingled fear and suspicion. "Denis, as a friend, I bid you mind yourself this day, an' see you don't bring aither of us into throuble."

There lay before the Cassidys' houses a small flat of common, trodden into rings by the young horses they were in the habit of training. On this level space were assembled those who came, either to clear their own character from suspicion or to witness the ceremony. The day was dark and lowering, and heavy clouds rolled slowly across the peaks of the surrounding mountains; scarcely a breath of air could be felt ; and, as the country people silently approached, such was the closeness of the day, their haste to arrive in time, and their general anxiety, either for themselves or their friends, that almost every man, on reaching the spot, might be seen taking up the skirts of his "cothamore," or "big coat" (the peasant's handkerchief), to wipe the sweat from his brow ; and as he took off his dingy woollen hat, or caubeen, the perspiration rose in strong exhalations from his head.

"Michael, am I in time?" might be heard from such persons as they arrived: "did this business begin yit?"

"Full time, Larry ; myself's here an hour ago, but no appearance of anything as yit. Father

Farrell and Squire Nicholson are both in Cassidy's waitin' till they all *gother*, whin they'll begin to put them through their facin's. You hard about what they've got?"

"No; for I'm only on my way home from the berril of a *cleaven* of mine, that we put down this mornin' in Tullyard. What is it?"

"Why, man alive, it's through the whole parish *inready*." He then went on, lowering his voice to a whisper, and speaking in a tone bordering on dismay.

The other crossed himself, and betrayed symptoms of awe and astonishment, not unmingled with fear.

"Well," he replied, "I dunna whether I'd come here, if I'd known that; for, innocent or guilty, I wouldn't wish to be near it. Och, may God pity thim that's to come acrass it, espishily if they dare to do it in a lie!"

"They needn't, I can tell yez both," observed a third person, "be a hair afeard of it, for the best raison livin', that there's no thruth at all in the report, nor the Cassidys' never thought of sindin' for anything o' the kind; I have it from Larry Cassidy's own lips, an' he ought to know best."

The truth is, that two reports were current among the crowd; one that the oath was to be simply on the Bible; and the other that a more awful means of expurgation was resorted to by the Cassidys. The people consequently, not knowing which to credit, felt that most painful of all sensations—uncertainty.

During the period which intervened between their assembling and the commencement of the ceremony, a spectator, interested in contemplating the workings of human nature in circumstances of deep interest, would have ample scope for observation. The occasion was to them a solemn one. There was little conversation among them ; for, when a man is wound up to a pitch of great interest, he is seldom disposed to relish discourse. Every brow was anxious, every cheek blanched, and every arm folded ; they scarcely stirred, or, when they did, only with slow abstracted movements, rather mechanical than voluntary. If an individual made his appearance about Cassidy's door, a sluggish stir among them was visible, and a low murmur of a peculiar character might be heard ; but on perceiving that it was only some ordinary person, all subsided again into a brooding stillness that was equally singular and impressive.

Under this peculiar feeling was the multitude, when Meehan and his brother were seen approaching it from their own house. The elder, with folded arms, and hat pulled over his brows, stalked grimly forward, having that remarkable scowl upon his face which had contributed to establish for him so diabolical a character. Denis walked by his side, with his countenance strained to inflation ;—a miserable parody of that sullen effrontery which marked the unshrinking miscreant beside him. He had not heard of the ordeal, owing to the caution of Anthony: but, notwithstanding his effort at indifference, a keen eye might have observed the latent anxiety of a man who was habitually villanous and naturally timid.

When this pair entered the crowd, a few secret glances, too rapid to be noticed by the people, passed between them and their accomplices. Denis, on seeing them present, took fresh courage, and looked with the heroism of a blusterer upon those who stood about him, especially whenever he found himself under the scrutinizing eye of his brother. Such was the horror and detestation in which they were held, that, on advancing into the assembly, the persons on each side turned away, and openly avoided them; eyes full of fierce hatred were bent on them vindictively, and "curses, not loud, but deep," were muttered with indignation which nothing but a divided state of feeling could repress within due limits. Every glance, however, was paid back by Anthony with interest, from eyes and black shaggy brows tremendously ferocious; and his curses, as they rolled up half smothered from his huge chest, were deeper and more diabolical by far than their own. He even jeered at them; but, however disgusting his frown, there was something truly appalling in the dark gleam of his scoff, which threw them at an immeasurable distance behind him, in the power of displaying on the countenance the worst human passions.

At length Mr. Nicholson, Father Farrell, and his curate, attended by the Cassidys and their friends, issued from the house; two or three servants preceded them, bearing a table and chairs for the magistrate and priests, who, however, stood during the ceremony. When they entered one of the rings before alluded to, the table and chairs were placed in the centre of it, and Father Farrell, as possessing most influence over the people, addressed them very impressively.

"There are," said he, in conclusion, "persons in this crowd whom we know to be guilty; but we will have an opportunity of now witnessing the lengths to which crime, long indulged in, can carry them. To such people I would say, *beware!* for they know not the situation in which they are placed."

During all this time there was not the slightest allusion made to the mysterious ordeal which had excited so much awe and apprehension among them—a circumstance which occasioned many a pale, downcast face to clear up, and reassume its usual cheerful expression. The crowd now were assembled around the ring, and every man on whom an imputation had been fastened came forward, when called upon, to the table at which the priest and magistrate stood uncovered. The form of the oath was framed by the two clergymen, who, as they knew the reservations and evasions commonest among such characters, had ingeniously contrived not to leave a single loophole through which the consciences of those who belonged to this worthy fraternity might escape.

To those acquainted with Irish courts of justice there was nothing particularly remarkable in the swearing. Indeed, one who stood among the crowd might hear from those who were stationed at the greatest distance from the table, such questions as the following:—

" Is the *thing* in it, Art?"

" No; 'tis nothin' but the *law* Bible, the magistrate's own one."

To this the querist would reply, with a satisfied nod of the head, " Oh! is that all? I heard they war to have *it;*" on which he would push himself through the crowd until he reached the table, where he took his oath as readily as another.

"Jem Hartigan," said the magistrate, to one of those persons, "are *you* to swear?"

"Faix, myself doesn't know, you honor; only that I hard them say that the Cassidys mintioned our names along wid many other honest people; an' one wouldn't, in' that case, lie under a false report, your honor, from any one, when we're as clear as them that never saw the light of anything of the kind."

The magistrate then put the book into his hand, and Jem, in return, fixed his eye, with much apparent innocence, on his face: " Now, Jem

Hartigan," etc. etc., and the oath was accordingly administered. Jem put the book to his mouth, with his thumb raised to an acute angle on the back of it; nor was the smack by any means a silent one which he gave it (his thumb).

The magistrate set his ear with the air of a man who had experience in discriminating such sounds. "Hartigan," said he, "you'll condescend to kiss the *book*, sir, if you please; there's a hollowness in that smack, my good fellow, that can't escape *me*."

"Not kiss it, your honor? Why, by this staff in my hand, if ever a man kissed—"

"Silence! you impostor," said the curate; "I watched you closely, and am confident your lips never touched the book."

"My lips *never* touched the book!—Why, you know I'd be sarry to conthradict either o' yez; but I was jist goin' to obsarve, wid simmission, that my own lips ought to know best; an' don't you hear them tellin' you that they *did* kiss it?" And he grinned with confidence in their faces.

"You double-dealing reprobate!" said the parish priest, " I'll lay my whip across your jaws. I saw you, too, an' you did *not* kiss the book."

"By dad, an' may be I did *not*, sure enough," he replied; "any man may make a mistake unknownst to himself; but I'd give my oath, an' be the five crasses, I kissed it as sure as—however, a good thing's never the worse o' bein' twice done, gintlemen; so here goes, jist to satisfy yez.'

And, placing the book near his mouth, and altering his position a little, he appeared to comply, though, on the contrary, he touched neither it nor his thumb. " It's the same thing to me," he continued, laying down the book with an air of confident assurance ; " it's the same thing to me if I kissed it fifty times over, which I'm ready to do if *that* doesn't satisfy yez."

As every man acquitted himself of the charges brought against him, the curate immediately took down his name. Indeed, before the " clearing " commenced, he requested that such as were to swear would stand together within the ring, that, after having sworn, he might hand each of them a certificate of the fact, which they appeared to think might be serviceable to them, should they happen to be subsequently indicted for the same crime in a court of justice. This, however, was only a plan to keep them together for what was soon to take place.

The detections of thumb-kissing were received by those who had already sworn, and by several in the outward crowd, with much mirth. It is but justice, however, to the majority of those assembled to state that they appeared to entertain a serious opinion of the nature of the ceremony, and no small degree of abhorrence against those who seemed to trifle with the solemnity of an oath.

Standing on the edge of the circle, in the innermost row, were Meehan and his brother. The former eyed, with all the hardness of a stoic, the successive individuals as they passed up to the table. His accomplices had gone forward, and to the surprise of many who strongly suspected them, in the most indifferent manner "cleared" themselves, in the trying words of the oath, of all knowledge of, and participation in, the thefts that had taken place.

The grim visage of the elder Meehan was marked by a dark smile, scarcely perceptible; but his brother, whose nerves were not so firm, appeared somewhat confused and distracted by the imperturbable villany of the perjurers.

At length they were called up. Anthony advanced slowly but collectedly to the table, only turning his eye slightly about to observe if his brother accompanied him. "Denis," said he, "which of us will swear first? You may." For, as he doubted his brother's firmness, he was prudent enough, should he fail, to guard against having the sin of perjury to answer for, along with those demands which his country had to make for his other crimes. Denis took the book, and cast a slight glance at his brother as if for encouragement; their eyes met, and the darkened brow of Anthony hinted at the danger of flinching in this crisis. The tremor of his hand was not, perhaps, visible to any but Anthony, who, however, did not overlook this circumstance. He held the book, but raised not his eye to meet the looks of either the magistrate or the priest's; the color also left his face, as with shrinking lips he touched the Word of God in deliberate falsehood. Having then laid it down, Anthony received it with a firm grasp, and, whilst his eye turned boldly in contemptuous mockery upon those who presented it, he impressed it with the kiss of a man whose depraved conscience seemed to goad him only to evil. After " clearing " himself, he laid the Bible upon the table with the affected air of a person who felt hurt at the imputation of theft, and joined the rest, with a frown upon his countenance, and a smothered curse upon his lips.

Just at this moment, a person from Cassidy's house laid upon the table a small box covered with black cloth; and our readers will be surprised to hear that, if fire had come down visibly from heaven, greater awe and fear could not have been struck into their hearts or depicted upon their countenances. The casual conversation and the commentaries upon the ceremony they had witnessed, instantly settled into a most profound silence, and every eye was turned towards it with an interest absolutely fearful.

"Let," said the curate, "none of those who have sworn depart from within the ring, until they *once more* clear themselves upon this;" and as he spoke, he held it up—" Behold," said he, " and tremble—behold THE DONAGH!!!"

A low murmur of awe and astonishment burst from the people in general, whilst those within the ring, who with few exceptions were the worst characters in the parish, appeared ready to sink into the earth. Their countenances, for the most part, paled into the condemned hue of guilt; many of them became almost unable to stand; and altogether the state of trepidation and terror in which they stood was strikingly wild and extraordinary.

The curate proceeded: "Let him now who is guilty depart; or, if he wishes, advance, and challenge the awful penalty annexed to perjury upon THIS! Who has ever been known to swear falsely upon the Donagh, without being visited by a tremendous punishment, either on the spot, or in twenty-four hours after his perjury? If we ourselves have not seen such instances with our own eyes, it is because none liveth who dare incur such dreadful penalty; but we have heard of those who did, and of their awful punishment afterwards. Sudden death, madness, paralysis, self-destruction, or the murder of some one dear to them, are the marks by which perjury upon the Donagh is known and visited. Advance now, ye who are innocent, but let the guilty withdraw; for we do not desire to witness the terrible vengance which would attend a false oath upon the DONAGH. Pause, therefore, and be cautious! for if this grievous sin be committed, a heavy punishment will fall, not only upon you, but upon the parish in which it occurs!"

The words of the priest sounded to the guilty like the death sentence of a judge. Before he concluded, all except Meehan and his brother, and a few who were really innocent, had slunk back out of the circle into the crowd. Denis, however, became pale as a corpse, and from time to time wiped the large drops from his haggard brow; even Anthony's cheek, despite of his natural callousness, was less red; his eyes became disturbed, but by their influence he contrived to keep Denis in sufficient dread to prevent him from mingling, like the rest, among the people. The few who remained along with them advanced, and notwithstanding their innocence, when the Donagh was presented and the figure of Christ and the Twelve Apostles displayed in the solemn tracery of its carving, they exhibited symptoms of fear. With trembling hands they touched the Donagh, and with trembling lips kissed the Crucifix, in attestation of their guiltlessness of the charge with which they had been accused.

"Anthony and Denis Meehan, come forward," said the curate, "and declare your innocence of the crimes with which you are charged by the Cassidys and others."

Anthony advanced, but Denis stood rooted to the ground; on perceiving which, the former sternly returned a step or two, and catching him by the arm with an admonitory grip that could not easily be misunderstood, compelled him to proceed with himself step by step to the table. Denis, however, could feel the strong man tremble, and perceive that, although he strove to lash himself into the energy of despair, and the utter disbelief of all religious sanction, yet the trial before him called every slumbering prejudice and apprehension of his mind into active power. This was a death-blow to his own resolution, or, rather it confirmed him in his previous determination not to swear on the Donagh, except to acknowledge his guilt, which he could scarcely prevent himself from doing, such was the vacillating state of mind to which he felt himself reduced.

When Anthony reached the table, his huge form seemed to dilate by his effort at maintaining the firmness necessary to support him in this awful struggle between conscience and superstition, on the one hand, and guilt, habit, and infidelity, on the other. He fixed his deep, dilated eyes upon the Donagh, in a manner that betokened somewhat of irresolution; his countenance fell, his color came and went, but eventually settled in a flushed red; his powerful hands and arms trembled so much, that he folded them to prevent his agitation from being noticed; the grimness of his face ceased to be stern, while it retained the blank expression of guilt; his temples swelled out with the terrible play of their blood-vessels, his chest, too, heaved up and down with the united pressure of guilt, and the tempest which shook him within. At length he saw Denis's eye upon him, and his passions took a new direction; he knit his brows at him with more than usual fierceness, ground his teeth, and, with a step and action of suppressed fury, he placed his foot at the edge of the table, and, bowing down under the eye of God and man, took the awful oath on the mysterious Donagh, in a falsehood! When it was finished, a feeble groan broke from his brother's lips. Anthony bent his eye on him with a deadly glare, but Denis saw it not. The shock was beyond his courage—he had become insensible.

Those who stood at the outskirts of the crowd, seeing Denis apparently lifeless, thought he must have sworn falsely on the Donagh, and exclaimed, "He's dead! gracious God! Denis Meehan's struck dead by the Donagh! He swore in a lie, and is now a corpse!" Anthony paused, and calmly surveyed him, as he lay with his head resting upon the hands of those who supported him. At this moment a silent breeze came over where he stood; and, as the Donagh lay upon the table, the black ribbons with which it was ornamented fluttered with a melancholy appearance that deepened the sensations of the people into something peculiarly solemn and preternatural. Denis at length revived, and stared wildly and vacantly about him. When composed sufficiently to distinguish and recognize individual objects, he looked upon the gloomy visage and threatening eye of his brother, and shrank back with a terror almost epileptical. "Oh!" he exclaimed, "save me! save me from that man, and I'll discover all!"

Anthony calmly folded one arm into his bosom,

and his lip quivered, with the united influence of hatred and despair.

"Hould him!" shrieked a voice which proceeded from his daughter. "Hould my father, or he'll murdher him! Oh! oh! merciful heaven!"

Ere the words were uttered, she had made an attempt to clasp the arms of her parent whose motions she understood; but only in time to receive from the pistol which he had concealed in his breast the bullet aimed at her uncle! She tottered, and the blood spouted out of her neck upon her father's brows, who hastily put up his hand and wiped it away, for it had actually blinded him.

The elder Meehan was a tall man, and, as he stood elevated nearly a head above the crowd, his grim brows red with his daughter's blood—which, in attempting to wipe away, he had deeply streaked across his face—his eyes shooting fiery gleams of his late resentment, mingled with the wildness of unexpected horror—as he thus stood, it would be impossible to contemplate a more revolting picture of that state to which the principles that had regulated his life must ultimately lead, even in this world.

On perceiving what he had done, the deep working of his powerful frame was struck into sudden stillness, and he turned his eyes on his bleeding daughter, with a fearful perception of her situation. Now was the harvest of his creed and crimes reaped in blood; and he felt that the stroke which had fallen upon him was one of those by which God will sometimes bare his arm and vindicate his justice. The reflection, however, shook him not; the reality of his misery was too intense and pervading, and grappled too strongly with his hardened and unbending spirit, to waste its power upon a nerve or a muscle. It was abstracted, and beyond the reach of bodily suffering. From the moment his daughter fell, he moved not; his lips were half open with the conviction produced by the blasting truth of her death, effected prematurely by his own hand.

Those parts of his face which had not been stained with her blood assumed an ashy paleness, and rendered his countenance more terrific by the contrast. Tall, powerful, and motionless he appeared to the crowd, glaring at the girl like a tiger anxious to join his offspring, yet stunned with the shock of the bullet which has touched a vital part. His iron-gray hair, as it fell in thick masses about his neck, was moved slightly by the blast, and a lock which fell over his temple was blown back with a motion rendered more distinct by his statue-like attitude, immovable as death.

A silent and awful gathering of the people around this impressive scene intimated their knowledge of what they considered to be a judicial punishment annexed to perjury upon the Donagh. This relic lay on the table, and the eyes of those who stood within view of it turned from Anthony's countenance to it, and again back to his blood-stained visage, with all the overwhelming influence of superstitious fear. Shudderings, tremblings, crossings, and ejaculations marked their conduct and feeling; for though the incident itself was simply a fatal and uncommon one, yet *they* considered it supernatural and miraculous.

At length a loud and agonizing cry burst from the lips of Meehan—"O God! God of heaven an' earth!—have I murdhered my daughter?" And he cast down the fatal weapon with a force which buried it some inches into the wet clay.

The crowd had closed upon Anne, but with the strength of a giant he flung them aside, caught the girl in his arms, and pressed her bleeding to his bosom. He gasped for breath. "Anne," said he—"Anne, I am without hope, an' there's none to forgive me except you—none at all; from God to the poorest of his creatures, I am hated an' cursed by all, except you! Don't curse me, Anne, don't curse me! Oh! isn't it enough, darlin', that my sowl is now stained with *your* blood, along with my other crimes? In hell, on earth, an' in heaven there's none to forgive your father but yourself!—NONE, NONE! Oh! what's com· in' over me! I'm dizzy an' shiverin'! How cowld the day's got of a sudden! Hould up, *avourneen machree!* I *was* a bad man; but to *you*, Anne, I was *not* as I was to every one! Darlin', oh! look at me with forgiveness in your eye, or, anyway, don't *curse* me! Oh! I'm far cowlder now! Tell me that you forgive me, *acushla, oge machree!—Manim asthee hu,** darlin', say it. I DAR'N'T LOOK TO GOD! But, oh! do *you* say the forgivin' word to your father before you die!"

"Father," said she, "I deserve this—it's only just; I have plotted with that divilish Martin to betray them all, except yourself, an' to get the reward; an' then we intended to go—an'—live at a distance—an' in wickedness—where we—might not be known—he's at our house—let him be—secured. Forgive me, father—you said so often that there was no thruth in religion—that I began to—think so. O—God! have mercy upon me!" And with these words she expired.

Meehan's countenance, on hearing this, was overspread with a ghastly look of the most desolating agony; he staggered back, and the body of his daughter, which he strove to hold, would have fallen from his arms, had it not been caught by the by-standers. His eye sought out his brother, but not in resentment. "Oh! she died, but didn't say, 'I FORGIVE YOU!' Denis," said he, "Denis, bring me home—I'm sick—very sick—oh! but it's cowld—everything's reeling—how cowld—cowld it is!" And, as he uttered the last words, he shuddered, fell down in a fit of apoplexy, never to rise again; and the bodies of his daughter and himself were both waked and buried together.

The result is brief. The rest of the gang were

* Young pulse of my heart!—my soul is within thee!

secured; Denis became approver, by whose evidence they suffered that punishment decreed by law to the crimes of which they had been guilty. The two events which we have just related of course added to the supernatural fear and reverence previously entertained for this terrible relic. It is still used as an ordeal of expurgation, in cases of stolen property; and we are not wrong in asserting that many of these misguided creatures, who too frequently hesitate not to swear falsely on the Word of God, would suffer death itself sooner than commit a perjury on the Donagh.

LARRY McFARLAND'S WAKE.

AS DESCRIBED BY TOM McROARKIN.

THE squire very kindly lent sheets for them both to be laid out in, and mould candlesticks to hould the lights; and, God he knows! 'twas a grievous sight to see the father and mother both stretched beside one another in their poor place, and their little orphans about them; the gorsoons—them that had sense enough to know their loss—breaking their hearts, the crathurs, and so hoarse that they weren't able to cry or spake. But, indeed, it was worse to see the two young things going over, and wanting to get acrass to waken their daddy and mammy, poor desolit childher!

When the corpses were washed and dressed, they looked uncommonly well, consitherin'. Larry, indeed, didn't bear death so well as Sally; but you couldn't meet a purtier corpse than she was in a day's travelling. I say, when they were washed and dressed, their friends and neighbors knelt down round them, and offered up a Pather and Ave apiece, for the good of their sowls; when this was done, they all raised the keena, stooping over them at a half bend, clapping their hands, and praising them as far as they could say anything good of them; and, indeed, the crathurs, they were never any one's enemy but their own, so that nobody could say an ill-word of either of them. Bad luck to it for potteen-work every day it rises! only for it, that couple's poor orphans wouldn't be left without father or mother as they were; nor poor Hurrish go the gray gate he did, if he had his father living, may be: but, having nobody to bridle him in, he took to horse-riding for the squire, and then to staling them for himself. He was hanged afterwards, along with Peter Doraghy Crolly, that shot Ned Wilson's uncle of the Black Hills.

After the first keening, the friends and neighbors took their sates about the corpse. In a short time, whiskey, pipes, snuff, and tobacco came, and every one about the place got a glass and a fresh pipe. Tom, when he held his glass in his hand, looking at his dead brother, filled up to the eyes, and couldn't for some time get out a word; at last, when he was able to spake, "Poor Larry," says he, "you're lying there low before me, and many a happy day we spint with one another. When we were childher," said he, turning to the rest, "we were never asunder; he was oulder nor me by two years, and can I ever forget the leathering he gave Dick Rafferty long ago, for hitting me with the rotten egg, although Dick was a great dale bigger than either of us? God knows, although you didn't thrive in life, either of you, as you might and could have done, there wasn't a more neighborly or friendly couple in the parish they lived in; and now God help them both and their poor orphans over them! Larry, acushla, your health, and Sally, yours; and may God Almighty have marcy on both your sowls!"

After this, the neighbors began to flock in more generally. When any relation of the corpses would come, as soon, you see, as they'd get inside the door, whether man or woman, they'd raise the shout of a keena, and all the people about the dead would begin along with them, stooping over them and clapping their hands as before.

Well, I said, it's it that was the merry wake, and that was only the thruth, neighbors. As soon as night came, all the young boys and girls from the country-side about them flocked to it in scores. In a short time the house was crowded; and may be there wasn't laughing, and story-telling, and singing, and smoking, and drinking, and crying—all going on, helter-skelter, together. When they'd be all in full chorus this way, may be some new friend or relation that wasn't there before would come in and raise the keena; of coorse the youngsters would then keep quiet; and if the person coming in was from the one neighborhood with any of them that were so merry, as soon as he'd raise the shout the merry folks would rise up, begin to pelt their hands together, and cry along with him till their eyes would be as red as a ferret's. That once over, they'd be down again at the songs, and divarsion, and divilment, just as if nothing of the kind had taken place; the other would then shake hands with the friends of the corpses, get a glass or two, and a pipe, and in a few minutes be as merry as the best of them.

" Well," said Andy Morrow, " I should like to know if the Scotch and English are such heerum-skeerum kind of people as we Irishmen are?"

" Musha, in throth I'm sure they're not," says Nancy; "for I believe that Irishmen are like nobody in the wide world but themselves ; quare crathurs that'll laugh, or cry, or fight with any one, just for nothing else, good or bad, but company."

Indeed, and you all know that what I'm saying's thruth, except Mr. Morrow there that I'm telling it to bekase he's not in the habit of going to wakes ; although, to do him justice, he's very friendly in going to a neighbor's funeral ; and, indeed, *kind father for you.** Mr. Morrow, for it's he that was a real good hand at going to such places himself.

Well, as I was telling you, there was great sport going on. In one corner, you might see a knot of ould men sitting together, talking over ould times—ghost-stories, fairy-tales, or the great rebellion of '41, and the strange story of Lamh Dearg, or the *bloody hand*—that may be I'll tell

---

* That is, in this point you are of the same *kind* as your father; possessing that prominent trait in his disposition or character.

you all some other night, plase God; there they'd sit smoking—their faces quite plased with the pleasure of the pipe—amusing themselves and a crowd of people that would be listening to them with open mouth. Or, it's odds, but there would be some droll young fellow among them taking a *rise* out of them; and, positively, he'd often find them able enough for him, particularly old Ned Mangin that wanted at the time only four years of a hundred. The Lord be good to him, and rest his sowl in glory! it's he that was the pleasant ould man, and could tell a story with any one that ever got up.

In another corner, there was a different set, bent on some piece of divilment of their own. The boys would be sure to get beside their sweethearts, anyhow; and, if there was a purty girl, as you may set it down there was, it's there the *skroodging*,* and the pushing, and the shoving, and sometimes the knocking down itself would be about seeing who'd get her. There's ould Katty Duffy, that's now as crooked as the hind leg of a dog, and it's herself was then as straight as a rush, and as blooming as a rose—Lord bless us! what an alteration time makes upon the strongest and fairest of us!—it's she that was the purty girl that night, and it's myself that gave Frank M'Shane, that's still alive to acknowledge it, the broad of his back upon the flure when he thought to pull her off my knee. The very gor-

* The pressure in a crowd.

soons and girshas were coorting away among themselves, and learning one another to smoke in the dark corners. But all this, Mr. Morrow, took place in the corpse-house, before ten or eleven o'clock at night; after that time, the house got too throng entirely, and couldn't hould the half of them; so, by jing, off we set, maning all the youngsters of us, both boys and girls, out to Tom's barn that was *red** up for us there, to commence the plays. When we were gone, the ould people had more room, and they moved about on the sates we had left them. In the manetime, lashings of tobacco and snuff, cut in platefuls, and piles of fresh new pipes, were laid on the table for any one that wished to use them.

When we got to the barn, it's then we *took our pumps off*† in airnest—by the hokey, such sport you never saw. The first play we began was *Hot-loof;* and may be there wasn't skelping then. It was the two parishes of Errigle-Keeran and Errigle-Truagh against one another. There was the Slip from Althadhawan for Errigle-Truagh, against Pat M'Ardle, that had married Lanty Gorman's daughter of Cargach, for Errigle-Keeran. The way they play it, Mr. Morrow, is this: Two young men out of each parish go out upon the flure; one of them stands up, then bends himself, sir, at a nalf bend, placing his left hand behind on the back part of his ham, keeping it there to receive what it's to get. Well, there he stands,

* Cleared up—set in order. † Threw aside all restraint.

and the other, coming behind him, places his left foot out before him, doubles up the cuff of his coat, to give his hand and wrist freedom; he then rises his right arm, coming down with the heel of his hand upon the other fellow's palm under him with full force. By jing, it's the divil's own divarsion; for you might as well get a stroke of a sledge as a blow from one of them able, hard-working fellows, with hands upon them like limestone. When the fellow that's down gets it hot and heavy, the man that struck him stands bent in his place, and some friend of the other comes down upon him, and pays him for what the other fellow got.

The next play they went to was the *Sitting Brogue*. This is played by a ring of them sitting down upon the bare ground, keeping their knees up. A shoemaker's leather apron is then got, or a good stout brogue, and sent round under their knees. In the manetime, one stands in the middle; and, after the brogue is sent round, he is to catch it as soon as he can. While he stands there, of coorse his back must be to some one, and accordingly those that are behind him thump him right and left with the brogue, while he all the time is trying to catch it. Whoever he catches this brogue with must stand up in his place, while he sits down where the other had been, and then the play goes on as before.

There's another play called the *Standing Brogue*—where one man gets a brogue of the same kind, and another stands up facing him with his hands locked together, forming an arch turned upside down. The man that houlds the brogue then strikes him with it betune the hands; and even the smartest fellow receives several pelts before he is able to close his hands and catch it; but when he does, he becomes brogueman, and the man who held the brogue stands for him until he catches it. The same thing is gone through, from one to another, on each side, until it is over.

The next is *Frimsy Framsy*, and is played in this manner: a chair or stool is placed in the middle of the flure, and the man who manages the play sits down upon it, and calls his sweetheart, or the prettiest girl in the house. She accordingly comes forward, and must kiss him. He then rises up, and she sits down. "Come now," he says, "fair maid—*Frimsy Framsy*, who's your fancy?" She then calls them she likes best, and, when the young man she calls comes over and kisses her, he then takes her place, and calls another girl—and so on, smacking away for a couple of hours. Well, throth, it's no wonder that Ireland's full of people; for I believe they do nothing but coort from the time they're the hoight of my leg. I dunna is it true, as I hear Captain Sloethorn's steward say, that the Englishwomen are so fond of Irishmen?

"Well," said Andy Morrow, "have you any more of their sports, Tom?"

"Ay have I; one of the best and pleasantest you heard yet."

"I hope there's no more coorting in it," says Nancy. "God knows, we're tired of their kissing an' marrying."

"Were you always so?" says Ned, across the fire to her.

"Behave yourself, Ned," says she; "don't *you* make me spake; sure you were set down as the greatest brine-oge that was ever known in the parish for such things."

"No; but don't you make *me* spake," replies Ned.

"Here, Biddy," said Nancy, "bring that uncle of yours another pint; that's what he wants most at the present time, I'm thinking."

Biddy accordingly complied with this.

"Don't make *me* spake," continued Ned.

"Come, Ned," she replied, "you've a fresh pint now; so drink it, and give no more *gosther*."*

"*Shuid-urth!*" † says Ned, putting the pint to his head, and winking slyly at the rest.

"Ay, wink; in troth I'll be up to you for that, Ned," says Nancy, by no means satisfied that Ned should enter into particulars. "Well, Tom," says she, diverting the conversation, "go on, and give us the remainder of your wake."

Well, says Tom, the next play is in the mil-

* Idle talk—gossip.
† Shuid-urth—This to you, or upon you; a form of drinking healths.

intary line. You see, Mr. Morrow, the man that leads the sports places them all on their sates, gets from some of the girls a white handkerchief, which he ties round his hat as you would tie a piece of mourning; he then walks round them two or three times singing—

> Will you list and come with me, fair maid?
> Will you list and come with me, fair maid?
> Will you list and come with me, fair maid,
> And folly the lad with the white cockade?

When he sings this, he takes off his hat, and puts it on the head of the girl he likes best, who rises up and puts her arm round him, and then they both go about in the same way, singing the same words. She then puts the hat on some young man, who gets up and goes round with them singing as before. *He* next puts it on the girl *he* loves best, who, after singing and going round in the same manner, puts it on another, and *he* on *his* sweetheart, and so on. This is called the *White Cockade*. When it's all over, that is, when every young man has pitched upon the girl that he wishes to be his sweetheart, they sit down, and sing songs, and coort, as they did at the marrying.

After this comes the *Weds* or *Forfeits*, or what they call putting round the button. Every one gives in a forfeit—the boys a neck-handkerchief or a pen-knife, and the girls a pocket-handkerchief or something that way. The forfeit is held over them, and each of them stoops in turn. They are then compelled to command the person that owns that forfeit to sing a song, to kiss such and such a girl, or to carry some ould man, with his legs about their neck three times around the house, and this last is always great fun. Or may be a young, upsetting fellow will be sent to kiss some toothless, slavering ould woman, just to punish him; or, if a young woman is any way saucy, she'll have to kiss some ould, withered fellow, his tongue hanging with age half-way down his chin, and the tobacco-water trickling from each corner of his mouth.

By jingo, many a time when the friends of the corpse would be breaking their very hearts with grief and affliction I have seen them obligated to laugh out in spite of themselves, at the drollery of the mock priest, with his ould black coat and wig upon him; and, when the laughing-fit would be over, to see them rocking themselves again with the sorrow—so sad. The best man for managing such sports in this neighborhood for many a year was Roger M'Cann, that lives up as you go to the mountains. You wouldn't begrudge to go ten miles the coldest winter night that ever blew, to see and hear Roger.

There's another play that they call the *Priest of the Parish*, which is remarkably pleasant. One of the boys gets a wig upon himself, as before, goes out on the flure, places the boys in a row, calls one his *man Jack*, and says to each, "What will you be?" One answers, "I'll be *black cap*";

another, "*red cap*"; and so on. He then says, "The priest of the parish has lost his considhering cap—some says this and some says that, but I say my man Jack!" Man Jack, then, to put it off himself, says, "Is it me, sir?" "Yes, you, sir!" "You lie, sir!" "Who then, sir?" "Black cap!" If black cap then doesn't say, "Is it me, sir?" before the priest has time to call him, he must put his hand on his ham, and get a pelt of the brogue. A body must be supple with the tongue in it.

After this comes one they call *Horns*, or the *Painter*. A droll fellow gets a lump of soot or lampblack, and, after fixing a ring of the boys and girls about him, he lays his two fore-fingers on his knees, and says, "Horns, horns, cow-horns!" and then raises his fingers by a jerk up above his head; the boys and girls in the ring then do the same, for the meaning of the play is this: the man with the black'ning *always* raises his finger every time he names an animal; but if he names any that has *no* horns, and that the others jerk up their fingers, then they must get a stroke over the face with the soot. "Horns, horns, goat-horns!" then he ups with his finger like lightning; they must all do the same, bekase a goat *has* horns. "Horns, horns, horse-horns!"—he ups with them again, but the boys and girls ought not, bekase a horse has *not* horns; however, any one that raises them *then*, gets a slake. So that it all comes to this: any one, you see, that lifts his finger when an animal is named that has *no* horns, or any one that does *not* raise them when a baste is mintioned that *has* horns, will get a mark. It's a purty game, and requires a keen eye and a quick hand; and may be there's not fun in straiking the soot over the purty, warm, rosy cheeks of the colleens, while their eyes are dancing with delight in their heads, and their sweet breath comes over so pleasant about one's face, the darlings!—och! och!

There's another game they call the *Silly ould Man* that's played this way: a ring of the boys and girls is made on the flure—boy and girl about—holding one another by the hands; well and good. A young fellow gets into the middle of the ring, as "the silly ould man." There he stands looking at all the girls, to choose a wife, and, in the manetime, the youngsters of the ring sing out—

> Here's a silly ould man that lies all alone,
>   That lies all alone,
>   That lies all alone,
> Here's a silly ould man that lies all alone,
> He wants a wife, and he can get none.

When the boys and girls sing this, the silly ould man must choose a wife from some of the colleens belonging to the ring. Having made choice of her, she goes into the ring along with him, and they all sing out—

> Now, young couple, you're married together,
>   You're married together,
>   You're married together,
> You must obey your father and mother,
> And love one another like sister and brother—
> I pray, young couple, you'll kiss together!

And you may be sure this part of the marriage is not missed, anyway.

"I doubt," said Andy Morrow, "that good can't come of so much kissing, marrying, and coorting."

The narrator twisted his mouth knowingly, and gave a significant groan.

"*Be dhe husth*,* hould your tongue, Misther Morrow," said he. "Biddy avourneen," he continued, addressing Biddy and Bessy, "and Bessy, alannah, just take a friend's advice, and never mind going to wakes; to be sure, there's plinty of fun and divarsion at such places, but—healths apiece!" putting the pint to his lips—"and that's all I say about it."

"Right enough, Tom," observed Shane Fadh. "Sure most of the matches are planned at them, and, I may say, most of the *runaways*, too—poor young, foolish crathurs, going off and getting themselves married, then bringing small, helpless families upon their hands, without money or manes to begin the world with, and afterwards likely to eat one another out of the face for their folly; however, there's no putting ould heads upon young shoulders, and I doubt, except the wakes are stopped altogether, that it'll be the ould case still."

"I never remember being at a counthry wake," said Andy Morrow. "How is everything laid out in the house?"

* The translation follows it above.

Sure it's to you I'm telling the whole story, Mr. Morrow; these thieves about me here know all about it as well as I do—the house, eh? Why, you see, the two corpses were stretched beside one another, washed, and laid out. There were long deal boords, with their ends upon two stools, laid over the bodies; the boords were covered with a white sheet got at the big house, so the corpses wern't to be seen. On these, again, were placed large mould candles, plates of cut tobacco, pipes, and snuff, and so on. Sometimes corpses are waked in a bed, with their faces visible; when that is the case, white sheets, crosses, and sometimes flowers are pinned up about the bed, except in the front; but when they're undher boord, a set of ould women sit smoking and rocking themselves from side to side, quite sorrowful—these are *keeners*—friends or relations; and when every one connected with the dead comes in, they raise the *keene*, like a *song* of sorrow, wailing and clapping their hands.

The furniture is mostly removed, and sates made round the walls, where the neighbors sit smoking, chatting, and gosthering. The best of aiting and dhrinking that they can afford is provided; and, indeed, there is generally open house, for it's unknown how people injure themselves by their kindness and waste at christening, weddings, and wakes.

In regard to poor Larry's wake—we had all this, and more at it; for, as I observed a while agone, the man had made himself no friends when he was living, and the neighbors gave a loose to all kinds of divilment when he was dead. Although there's no man would be guilty of any disrespect where the dead are, yet, when a person has led a good life, and conducted themselves dacently and honestly, the young people of the neighborhood show their respect by going through their little plays and divarsions quieter and with less noise, lest they may give any offince; but, as I said, whenever the person didn't live as they ought to do, there's no stop to their noise and *rollikin.**

When it drew near morning, every one of us took his sweetheart, and, after convoying her home, we went to our own houses to get a little sleep. So that was the end of poor Larry McFarland and his wife Sally Lowry.

"Success, Tom!" said Bill M'Kinny; "take a pull of the malt now, afther the story, your soul! But what was the funeral like?"

"Why, then, a poor berrin it was," said Tom "a miserable sight, God knows—just a few of the neighbors; for those that used to take his thrate, and while he had a shilling in his pocket blarney him up, not one of the skulking thieves showed their faces at it—a good warning to foolish men that throw their money down throats that haven't hearts anundher them. But, boys, *I* desarve another thrate, I think, afther my story!" This,

---

* Uproariousness.

we need scarcely add, he was supplied with, and, after some further desultory chat, they again separated, with the intention of reassembling at Ned's on the following night.

CHARLES LEVER.

Charles Lever.

THE DOCTOR'S TALE.*

IT is now fifteen years since—if it wasn't for O'Shaughnessy's wrinkles, I could not believe it five—we were quartered in Loughrea; there were, besides our regiment, the Fiftieth, and the Seventy-third, and a troop or two of horse-artillery, and the whole town was literally a barrack, and, as you may suppose, the pleasantest place imaginable. All the young ladies, and indeed all those that had got their brevet some years before, came flocking into the town, not knowing but the devil might persuade a raw ensign or so to marry some of them.

Such dinner parties, such routs, and balls never were heard of west of Athlone. The gaieties were incessant; and, if good feeling, plenty of claret, short whist, country dances, and kissing could have done the thing, there wouldn't have

* I cannot permit the reader to fall into the same blunder with regard to the worthy "Maurice" that my friend Charles O'Malley has done. It is only fair to state that the doctor, in the following tale, was hoaxing the dragoon. A braver and a better fellow than Quill never existed; equally beloved by his brother officers, as delighted in for his convivial talents. His favorite amusement was to invent some story or adventure, in which, mixing up his own name with that of some friend or companion, the veracity of the whole was never questioned. Of this nature was the pedigree he devised in the last chapter to impose upon O'Malley, who believed implicity all he told him.   H. L.

been a bachelor with a red coat for six miles around.

You know the west, O'Mealy, so I needn't tell you what the Galway girls are like; fine, hearty, free-and-easy, talking, laughing devils, but as deep and as cute as a master in chancery; ready for any fun or merriment, but always keeping a sly lookout for a proposal or a tender acknowledgment, which—what between the heat of a ball-room, whiskey-negus, white satin shoes, and a quarrel with your guardian—it's ten to one you fall into before you're a week in the same town with them.

As for the men, I don't admire them so much; pleasant and cheerful enough, when they're handicapping the coat off your back and your new tilbury for a spavined pony and a cotton umbrella, but regular devils if you come to cross them the least in life; nothing but ten paces—three shots apiece—to begin and end with something like Roger de Coverly, when every one has a pull at his neighbor. I'm not saying they're not agreeable, well informed, and mild in their habits; but they lean overmuch to corduroys and coroner's inquests for one's taste further south. However, they're a fine people, take them all in all; and, if they were not interfered with, and their national customs invaded with road-making, petty sessions, grand-jury laws, and a stray commission now and then, they are capable of great things and would astonish the world.

But, as I was saying, we were ordered to Loughrea, after being fifteen months in detachments about Biri, Tullamore, Kilbeggan, and all that country; the change was indeed a delightful one, and we soon found ourselves the centre of the most marked and determined civilities. I told you they were wise people in the west; this was their calculation; the line—ours was the Roscommon militia—are here to-day, there to-morrow; they may be flirting in Tralee this week, and fighting on the Tagus the next; not that there was any fighting there in those times, but then there was always Nova Scotia, and St. John's, and a hundred other places that a Galway young lady knew nothing about, except that people never came back from them. Now, what good, what use was there in falling in love with them, mere transitory and passing pleasures that was? But as for us, there we were; if not in Kilkenny, we were in Cork. Save cut and come again, no getting away under pretence of foreign service; no excuse for not marrying by any cruel pictures of the colonies, where they make spatch-cocks of the officers' wives, and scrape their infant families to death with a small tooth comb. In a word, my dear O'Mealey, we were at a high premium; and even O'Shaughnessy, with his red head and the legs you see, had his admirers—there now, don't be angry, Dan, the men, at least, were mighty partial to you.

Loughrea, if it was a pleasant, was a very expensive place. White gloves and car-hire—there wasn't a chaise in the town—short whist, too (God forgive me, if I wrong them! but I wonder were they honest?), cost money; and as our popularity rose our purses fell, till at length, when the one was at the flood, the other was something very like low water:

Now, the Roscommon was a beautiful corps; no petty jealousies, no little squabbling among the officers, no small spleen between the major's wife and the paymaster's sister; all was amiable, kind, brotherly, and affectionate. To proceed. I need only mention one fine trait of them—no man ever refused to endorse a brother officer's bill. To think of asking the amount, or even the date, would be taken personally; and thus we went on mutually aiding and assisting each other, the colonel drawing on me, I on the major, the senior captain on the surgeon, and so on, a regular cross-fire of "promises to pay," all stamped and regular.

Not but that the system had its inconveniences; for sometimes an obstinate tailor or bootmaker would make a row for his money, and then we'd be obliged to get up a little quarrel between the drawer and accepter of the bill; they couldn't speak for some days; and a mutual friend to both would tell the creditor that the slightest imprudence on his part would lead to bloodshed; and —the Lord help him!—if there was a duel, he'd be proved the whole cause of it. This and twenty other plans were employed, and finally the matter would be left to arbitration among our brother officers; and, I need not say, they behaved like trumps. But, notwithstanding all this, we were frequently hard pressed for cash; as the colonel said, "It's a mighty expensive corps." Our dress was costly, not that it had much lace and gold on it, but that, what between falling on the road at night, shindies at mess, and other devilment, a coat lasted no time. Wine, too, was heavy on us; for, though we often changed our wine merchant, and rarely paid him, there was an awful consumption at the mess!

Now, what I have mentioned may prepare you for the fact that, before we were eight weeks in garrison, Shaugh and myself, upon an accurate calculation of our conjoint finances, discovered that, except some vague promises of discounting here and there through the town, and seven and fourpence in specie, we were innocent of any pecuniary treasures. This was embarrassing; we had both embarked in several small schemes of pleasurable amusement—had a couple of hunters each, a tandem, and a running account—I think it galloped—at every shop in the town.

Let me pause for a moment here, O'Mealey, while I moralize a little in a strain I hope may benefit you. Have you ever considered—of course you have not, you're too young and unreflecting—how beautifully every climate and every soil possesses some one antidote or another to its own noxious influences? The tropics have their succulent and juicy fruits, cooling and refreshing; the northern latitudes have their beasts with fur and warm skins to keep out the frost-bites; and so it is in Ireland. Nowhere on the face of the habitable globe does a man contract such habits of small debt, and nowhere, I'll be sworn, can he so easily get out of any scrape concerning them. They have their tigers in the east, their antelopes in the south, their white bears in Norway, their buffaloes in America; but we have an animal in Ireland that beats them all hollow—a country attorney.

Now, let me introduce you to Mr. Matthew Donevan. Mat, as he was familiarly called by his numerous acquaintances, was a short, florid, rosy little gentleman, of some four or five and forty, with a well-curled wig of the fairest imaginable auburn, the gentle wave of the front locks which played in infantine loveliness upon his little bullet forehead contrasting strongly enough with a cunning leer of his eye, and a certain *nisi prius* laugh that, however it might please a client, rarely brought pleasurable feelings to his opponent in a cause.

Mat was a character in his way; deep, double, and tricky in everything that concerned his profession, he affected the gay fellow—liked a jolly dinner at Brown's hotel, would go twenty miles to see a steeple-chase and a coursing-match, bet with any one when the odds were strong in his favor, with an easy indifference about money that made him seem, when winning, rather the victim of good luck than anything else. As he kept a rather pleasant bachelor's house, and liked the military much, we soon became acquainted. Upon him, therefore, for reasons I can't explain, both our hopes reposed; and Shaugh and myself at once agreed that, if Mat could not assist us in our distresses, the case was a bad one.

A pretty little epistle was accordingly concocted, inviting the worthy attorney to a small dinner at five o'clock the next day, intimating that we were to be perfectly alone, and had a little business to discuss. True to the hour, Mat was there, and, as if instantly guessing that ours was no party of pleasure, his look, dress, and manner were all in keeping with the occasion—quiet, subdued, and searching.

When the claret had been superseded by the whiskey, and the confidential hours were approaching, by an adroit allusion to some heavy wager then pending we brought our finances upon the tapis. The thing was done beautifully; an easy *adagio* movement—no violent transition—but hang me if old Mat didn't catch the matter at once.

"Oh! it's there ye are, captain," said he, with his peculiar grin; "two and sixpence in the pound, and no assets."

"The last is nearer the mark, my old boy," said Shaugh, blurting out the whole truth at once. The wily attorney finished his tumbler slowly, as if giving himself time for reflection, and then, smacking his lips in a preparatory manner, took a quick survey of the room with his piercing green eye.

"A very sweet mare of yours that little mouse-colored one is, with the dip in the back; and she has a trifling curb—may be it's a spavin, indeed—in the near hind leg. You gave five and twenty for her, now, I'll be bound?"

"Sixty guineas, as sure as my name's Dan!" said Shaugh, not at all pleased at the value put upon his hackney; "and, as to spavin or curb, I'll wager double the sum she has neither the slightest trace of one nor the other."

"I'll not take the bet," said Mat dryly; "money's scarce in these parts."

This hit silenced us both, and our friend continued:

"Then there's the bay horse, a great strapping, leggy beast he is for a tilbury; and the hunters, worth nothing here; they don't know this country—them's neat pistols—and the tilbury is not bad—"

"Confound you!" said I, losing all patience. "We didn't ask you here to appraise our movables; we want to raise the wind without that."

"I see—I perceive," said Mat, taking a pinch of snuff very leisurely as he spoke—"I see. Well, that is difficult, very difficult just now. I've mortgaged every acre of ground in the two counties near us, and a sixpence more is not to be had that way. Are you lucky at the races?"

" Never win a sixpence."

" What can you do at whist ? "

" Revoke, and get cursed by my partner; devil a more."

" That's mighty bad, for otherwise we might arrange something for you. Well, I only see one thing for it; you must marry; a wife with some money will get you out of your present difficulties, and we'll manage that easily enough."

" Come, Dan," said I, for Shaugh was dropping asleep, " cheer up, old fellow ! Donevan has found the way to pull us through our misfortunes. A girl with forty thousand pounds, the best cock-shooting in Ireland, an old family, a capital cellar, all await ye—rouse up there ! "

" I'm convanient," said Shaugh, with a look intended to be knowing, but really very tipsy.

" I didn't say much for her personal attractions, captain," said Mat; " nor, indeed, did I specify the exact sum; but Mrs. Rogers Dooley, of Clonakilty, might be a princess—"

" And so she shall be, Mat; the O'Shaughnessys were kings of Ennis in the time of Nero ; and I'm only waiting for a trifle of money to revive the title. What's her name ? "

" Mrs. Rogers Dooley."

" Here's her health, and long life to her—

' And may the devil cut the toes
Of all her foes,
That we may know them by their limping.' "

This benevolent wish uttered, Dan fell flat

upon the hearth-rug, and was soon sound asleep. I must hasten on; so need only say that, before we parted that night, Mat and myself had finished the half-gallon bottle of Loughrea whiskey, and concluded a treaty for the hand and fortune of Mrs. Rogers Dooley; he being guaranteed a very handsome percentage on the property, and the lady being reserved for choice between Dan and myself, which, however, I was determined should fall upon my more fortunate friend.

The first object which presented itself to my aching senses the following morning was a very spacious card of invitation from Mr. Jonas Malone, requesting me to favor him with the seductions of my society the next evening at a ball; at the bottom of which, in Mr. Donevan's hand, I read:

"Don't fail; you know who is to be there. I've not been idle since I saw you. Would the captain take twenty-five for the mare?"

So far so good, thought I, as, entering O'Shaughnessy's quarters, I discovered him endeavoring to spell out his card, which, however, had no postscript. We soon agreed that Mat should have his price; so, sending a polite answer to the invitation, we despatched a still more civil note to the attorney, and begged of him, as a weak mark of esteem, to except the mouse-colored mare as a present.

Here O'Shaughnessy sighed deeply, and even seemed affected by the souvenir.

"Come, Dan, we did it all for the best. O

O'Mealey, he was a cunning fellow—but no matter. We went to the ball, and, to be sure, it was a great sight. Two hundred and fifty souls, where there was not good room for the odd fifty; such laughing, such squeezing, such pressing of hands and waists in the staircase! And then such a row and riot at the top—four fiddles, a key bugle, and a bagpipe playing "Haste to the wedding," amid the crash of refreshment trays, the tramp of feet, and the sounds of merriment on all sides!

It's only in Ireland, after all, people have fun. Old and young, merry and morose, the gay and cross-grained—are crammed into a lively country dance; and, ill-matched, ill-suited, go jigging away together to the blast of a bad band, till their heads, half turned by the noise, the heat, the novelty, and the hubbub, they all get as tipsy as if they were really deep in liquor.

Then there is that particularly free-and-easy tone in every one about; here go a couple capering daintily out of the ball-room to take a little fresh air on the stairs, where every step has its own separate flirtation party; there a riotous old gentleman, with a boarding-school girl for his partner, has plunged smack into a party at loo, upsetting cards and counters, and drawing down curses innumerable; here are a merry knot round the refreshments, and well they may be; for the negus is strong punch, and the biscuit is tipsy cake—and all this with a running fire of good stories, jokes, and witticisms on all sides, in the laughter at which even the droll-looking servants join as heartily as the rest.

We were not long in finding out Mrs. Rogers, who sat in the middle of a very high sofa, with her feet just touching the floor. She was short, fat, wore her hair in a drop, had a species of shining-yellow skin, and a turned-up nose, all of which were by no means prepossessing. Shaugh and myself were too hard-up to be particular, and so we invited her to dance alternately for two consecutive hours, plying her assiduously with negus during the lulls of the music.

Supper was at last announced, and enabled us to recruit for new efforts; and so, after an awful consumption of fowl, pigeon-pie, ham, and brandied cherries, Mrs. Rogers brightened up considerably, and professed her willingness to join the dancers. As for us, partly from exhaustion, partly to stimulate our energies, and in some degree to drown reflection, we drank deep, and, when we reached the drawing-room, not only the agreeable guests themselves, but even the furniture, the venerable chairs, and the stiff old sofa seemed performing "Sir Roger de Coverley." How we conducted ourselves till five in the morning let our cramps confess; for we were both bed-ridden for ten days after. However, at last, Mrs. Rogers gave in; and, reclining gracefully upon a window-seat, pronounced it a most elegant party and asked me to look for her shawl. While I perambulated the staircase with her bonnet on my head, and more wearing apparel than would stock a magazine, Shaugh was roaring himself hoarse calling Mrs. Rogers's coach.

"Sure, captain," said the lady, with a tender leer, "it's only a chair."

"And here it is," said I, surveying a very portly looking old sedan, newly painted and varnished, which blocked up half the hall.

"You'll catch cold, my angel," said Shaugh, in a whisper, for he was coming it very strong by this; "get into the chair. Maurice, can't you find those fellows?" said he to me; for the chairmen had gone down-stairs, and were making very merry among the servants.

"She's fast now," said I, shutting the door to. "Let us do the gallant thing, and carry her home ourselves.' Shaugh thought this a great notion; and, in a minute, we mounted the poles, and sallied forth, amid a great chorus of laughing from all the footmen, maids, and tea-boys that filled the passage.

"The big house with the bow window and the pillars, captain," said a fellow, as we issued upon our journey.

"I know it," said I. "Turn to the left after you pass the square."

"Isn't she heavy?" said Shaugh, as he meandered across the narrow street with a sidelong motion that must have suggested to our fair inside passenger some notions of a sea voyage. I truth, I must confess, her progress was rather a devious one; now zigzagging from side to side, now getting into a sharp trot, and then suddenly pulling up at a dead stop, or running the machine chuck against a wall, to enable us to stand still and gain breath.

" Which way now?" cried he, as we swung round the angle of the street, and entered the large market-place. " I'm getting terribly tired."

"Never give in, Dan; think of Clonakilty, and the old lady herself"—and here I gave the chair a hoist that evidently astonished our fair friend, for a very imploring cry issued forth immediately after.

" To the right, quick-step, forward—charge!" cried I; and we set off at a brisk trot down a steep, narrow lane.

"Here it is now—the light in the window; cheer up!"

As I said this, we came shortly up to a fine, portly looking doorway with great stone pillars and cornice.

" Make yourself at home, Maurice," said he; " bring her in." And so saying, we pushed forward, for the door was open, and passed boldly into a great flagged hall, silent and cold, and dark as the night itself.

" Are you sure we're right?" said he.

" All right," said I; " go ahead."

And so we did till we came in sight of a small candle that burned dimly at a distance from us.

" Make for the light," said I; but, just as I said

so, Shaugh slipped and fell flat on the flagway; the noise of his fall sent up a hundred echoes in the silent building, and terrified us both dreadfully; and, after a minute's pause, by one consent, we turned and made for the door, falling almost at every step, and frightened out of our senses; we came tumbling together into the porch, and out into the street, and never drew breath till we reached the barracks. Meanwhile, let me return to Mrs. Rogers. The dear old lady, who had passed an awful time since she left the ball, had just rallied out of a fainting fit when we took to our heels; so, after screaming and crying her best, she at last managed to open the top of the chair, and, by dint of great exertions, succeeded in forcing the door, and at length freed herself from bondage. She was leisurely groping her way round it in the dark, when her lamentations being heard without woke up the old sexton of the chapel—for it was there we placed her—who, entering cautiously with a light, no sooner caught a glimpse of the great black sedan and the figure beside it than he also took to his heels, and ran like a madman to the priest's house.

"Come, your reverence, come, for the love of marcy! Sure didn't I see him myself? O wirra, wirra!"

"What is it, ye ould fool?" said M'Kenny.

"It's Father Con Doran, your reverence, that was buried last week, and there he is up now, coffin and all, saying a midnight mass as lively as ever!"

Poor Mrs. Rogers, God help her! It was a trying sight for her, when the priest and the two coadjutors, and the three little boys and the sexton, all came in to lay her spirit; and the shock she received that night they say she never got over.

Need I say, my dear O'Mealey, that our acquaintance with Mrs. Rogers was closed? The dear woman had a hard struggle for it afterwards: her character was assailed by all the elderly ladies in Loughrea for going off in our company, and her blue satin piped with scarlet, utterly ruined by a deluge of holy water bestowed on her by the pious sexton. It was in vain that she originated twenty different reports to mystify the world; and even ten pounds spent in masses for the eternal repose of Father Con Doran only increased the laughter this unfortunate affair gave rise to. As for us, we exchanged into the line, and foreign service took us out of the road of duns, debts, and devilment, and we soon reformed, and eschewed such low company.

THE ADJUTANT'S COURTSHIP.

IT is now about eight years, may be ten years, since that we were ordered to march from Belfast and take up our quarters in Londonderry. We had not been more than a few weeks altogether in Ulster when the order came; and as we had been, for the preceding two years, doing duty in the south and west, we concluded that the island was tolerably the same in all parts. We opened our campaign in the maiden city exactly as we had been doing with "unparalleled success" in Cashel, Fermoy, Tuam, etc.; that is to say, we announced garrison balls, and private theatricals; offered a cup to be run for in steeplechase; turned out a four-in-hand drag, with mottled grays; and brought over two deal boats to challenge the north.

"The 18th found the place stupid," said we.

To be sure they did; slow fellows like them must find any place stupid. No dinners; but they gave none. No fun; but they had none in themselves. In fact, we knew better; we understood how the thing was to be done, and resolved that, as a mine of rich ore lay unworked, it was reserved for us to produce the shining metal that others less discerning had failed to discover. Little we knew of the matter; never was there a blunder like ours. Were you ever in Derry?

"Never," said the listeners.

Well, then, let me inform you that the place has its own peculiar features. In the first place, all the large towns in the south and west have, besides the country neighborhood that surrounds them, a certain sprinkling of gentlefolk who, though with small fortunes and not much usage of the world, are still a great accession to society, and make up the blank which, even in the most thickly peopled country, would be sadly felt without them. Now, in Derry, there is none of this. After the great guns—and, per Baccho! what great guns are they!—you have nothing but the men engaged in commerce—sharp, clever, shrewd, well-informed fellows; they are deep in flax-seed, cunning in molasses, and not to be excelled in all that pertains to coffee, sassafras, cinnamon, gum, oakum, and elephants' teeth. The place is a rich one, and the spirit of commerce is felt throughout it. Nothing is cared for, nothing is talked of, nothing alluded to, that does not bear upon this; and, in fact, if you haven't a venture in Smyrna figs, Memel timber, Dutch dolls, or some such commodity, you are absolutely nothing, and might as well be at a ball with a cork leg, or go deaf to the opera.

Now, when I've told this much, I leave you to guess what impressions our triumphal entry into the city produced. Instead of the admiring crowds that awaited us elsewhere, as we marched gaily into quarters, here we saw nothing but grave, sober-looking, and, I confess it, intelligent-looking faces, that scrutinized our appearance closely enough, but evidently with no great approval and less enthusiasm. The men passed on hurriedly to their counting-houses and the wharfs; the women, with almost as little interest, peeped at us from the windows, and walked away again. Oh! how we wished for Galway, glorious Galway! That Paradise of the infantry that lies west of the Shannon. Little we knew, as we ordered the band, in lively anticipation of the gaieties before us, to strike up "Payne's first set," that to the ears of the fair listeners in Ship Quay Street the rumble of a sugar hogshead, or the crank, crank of a weighing-crane, was more delightful music.

"By Jove," interrupted Power, "you are quite right. Women are strongly imitative in their tastes. The lovely Italian, whose very costume is a natural following of a Raphael, is no more like the pretty Liverpool damsel than Genoa is to Glassnevin; and yet what the deuce have they, dear souls, with their feet upon the soft carpet, and their eyes upon the pages of Scott or Byron, to do with all the cotton or dimity that ever was printed? But let us not repine; that very plastic character is our greatest blessing."

"I'm not so sure that it always exists," said the

doctor dubiously, as though his own experience pointed otherwise.

"Well, go ahead," said the Skipper, who evidently disliked the digression thus interrupting the adjutant's story.

Well, we marched along, looking right and left at the pretty faces—and there was plenty of them, too—that a momentary curiosity drew to the windows; but, although we smiled, and ogled, and leered as only a newly arrived regiment can smile, ogle, or leer, by all that's provoking, we might as well have wasted our blandishments upon the Presbyterian meeting-house that frowned upon us with its high pitched roof and round windows.

"Droll people these," said one. "Raythur rum ones," cried another. "The black north, by Jove," said a third; and so we went along to the barracks, somewhat displeased to think that, though the 18th were slow, they might have met their match.

Disappointed as we undoubtedly felt at the little enthusiasm that marked our *entrée*, we still resolved to persist in our original plan, and, accordingly, early the following morning announced our intention of giving amateur theatricals. The mayor, who called upon our colonel, was the first to learn this, and received the information with pretty much the same kind of look as the Archbishop of Canterbury might be supposed to assume if requested by a friend to ride for the

Derby. The incredulous expression of the poor man's face, as he turned from one of us to the other, evidently canvassing in his mind whether we might not by some special dispensation of Providence be all insane, I shall never forget.

His visit was a very short one; whether concluding that we were not quite safe company, or whether our notification was too much for his nerves, I know not.

We were not to be balked, however; our plans for gaiety, long planned and conned over, were soon announced in all form; and, though we made efforts almost superhuman in the cause, our plays were performed to empty benches, our balls were unattended, our picnic invitations politely declined, and, in a word, all our advances treated with a cold and chilling politeness that plainly said, "We'll none of you."

Each day brought some new discomfiture, and, as we met at mess, instead of having, as heretofore, some prospect of pleasure and amusement to chat over it was only to talk gloomily over our miserable failures, and lament the dreary quarters that our fates had doomed us to.

Some months wore on in this fashion, and at length—what will not time do?—we began by degrees to forget our woes. Some of us took to late hours and brandy and water; others got sentimental, and wrote journals, and novels, and poetry; some few made acquaintances among the towns-people, and cut into a quiet rubber to pass the evening, while another detachment, among which I was, got up a little love affair to while away the tedious hours, and cheat the lazy sun.

I have already said something of my taste in beauty. Now, Mrs. Boggs was exactly the style of woman I fancied. She was a widow, she had black eyes—not your jet black, sparkling, Dutch-doll eyes that roll about and tremble, but mean nothing—no; hers had a soft, subdued, downcast, pensive look about them, and were fully as melting a pair of orbs as any blue eyes you ever looked at.

Then she had a short upper lip, and sweet teeth; by Jove, they were pearls! and she showed them, too, pretty often. Her figure was well rounded, plump, and what the French call *nette*. To complete all, her instep and ankle were unexceptionable; and, lastly, her jointure was seven hundred pounds per annum, with a trifle of eight thousand more that the late lamented Boggs bequeathed when, after four months of uninterrupted bliss, he left Derry for another world.

When chance first threw me in the way of the fair widow, some casual coincidence of opinion happened to raise me in her estimation, and I soon afterward received an invitation to a small evening party at her house, to which I alone of the regiment was asked.

I shall not weary you with the details of my intimacy; it is enough that I tell you I fell desperately in love. I began by visiting twice or thrice a week, and in less than two months spent every morning at her house, and rarely left it till the "roast beef" announced mess.

I soon discovered the widow's cue: she was serious. Now, I had conducted all manner of flirtations in my previous life; timid young ladies, manly young ladies, musical, artistical, poetical, and hysterical. Bless you, I knew them all by heart; but never before had I to deal with a serious one, and a widow to boot. The case was a trying one. For some weeks it was all very up-hill work; all the red shot of warm affection I used to pour in on other occasions was of no use here. The language of love, in which I was no mean proficient, availed me not. Compliments and flattery, those rare skirmishers before the engagement, were denied me; and I verily think that a tender squeeze of the hand would have cost me my dismissal.

"How very slow all this," thought I, as, at the end of two months' siege, I still found myself seated in the trenches, and not a single breach in the fortress. "But, to be sure, it's the way they have in the north, and one must be patient."

While thus I was in no very sanguine frame of mind as to my prospects, in reality my progress was very considerable, having become a member of Mr. M'Phun's congregation. I was gradually rising in the estimation of the widow and her friends, whom my constant attendance at meeting, and my very serious demeanor, had so far impressed that very grave deliberation was held whether I should not be made an elder at the next brevet.

If the Widow Boggs had not been a very lovely and wealthy widow, had she not possessed the eyes, lips, hips, ankles, and jointure aforesaid, I honestly avow that not the charms of that sweet man, Mr. M'Phun's eloquence, nor even the flattering distinction in store for me, would have induced me to prolong my suit. However, I was not going to despair when in sight of land. The widow was evidently softened; a little time longer, and the most scrupulous moralist, the most rigid advocate for employing time wisely, could not have objected to my daily system of courtship. It was none of your sighing, dying, ogling, hand-squeezing, waist-pressing, oath-swearing, everlasting-adoring affairs, with an interchange of rings and lockets; not a bit of it. It was confoundedly like a controversial meeting at the Rotunda, and I myself had a far greater resemblance to Father Tom Maguire than a gay Lothario.

After all, when mess-time came, when the roast beef played, and we assembled at dinner, and the soup and fish had gone round, with the glasses of sherry in, my spirits rallied, and a very jolly evening consoled me for all my fatigues and exertions, and supplied me with energy for the morrow; for let me observe here that I only made love before dinner. The evenings I reserved for myself, assuring Mrs. Boggs that my regimental duties required all my time after mess-hour, in which I was perfectly correct; for at six we dined, at seven I opened the claret No. 1, at eight I had uncorked my second bottle, by half-past eight I was returning to the sherry, and at nine, punctual to the moment, I was returning to my quarters on the back of my servant, Tim Daly, who had carried me safely for eight years without a single mistake, as the fox hunters say. This was a way we had in the —th; every man was carried away from mess, some sooner, some later; I was always an early riser, and went betimes.

Now, although I had very abundant proof, from circumstantial evidence, that I was nightly removed from the mess-room to my bed in the mode I mention, it would have puzzled me sorely to prove the fact in any direct way; inasmuch as, by half-past nine, as the clock chimed, Tim entered to take me. I was very innocent of all that was going on, and, except a certain vague sense of regret at leaving the decanter, felt nothing whatever.

It so chanced—what mere trifles are we ruled by in our destinies!—that, just as my suit with the widow had assumed its most favorable footing, old General Hinks, that commanded the district, announced his coming over to inspect our regiment. Over he came accordingly, and, to be sure, we had a day of it. We were paraded for six mortal hours; then we were marching and counter-marching; moving into line, back again into column, now forming open column, then into square; till at last we began to think that the old general was like the Flying Dutchman, and was probably condemned to keep on drilling us to the day of judgment. To be sure, he enlivened the proceeding to me, by pronouncing the regiment the worst drilled and appointed corps in the service, and the adjutant (me!) the stupidest dunderhead—these were his words—he had ever met with.

"Never mind," thought I, "a few days more, and it's little I'll care for the eighteen manœuvres. It's small trouble your eyes right or your left shoulders forward will give me. I'll sell out, and with the Widow Boggs and seven hundred a year—but no matter."

This confounded inspection lasted till half-past five in the afternoon, so that our mess was delayed a full hour in consequence, and it was past seven as we sat down to dinner. Our faces were grim enough as we met together at first; but what will not a good dinner and good wine do for the surliest party? By eight o'clock we began to feel somewhat more convivially disposed; and, before nine, the decanters were performing a quick-step round the table, in a fashion very exhilarating and very jovial to look at.

"No flinching to-night," said the senior major; "we've had a severe day, let us also have a merry evening."

"By Jove, Ormond," cried another, "we must not leave this to-night. Confound the old humbugs and their misty whist party, throw them over!"

"I say, Adjutant," said Forbes, addressing me, "you've nothing particular to say to the fair widow this evening; you'll not bolt, I hope."

"That he sha'n't," said one near me; "he must make up for his absence to-morrow, for to-night we all stand fast."

"Besides," said another, "she's at meeting by this. Old what-d'ye-call-him is at fourteenthly before now."

"A note for you, sir," said the mess waiter, presenting me with a rose-colored three-cornered billet. It was from *la chère* Boggs herself, and ran thus:

"DEAR SIR—Mr. M'Phun and a few friends are coming to tea at my house after meeting; perhaps you will also favor us with your company.
 "Yours truly,   ELIZA BOGGS.'

What was to be done? Quit the mess, leave a jolly party just at the jolliest moment, exchange Lafitte and red hermitage for a *soirée* of elders presided over by that sweet man Mr. M'Phun? It was too bad; but then, how much was in the scale? What would the widow say if I declined? What would she think? I well knew that the invitation meant nothing less than a full-dress parade of me before her friends, and that to decline was perhaps to forfeit all my hopes in that quarter for ever.

"Any answer, sir?" said the waiter.

"Yes," said I, in a half whisper, "I'll go; tell the servant I'll go."

At this moment, my tender epistle was abstracted from before me and, ere I turned round, had made the tour of half the table. I never perceived the circumstance, however, and, filling my glass, professed my resolve to sit to the last, with a mental reserve to take my departure at the very first opportunity. Ormond and the paymaster quitted the room for a moment, as if to give orders for a broil at twelve, and now all seemed to promise a very convivial and well-sustained party for the night.

"Is that all arranged?" inquired the major, as Ormond entered.

"All right," said he; "and now let us have a bumper and a song. Adjutant, old boy, give us a chant."

"What shall it be, then?" inquired I, anxious to cover my intended retreat by an appearance of joviality.

"Give us—

'When I was in the Fusileers,
Some fourteen years ago.'"

"No, no, confound it! I've heard nothing else, since I joined the regiment. Let us have the Paymaster's Daughter."

"Ah! that's pathetic; I like that," lisped a young ensign.

"If I'm to have a vote," grunted out the senior major, "I pronounce for West India Quarters."

"Yes, yes," said half a dozen voices together, "let's have West India Quarters. Come, give him a glass of sherry, and let him begin."

I had scarcely finished off my glass, and cleared my throat for my song, when the clock on the chimney-piece chimed half-past nine, and the same instant I felt a heavy hand fall upon my shoulder; I turned and beheld my servant Tim. This, as I have already mentioned, was the hour at which Tim was in the habit of taking me home to my quarters, and, though we had dined an hour later, he took no notice of the circumstance, but, true to his custom, he was behind my chair. A very cursory glance at my "familiar" was quite sufficient to show me that we had somehow changed sides, for Tim, who was habitually the most sober of mankind, was, on the present occasion, exceedingly drunk, while I, a full hour before that consummation, was perfectly sober.

"What d'ye want, sir?" inquired I, with something of severity in my manner.

"Come home," said Tim, with a hiccup that set the whole table in a roar.

"Leave the room this instant," said I feeling wrathy at being thus made a butt of for his offences—"leave the room, or I'll kick you out of it." Now this, let me add in a parenthesis, was somewhat of a boast, for Tim was six feet three, and strong in proportion, and, when in liquor, fearless as a tiger.

"You'll kick me out of the room, eh! will you? Try, only try it; that's all." Here a new roar of laughter burst forth, while Tim, again placing an enormous paw upon my shoulder, continued: "Don't be sitting there, making a baste of yourself, when you've got enough. Don't you see you're drunk?"

I sprang to my legs on this, and made a rush to the fireplace to secure the poker; but Tim was beforehand with me, and, seizing me by the waist with both hands, flung me across his shoulders, as though I were a baby, saying, at the same time, "I'll take you away at half-past eight tomorrow, av you're as rampageous again." I kicked, I plunged, I swore, I threatened, I even begged and implored to be set down; but, whether my voice was lost in the uproar around me, or that Tim only regarded my denunciations in the light of cursing, I know not; but he carried me bodily down the stairs, steadying himself by one hand on the bannisters, while with the other he held me as in a vise. I had but one consolation all this while: it was this, that, as my quarters lay immediately behind the mess-room, Tim's excursion would soon come to an end, and I should be free once more; but guess my terror to find that the drunken scoundrel, instead of going, as usual, to the left, turned short to the right hand, and marched boldly into Ship Quay Street. Every window in the mess-room was filled with our fellows, absolutely shouting with laughter. "Go it, Tim—that's the fellow—hold him tight—never let go," cried a dozen voices, while the wretch, with the tenacity of drunkenness, gripped me still harder, and took his way down the middle of the street.

It was a beautiful evening in July, a soft summer night, as I made this pleasing excursion down the most frequented thoroughfare in the maiden city, my struggles every moment exciting roars of laughter from an increasing crowd of spectators, who seemed scarcely less amused than puzzled at the exhibition. In the midst of a torrent of imprecations against my torturer, a loud noise attracted me. I turned my head, and saw—horror of horrors!—the door of the meeting-house just flung open, and the congregation issuing forth *en masse*. Is it any wonder if I remember no more? There I was, the chosen one of the Widow Boggs—the elder elect—the favored friend and admired associate of Mr. M'Phun, taking an airing on a summer's evening on the back of a drunken Irishman! Oh! the thought was horrible; and, certainly, the short and pithy epithets by which I was characterized in the crowd neither improved my temper nor assuaged my wrath; and I feel bound to confess that my own language was neither serious nor becoming. Tim, however, cared little for all this, and pursued the even tenor of his way through the whole crowd, nor stopped till, having made half the circuit of the wall, he deposited me safe at my own door, adding, as he set me down, " Oh! av you're as throublesome every evening, it's a wheelbarrow I'll be obleeged to bring for you."

The next day I obtained a short leave of absence, and, ere a fortnight expired, exchanged into the —th, preferring Halifax itself to the ridicule that awaited me in Londonderry.

THE GHOST.

AS RELATED BY MICKEY FREE.

WELL, I believe your honor heard me tell long ago how my father left the army, and the way that he took to another line of life that was more to his liking. And so it was; he was happy as the day was long; he drove a hearse for Mr. Callaghan, of Cork, for many years, and a pleasant place it was; for ye see, my father was a cute man, and knew something of the world; and, though he was a droll devil, and, could sing a funny song when he was among the boys, no sooner had he the big black cloak on him, and the weepers, and he seated on the high box with the six long-tailed blacks before him, you'd really think it was his own mother was inside, he looked so melancholy and miserable. The sexton and grave-digger was nothing to my father; and he had a look about his eye—to be sure there was a reason for it—that you'd think he was up all night crying; though it's little indulgence he took that way.

"Well, of all Mr. Callaghan's men, there was none so great a favorite as my father; the neighbors were all fond of him.

"'A kind crayture every inch of him, the women would say. 'Did ye see his face at Mrs. Delany's funeral?'

"'True for you,' another would remark; 'he mistook the road with grief, and stopped at a shebeenhouse instead of Kilmurry Church.'

"I need say no more, only one thing, that it was principally among the farmers and the country people my father was liked so much. The great people and the quality—I ax your pardon—but sure isn't it true, Mister Charles, they don't fret so much after their fathers and brothers, and they care little who's driving them, whether it was a decent, respectable man like my father, or a chap with a grin on him like a rat-trap? And so it happened that my father used to travel half the country; going here and there wherever there was trade stirring; and, faix, a man didn't think himself rightly buried if my father wasn't there; for, ye see, he knew all about it; he could tell to a quart of sperits what would be wanting for a wake; he knew all the good cryers for miles round; and I've heard it was a beautiful sight to see him standing on a hill, arranging the procession, as they walked into the churchyard, and giving the word like a captain.

"'Come on, the *stiff*—now the friends of the *stiff*—now de pop'lace.'

"That's what he used to say; and, troth, he was always repeating it when he was a little gone in drink—for that's the time his spirits would rise—and he'd think he was burying half Munster.

"And sure it was a real pleasure and a pride to be buried in them times; for, av it was only a small farmer with a potato garden, my father would come down with the black cloak on him, and three yards of crape behind his hat, and set all the children crying and yelling for half a mile round; and then the way he'd walk before them with a spade on his shoulder, and, sticking it down in the ground, clap his hat on the top of it, to make it look like a chief mourner. It was a beautiful sight!"

"But, Mike, if you indulge much longer in this flattering recollection of your father, I'm afraid we shall lose sight of the ghost entirely."

"No fear in life, your honor, I'm coming to him now. Well, it was this way it happened: In the winter of the great frost, about forty-two or forty-three years ago, the ould priest of Tulloughmuray took ill and died; he was sixty years priest of the parish, and mightily beloved by all the people, and good reason for it; a pleasanter man and a more social crayture never lived: 'twas himself was the life of the whole countryside. A wedding nor a christening wasn't lucky av he wasn't there, sitting at the top of the table, with as much kindness in his eye as would make the fortunes of twenty hypocrites, if they had it among them. And then he was so good to the poor; the Priory was always full of ould men and ould women, sitting around the big fire in the kitchen, so that the cook could hardly get near it. There they were eating their meals, and burning their shins, till they were speckled like a trout's back, and grumbling all the time; but Father Dwyer liked them, and he would have them.

"'Where have they to go,' he'd say, 'av it wasn't to me? Give Molly Kinshela a lock of that bacon, Tim, it's a cowld morning; will ye have a taste of the "dew"?'

"Ah! that's the way he'd spake to them; but sure goodness is no warrant for living any more than devilment; and so he got cowld in his feet at a station, and he rode home in the heavy snow without his big coat—for he gave it away to a blind man on the road—and in three days he was dead.

"I see you're getting impatient; so I'll not stop to say what grief was in the parish when it was known; but troth there never was seen the like before; not a crayture would lift a spade for two days, and there was more whiskey sold in that time than at the whole spring fair. Well, on the third day, the funeral set out, and never was the equal of it in them parts: first, there was my father; he came special from Cork with the six horses all in new black and plumes like little poplar trees; then came Father Dwyer, followed by the two coadjutors in beautiful surplices, walking bare-headed, with the little boys of the Priory school, two and two."

"Well, Mike, I'm sure it was very fine; but for heaven's sake spare me all these descriptions, and get on to the ghost!"

"Faith, your honor's in a great hurry for the ghost; may be you won't like him when ye have him, but I'll go faster if you please. Well, Father Dwyer, ye see, was born at Aghan-lish, of an ould family, and he left it in his will that he was to be buried in the family vault; and, as Aghan-lish was eighteen miles up the mountains, it was getting late when they drew near. By that time, the great procession was all broke up and gone home. The coadjutors stopped to dine at the 'Blue Bellows' at the crossroads; the little boys took to pelting snow-balls; there was a fight or two on the way besides; and, in fact, except an ould deaf fellow that my father took to mind the horses, he was quite alone. Not that he minded that same; for, when the crowd was gone, my father began to song, and tould the deaf chap that it was a lamentation. At last they came in sight of Aghan-lish. It was a lonesome, melancholy-looking place, with nothing near it except two or three ould fir-trees, and a small slated house with one window, where the sexton lived, and even that same was shut up, and a padlock on the door. Well, my father was not over much pleased at the look of matters; but, as he was never hard put to what to do, he managed to get the coffin into the vestry; and then, when he unharnessed the horses, he sent the deaf fellow with them down to the village to tell the priest that the corpse was there, and to come up early in the morning and perform Mass. The next thing to do was to make himself comfortable for the night; and then he made a roaring fire on the old hearth —for there was plenty of bog-fir there—closed the windows with the black cloaks, and, wrapping two round himself, he sat down to cook a little supper he brought with him in case of need.

"Well, you may think it was melancholy enough to pass the night up there alone, with a corpse in an old ruined church in the middle of the mountains, the wind howling about on every side, and the snowdrift beating against the walls; but, as the fire burned brightly, and the little plate of rashers and eggs smoked temptingly before him, my father mixed a jug of the strongest punch, and sat down as happy as a king. As long as he was eating away he had no time to be thinking of anything else; but, when all was done, and he looked about him, he began to feel very low and melancholy in his heart. There was the great black coffin on three chairs in one corner; and then the mourning-cloaks that he had stuck up against the windows moved backward and forward like living things; and outside the wild cry of the plover as he flew past, and the night-owl sitting in a nook of the old church. 'I wish it was morning, anyhow,' said my father; 'for this is a lonesome place to be in; and, faix, he'll be a cunning fellow that catches me passing the night this way again.' Now, there was one thing distressed him most of all: my father used always to make fun of the ghosts and sperits the neighbors would tell of, pretending there was no such thing; and now the thought came to him, 'May be they'll revenge themselves on me to-night, when they have me up here alone.' And with that he made another jug stronger than the first, and tried to remember a few prayers in case of need; but somehow his mind was not too clear, and he said afterwards he was always mixing up ould songs and toasts with the prayers, and, when he thought he had just got hold of a beautiful psalm, it would turn out to be 'Tatter Jack Walsh,' or 'Limping' James,' or something like that. The storm, meanwhile, was rising every moment, and parts of the old abbey were falling, as the wind shook the ruin; and my father's sperits, notwithstanding the punch, were lower than ever.

"'I made it too weak,' said he, as he set to work on a new jorum; and troth this time that was not the fault of it, for the first sup nearly choked him.

"'Ah!' said he now, 'I knew what it was; this is like the thing; and, Mr. Free, you are beginning to feel easy and comfortable; pass the jug; your very good health and song. I'm a little hoarse, it's true, but if the company will excuse—'

"And then he began knocking on the table with his knuckles, as if there was a room full of people asking him to sing. In short, my father was drunk as a fiddler; the last brew finished him; and he began roaring away all kinds of droll songs, and telling all manner of stories, as if he was at a great party.

"While he was capering this way about the room, he knocked down his hat, and with it a pack of cards he put into it before leaving home, for he was mighty fond of a game.

"'Will ye take a hand, Mr. Free?' said he, as he gathered them up and sat down beside the fire.

"'I'm convanient,' said he, and began dealing out as if there was a partner fornenst him.

"When my father used to get this far in the story, he became very confused. He says that once or twice he mistook the liquor, and took a pull at the bottle of potteen instead of the punch; and the last thing he remembers was asking poor Father Dwyer if he would draw near to the fire, and not be lying there near the door.

"With that he slipped down on the ground, and fell fast asleep. How long he lay that way he could never tell. When he awoke and looked up, his hair nearly stood on end with fright. What do you think he seen fornenst him, sitting at the other side of the fire, but Father Dwyer himself; there he was, divil a lie in it, wrapped up in one of the mourning-cloaks, trying to warm his hands at the fire.

"'*Salve hoc nomine patri!*' said my father, crossing himself. 'Av it's your ghost, God presarve me!'

"'Good-evening t'ye, Mr. Free,' said the ghost; 'and, av I might be bould, what's in the jug?' For, ye see, my father had it under his arm fast, and never let it go when he was asleep.

"'*Pater noster qui es in*—potteen, sir,' said my father, for the ghost didn't look pleased at his talking Latin.

"'Ye might have the politeness to ax if one had a mouth on him,' then says the ghost

"'Sure I didn't think the like of you would taste sperits.'

"'Try me,' said the ghost; and with that he filled out a glass, and tossed it off like a Christian.

"'Beamish!' says the ghost, smacking his lips.

"'The same,' says my father; 'and sure what's happened you has not spoilt your taste?'

"'If you'd mix a little hot,' says the ghost, 'I'm thinking it would be better; the night is mighty sevare.'

"'Anything that your reverence pleases,' says my father, as he began to blow up a good fire to boil the water.

"'And what news is stirring?' says the ghost.

"'Devil a word, your reverence; your own funeral was the only thing doing last week. Times is bad; except the measles, there's nothing in our parts.'

"'And we're quite dead hereabouts too,' says the ghost.

"'There's some of us so, anyhow,' says my

father, with a sly look. 'Taste that, your reverence.'

"'Pleasant and refreshing,' says the ghost. 'And now, Mr. Free, what do you say to a little spoil five, or beggar my neighbor?'

"'What will we play for?' says my father; for a thought just struck him — 'May be it's some trick of the devil to catch my soul.'

"'A pint of Beamish,' says the ghost.

"'Done,' says my father; 'cut for deal—the ace of clubs—you have it.'

"Now, the whole time the ghost was dealing the cards my father never took his eyes off of him, for he wasn't quite asy in his mind at all; but when he saw him turn up the trump, and take a strong drink afterwards, he got more at ease, and began the game.

"How long they played it was never rightly known; but one thing is sure, they drank a cruel deal of spirits; three quart bottles my father brought with him were all finished, and by that time his brain was so confused with the liquor and all he lost—for somehow he never won a game—that he was getting very quarrelsome.

"'You have your own luck of it,' says he at last.

"'True for you; and, besides, we play a great deal where I come from.'

"'I've heard so,' says my father. 'I lead the knave, sir, spades; bad cess to it, lost again!'

"Now, it was really very distressing; for, by

this time, though they only began for a pint of Beamish, my father went on betting till he lost the hearse and all the six horses, mourning-cloaks, plumes, and everything.

"'Are you tired, Mr. Free? May be you'd like to stop?'

"'Stop! faith it's a nice time to stop; of course not.'

"'Well, what will ye play for now?'

"The way he said these words brought a trembling all over my father, and his blood curdled in his heart. 'O murther!' says he to himself. 'It's my sowl he is wanting all the time.'

"'I've mighty little left,' says my father, looking at him keenly, while he kept shuffling the cards quick as lightning.

"'Mighty little; no matter, we'll give you plenty of time to pay, and, if you can't do it, it shall never trouble you as long as you live.'

"'O you murthering devil!' says my father, flying at him with a spade that he had behind his chair. 'I've found you out.'

"With one blow he knocked him down; and now a terrible fight began, for the ghost was very strong too; but my father's blood was up, and he'd have faced the devil himself then. They rolled over each other several times, the broken bottles cutting them to pieces, and the chairs and tables crashing under them. At last the ghost took the bottle that lay on the hearth, and levelled my father to the ground with one blow; down he fell, and the bottle and the whiskey were both dashed into the fire; that was the end of it, for the ghost disappeared that moment in a blue flame that nearly set fire to my father as he lay on the floor.

"Och! it was a cruel sight to see him next morning, with his cheek cut open, and his hands all bloody, lying there by himself; all the broken glass and the cards all round him; the coffin, too, was knocked down off the chair; may be the ghost had trouble getting into it. However that was, the funeral was put off for a day, for my father couldn't speak; and as for the sexton, it was a queer thing, but when they came to call him in the morning he had two black eyes, and a gash over his ear, and he never knew how he got them. It was easy enough to know the ghost did it; but my father kept the secret, and never told it to any man, woman, or child in them parts."

SERVING A WRIT.

THE way of it was this, said Major O'Shaughnessy: my father, who, for reasons registered in the King's Bench, spent a great many years of his life in that part of Ireland geographically known as lying west of the law, was obliged for certain reasons of family to come up to Dublin. This he proceeded to do with due caution; two trusty servants formed an advance guard, and patrolled the country for at least five miles in advance; after them came a skirmishing body of a few tenants, who, for the consideration of never paying rent, would have charged the whole Court of Chancery, if needful. My father himself, in an old chaise, victualled like a fortress, brought up the rear; and, as I said before, he was a bold man who would have attempted to have laid siege to him. As the column advanced into the enemy's country, they assumed a closer order, the patrol and the picket falling back upon the main body; and in this way they reached that most interesting city called Kilbeggan. What a fortunate thing it is for us in Ireland that we can see so much of the world without foreign travel, and that any gentlemen for six and eightpence can leave Dublin in the morning and visit Timbuctoo against dinner-time! Don't stare! it's truth I'm telling! For dirt, misery, smoke, unaffected behavior, and black faces, I'll back Kilbeggan against all Africa. Free-and-easy, pleasant people ye are, with a skin as begrimed and as rugged as your own potatoes! But to resume. The sun was just rising in a delicious morning of June, when my father—whose loyal antipathies I have mentioned made him also an earlier riser—was preparing for the road. A stout escort of his followers were as usual under arms to see him safe in the chaise, the passage to and from which every day being the critical moment of my father's life.

"It's all right, your honor," said his own man, as, armed with a blunderbuss, he opened the bedroom door.

"Time enough, Tim," said my father; "close the door, for I haven't finished my breakfast."

Now, the real truth was that my father's attention was at that moment withdrawn from his own concerns by a scene which was taking place in a field beneath his window.

But a few minutes before a hack-chaise had stopped upon the roadside, out of which sprang three gentlemen, who, proceeding to the field, seemed bent upon something which, whether a survey or a duel, my father could not make out. He was not long, however, to remain in ignorance. One, with an easy, lounging gait, strode toward a distant corner, another took an opposite direction, while the third, a short, pursy gentleman, in a red handkerchief and a rabbit-skin waistcoat, proceeded to open a mahogany box, which, to the critical eyes of my respected father, was agreeably suggestive of bloodshed and murder.

"A duel, by Jupiter!" said my father, rubbing his hands. "What a heavenly morning the scoundrels have—not a leaf stirring, and a sod like a billiard-table!"

Meanwhile, the little man who officiated as second, it would appear, to *both* parties bustled about with activity little congenial to his shape; and, what between snapping the pistols, examining the flints, and ramming down the charges, had got himself into a sufficient perspiration before he commenced to measure out the ground.

"Short distance and no quarter!" shouted one of the combatants from the corner of the field.

"Across a handkerchief, if you like!" roared the other.

"Gentlemen every inch of them!" responded my father.

"Twelve paces!" cried the little man; "no more and no less. Don't forget that I am alone in this business!"

"A very true remark," observed my father; "and an awkward predicament yours will be if they are both shot!"

By this time the combatants had taken their places, and the little man, having delivered the pistols, was leisurely retiring to give the word. My father, however, whose critical eye was never at fault, detected a circumstance which promised an immense advantage to one at the expense of the other; in fact, one of the parties was so placed with his back to the sun that his shadow extended in a straight line to the very foot of his antagonist.

"Unfair! unfair!" cried my father, opening the window as he spoke, and addressing himself to him of the rabbit-skin. "I crave your pardon for the interruption," said he, "but I feel bound to observe that that gentleman's shadow is likely to be made a shade of him."

"And so it is," observed the short man; "a thousand thanks for your kindness; but the truth is I am totally unaccustomed to this kind of thing, and the affair will not admit of delay."

"Not an hour!" said one.

"Not five minutes!" growled the other of the combatants.

"Put them up north and south!" said my father.

"Is it thus?"

"Exactly so; but now again the gentleman in the brown coat is covered with the ash-tree."

"And so he is!" said rabbit-skin, wiping his forehead with agitation.

"Move them a little to the left," said he.

"That brings me upon an eminence," said the gentleman in blue. "I'll be d—d if I'll be made a cock-shot of."

"What an awkward little thing it is in the hairy waistcoat!" said my father. "He's lucky if he don't get shot himself."

"May I never! if I'm not sick of you both!" ejaculated rabbit-skin, in a passion. "I've moved you round every point of the compass, and the devil a nearer we are than ever."

"Give us the word!" said one.

"The word!"

"Downright murder!" said my father.

"I don't care," said the little man; "we shall be here till doomsday."

"I can't permit this," said my father. "Allow me—" So saying, he stepped upon the window-sill, and leaped down into the field.

"Before I can accept of your politeness," said he of the rabbit-skin, "may I beg to know your name and position in society?"

"Nothing more reasonable," said my father. "I'm Miles O'Shaughnessy, Colonel of the Royal Raspers; here is my card."

The piece of pasteboard was complacently handed from one to the other of the party, who saluted my father with a smile of most courteous benignity.

"Colonel O'Shaughnessy," said one.

"Miles O'Shaughnessy," said another.

"Of Killinahoula Castle," said the third.

"At your service," said my father, bowing, as he presented his snuff-box; "and now to business, if you please, for my time also is limited."

"Very true," observed he of the rabbit-skin; "and, as you observe, now to business; in virtue of which, Colonel Miles O'Shaughnessy, I hereby arrest you in the king's name. Here is the writ; it's at the suit of Barnaby Kelly of Loughrea, for the sum of £1,583 19s. 7½d., which—"

Before he could conclude the sentence, my father discharged one obligation by implanting his closed knuckles in his face. The blow, well aimed and well intentioned, sent the little fellow somerseting like a sugar hogshead. But, alas! it was of no use; the others, strong and able-bodied, fell both upon him, and after a desperate struggle succeeded in getting him down. To tie his hands and convey him to the chaise was the work of a few moments; and, as my father drove by the inn, the last object which caught his view was a bloody encounter between his own people and the myrmidons of the law, who in great numbers had laid siege to the house during his capture. Thus was my father taken; and thus, in reward for yielding to a virtuous weakness in his character, was he consigned to the ignominious durance of a prison. Was I not right, then, in saying that such is the melancholy position of our country, the most beautiful traits in our character are converted into the elements of ruin?

www.ingramcontent.com/pod-product-compliance
Lightning Source LLC
Chambersburg PA
CBHW030005240426
43672CB00007B/833